Third Edition

ANATOMY *of a* FOOD ADDICTION

◇

THE BRAIN CHEMISTRY OF OVEREATING

An Effective Program to Overcome Compulsive Eating

ANNE KATHERINE, M.A.

gürze books

Anatomy of a Food Addiction

The Brain Chemistry of Overeating

Third Edition

Cover design: Abacus Graphics, Oceanside, CA

Originally published by Fireside/Parkside

Published by:

Gürze Books
P.O. Box 2238
Carlsbad, CA 92018
(619) 434-7533

Library of Congress Cataloging-in-Publication Data

Katherine, Anne
Anatomy of a food addiction / The brain chemistry of overeating / by Anne Katherine.
p. cm.
Includes bibliographical references and index.
1. Eating disorders—popular works. I. Title.
RC552..E18K37 1991 90-20433
616.85'26—dc20 CIP

ISBN 0-936077-13-1

NOTE:

The author and publisher of this book intend for this publication to provide accurate information. It is sold with the understanding that it is meant to complement, not substitute for, professional medical and/or psychological services.

2 4 6 8 0 9 7 5 3

TO MOM

For all women and men whose lives
have been strangled by food

ACKNOWLEDGMENTS

◇

Thanks to Cody Sontag, M.A. (JoEllen Wahto); Sherry Ascher, M.A.; May C. Brown, Ph.D.; Alice Delaney, M.A.; Alliene Ellis; Frances West; Vickie Sears; Carol Conner Newman; Kathy Severson, Ph.D.; Amy Condon; Sandy Reno; Bob Reno, Ph.D.; Shirley Averett; and Jean Parker Cobb for soaring support, grand ideas, and faith.

CONTENTS

◇

Introduction *1*

1 ◇
Addiction Is an Illness *11*

2 ◇
Chemical Warfare *21*

3 ◇
Deprivation *48*

4 ◇
The Great Escape *70*

5 ◇
Nature's Telegrams *81*

6 ◇
How Healing Happens *95*

7 ◇
Achieving Abstinence *108*

8 ◇
Help! 131

9 ◇
Dear Beloved 137

10 ◇
Fat Prejudice 151

11 ◇
Anorexia and Bulimia 155

12 ◇
Timing, Choices, and Hitting Bottom 169

13 ◇
Relapse 174

14 ◇
Further Abstinence 187

15 ◇
Wait! 200

16 ◇
Fullness 223

Notes 229
Sources of Help 232
Index 233

PREFACE

When I took my first step toward recovery from binge eating in 1983, I had no idea that my life was unfulfilled because I was eating too much. What a wonder, then, that with each small step I took into recovery, my life gained more luster, my mind got clearer, and my energy grew.

I didn't realize that certain foods act in the body as if they are drugs, creating an addiction powerful enough to have held me in a pattern of binge eating despite my most fervent and spiritual efforts to break free. I call these foods "drug foods," which by themselves are not drugs, but through a series of chemical reactions eventually cause production of brain chemicals that can have a drug-like effect on the body. These chemicals cloud the mind, imprison the soul, and steal freedoms. All this from particular foods in interaction with a particular body type.

This susceptibility stems from the fact that many people have an inadequate supply of certain chemicals that can, among other things, alleviate pain. We learn, even as small children, to stimulate the release of these chemicals by eating sweets and we do this for a much more significant reason than to get a particular taste. We do this because, soon after, we feel better.

Thus, we discover how to manipulate our brain functioning by choosing to eat an abundance of certain types of foods. We make this adjustment without any consciousness of how or why it works; but, over time, such manipulation causes other brain changes, and we can unknowingly get trapped in a cycle of eating that causes more eating. This book explains that process.

If you suspect that you have a food addiction but aren't sure, try the test in the Introduction. You may not even realize how much of your life is influenced by drug foods. But if the very idea of giving up sugar seems impossible, if you fear that not having sweets would take all the color out of your life, or you feel that giving up desserts would be the hardest thing you could ever do, you are thinking like a junkie.

Do you have the same kind of emotional attachment to radishes that you do to chocolate? If someone said, "Radishes are now extinct and you'll never see another one," would it cause much of a ripple in your life? I like radishes and I'd miss them if they were gone, but I don't think much about radishes.

Chocolate, on the other hand, can raise passion. And what's the difference between chocolate and radishes? Chocolate is the perfect drug food. Its sweetness ultimately stimulates the release of dreamy brain chemicals, its fat is comforting, and another caffeine-like chemical in chocolate speeds up this whole process while providing a pleasurable reaction of its own. All this can be *highly* addictive.

A binge eater who is addicted to fat can easily consume a bag of "regular" potato chips, continuing to eat even after feeling full. However, the same person will get bored chewing healthy, nonfat chips. If there's no internal relief, what's the point? What's more, a food addict knows which foods hold a charge and which do not. No matter how good is the taste of the healthier version, the food that brings the sought-after bodily experience will be the one chosen.

I challenge you. Buy a package of baked, *nonfat* potato chips. Some taste better than others. Be sure you get chips that are potatoes only, not ground up potatoes with some form of sugar added. Better yet, try making your own from the following tasty recipe. Slice potatoes thin, spray with vegetable spray, sprinkle with Cajun or other seasoning, and bake, turning as needed. Do you eat the whole batch and want more, or find it half-full in the pantry six months later? What about "regular" chips?

Place a jar of nonfat mayo next to the regular mayo in the fridge. Which jar gets empty first? Which cereal calls loudest, frosted flakes or shredded wheat? Which frozen desert has that special glow around it—a nonfat, truly sugar-free, lightly fruit-sweetened frozen yogurt or the regular stuff? Do you know instincitvely which foods would draw you?

When I first started talking to clients in 1985 about their addiction to food, I had only a few uncorroborated studies to go on. When I wrote this book in 1987, I sought out obscure research reports from diverse disciplines, most of which weren't linked to each other. I made those links as I wrote. On the one hand, I knew I was climbing way out on a long limb. On the other hand, I knew from my own internal experience just how compelling a food craving can be, how powerful and irresistible.

Up till then, my food addiction had seemed like a curse, preventing me from feeling like a normal person. But when I understood that my experience was proof that food could be addictive, it helped me stand firm when I came under attack by some psychologists that said this was absolutely not possible. I *knew* that my relationship with certain foods was not normal. I *knew* that my thinking and obsessing, planning and hoarding, sneaking and hiding resembled the behavior of an addict. I *also* knew that only when I stopped eating the foods and quantities that kept me in a hazy prison, could I develop a normal relationship with food. Till then, drug foods acted just as addictive drugs do, they stimulated the desire for more. Finally, I knew that if I was food addicted, then others probably were, too.

Now, many of the original research studies on brain chemicals that regulate appetite have been abundantly replicated, and the effect of depletion of certain chemicals on eating is well-documented. I've worked with hundreds of binge eaters, some of whom have strong addictions to many foods, others who have mild addictions to some foods. Still others are addicted to the process of eating, capable of consuming large amounts of any food. All of them, however, have been helped by an understanding of the brain chemistry of eating and the practice of abstinence. I can safely crawl back from my limb and be grateful that I trusted my instincts.

Some people want to know if I lost weight as a result of my recovery. Well, what about weight? Is this a book about weight loss? No. It's a book that will tell you how to move drug foods out of your life and make room for clarity of mind and personal choice to move back in.

In fact, weight is an extremely complex issue, and worrying about one's weight is not helpful in recovery from food addiction. Focusing on weight loss creates tension that, more often than not, propels most people to binge. Focusing on recovery, though, creates moment-by-moment awareness, inner guidance, choice, and healthier alternatives. Actually, one can be in recovery and choose not to be concerned with weight loss at all, but few can sustain a weight loss without the long-term benefits of deep recovery.

In many ways, recovery from food addiction is a much more subtle process than, for instance, recovery from alcohol addiction which is much more clear cut—abstain from alcohol. A food addict *must* deal with food every day and cannot always be confident of the composition of meals he or she is served. What's more, the same food can be non-addictive in small doses and highly addictive when too much is eaten. Perfect abstinence from harmful foods is simply not possible.

So, I view recovery as the process of actively seeking freedom from the compulsion to eat. This means going on when accidentally triggered by an unsuspected ingredient, or getting back up when knocked down by a binge. It means constantly reminding ourselves of the goal of living a drug-free life. It does not necessarily mean having a thin body.

The rewards of recovery are profound and infinite. Clients who have just started this process often say to me with wonder, "My mind is so clear!" "I'm not sleepy all the time." "I have so much energy." They are astounded at the difference it makes to no longer feel drugged. Most have been in a kind of stupor for years and can't remember what life was like before their food addiction began.

A better life is very likely waiting for you as well, although getting there may be the hardest thing you've ever done. Yet, why wait? Why spend another week in the cloudy half-life of food addiction? Your own whole life is just ahead.

INTRODUCTION

◇

A spring breeze rippled through the filmy curtains of my office window. Two comfortable old rockers stood on the soft rug. A plant here and there, my desk against the wall, my credentials framed and shining—how proud I felt when I first opened my own office as a psychotherapist.

How sad the day my name came off the door.

My heart raced as I glanced a last time in the mirror. I patted my hair and smoothed my blouse. After a week apart, my fiancé would soon knock at the door and we would be together again. A light cheerful tap danced through the house. I ran to the door.

How sad were the long days when I adjusted to being completely alone, all the white-lace hopes erased. Oh, there were other losses, too. I had a large circle of good people as friends. I felt needed and wanted in the spiritual community I belonged to. I lost it all. How did it happen?

When I picture my decline, one scene seems to represent many others. I am in that office I was so proud of opening. My client is talking. I can barely focus on his words. I am under the influence of my drug and I hurt from trying to hold my face in a pose that shows I'm alert.

A spring breeze billows the curtains and whispers coolness across my arms. I don't appreciate the scent of spring. I don't perceive the restful greens of my office. I don't take in the frustration of my client. I'm tight with the effort of concentrating through my drug-induced fog and I want the hour to pass.

When my client leaves I feel my first energy. Now I am finally free to get my fix. I slip out of the office building to a nearby store, buy candy and two frozen desserts, and lock myself in the office so no one will catch me. Then I eat—not to taste, not to savor, but to get the substance into my body. I'm shooting up with sugar.

My practice dwindled to nothing. I cared about my clients and I learned to schedule them before the food had taken me over so that I could be present for them. Eventually, when I got into recovery, I had much, much more to offer and could finally return something to the clients who had stayed with me.

But before I understood I had a problem, oh, the agony of my secret life. I felt such shame representing myself as a whole, competent person when I knew that after my last client I'd hit the food stores and shove it down.

Then there are the people I lost. Intimates took a roller-coaster ride. My mood would be dreamy if I were satiated, barbed if it'd been too long since a binge. I didn't know I had a brain allergy to certain foods and that eating them caused a personality change. I'd rage at a beloved person for no significant reason, set up scenes so that I could withdraw and be cold. I had no control over how I acted and no idea it was chemically caused.

My addiction to eating made mincemeat out of my relationships. Some days I was so hung over from a binge I couldn't return calls, wouldn't answer the phone, was late for lunches and meetings. I was so desperate to feel complete that I took more from friends than I gave. Unconsciously, I manipulated friends to be there for me and gave to them mainly so they'd give to me. Often I was playing a part, trying to appear interesting and worthwhile so people would want to be with me. I was so out of touch with reality. I didn't see what I was doing.

It got worse. Toward the end, all I did was eat. I was the equivalent of the drunk in the gutter.

I barely crawled from bed. I ate all day curled on the couch, wearing a path between it and the kitchen. My cravings were instantaneous. If I wanted candy, I couldn't wait as long as it would take to get in the car and go to the store. Instead I would mix up some sugar-rich concoction, put it in the microwave, and burn my tongue because I would eat before it was cool enough.

I hid all this. I would clean up after each concoction so that no one would catch me at cooking and eating. I did this even when I lived alone, as if I were doing the kind of secretive thing that spies would be set to catch me doing.

I had no energy. My self-esteem was below sea level. I had no goals and no belief that I could reach goals if I had had them. I thought I might as well die. I felt dead.

I never thought to talk about my eating. It never occurred to me to tell anybody that I thought about eating day and night.

Whenever I went anywhere or did anything, the food was the major attraction. I went to the fair to eat the special foods that only fairs have. I went to the movies to eat popcorn. I went out with friends in order to have dinner or lunch. If there had been such a thing as a party without food, I probably wouldn't have gone.

At parties, I would eat secretly. If I liked a certain food a lot, I would take many servings, but I would disguise how much I was getting by hiding it under "good" food. I would drift by and casually lift extras of my favorite. I would eat carefully, steering from person to person or from room to room so that no one could detect how much I was eating. I wasn't focused on what people were saying to me or on what I was saying to them, but on the process of eating and disguising the amount I was eating. It never occurred to me that this was odd behavior. Although this vigilance about eating was constant, I was as unaware of it as I was of my constant food thoughts.

Today it's incredible to me when I realize how unaware I was then. How could my mind be so occupied with food and eating, yet not notice that this was so? How could I lose my practice, my lover, and my friends, even my religious community, and not realize that it was due to my involvement with food? How could all my aware, psychologically sophisticated, spiritual friends not notice I was slipping away?

How *could* this have happened? I was surrounded by therapists—aware, caring people. My lover was a therapist, my neighbors were therapists, my best friends were therapists, I saw a therapist every week for my own session. I saw a psychiatrist twice a month to consult about my clients. How could it happen that I slowly slipped out of life and lost everything without the heed of all of these perceptive therapists?

The answer is that we were then in the dark ages of disordered eating. As a doctoral candidate in psychology, I was exposed to less than a day's worth of instruction on alcoholism, nothing on addiction or the addiction process, and the term "eating disorder" had not yet been invented. Just ten years ago, no one in my circle of professional friends talked of eating disorders. (When we did get together, however, we spent a lot of time eating.)

If all this had happened fifty years ago, mine would have been another wasted life. Fortunately, I lived long enough to survive past the cusp of eating disorder unawareness. I finally told one friend, a sober alcoholic, that I ate sugar all the time, had no energy, and had little will to live. Our lives are blessed with these friends who hand us gently from one phase to the next. She said I sounded like her in her drinking days. She told me where to get help.

I went and kept on going. I started out angry, snappy, brittle, fearful, and sad. I was often codependent, egocentric, phony, and dramatic. But I got help despite showing my worst, most unattractive sides to the people who were helping me.

Early in my recovery I remember reading about a woman who, earlier in her life, had thought nonstop about eating. She had gained a normal life, and now she rarely thought about eating. She ate her three meals a day; she didn't turn to food when she felt bad. I remember reading that article as if it were about a person who had learned how to fly. I couldn't imagine a life that wasn't centered around food.

Now I too have a life that isn't centered around food. I can't believe the many changes. I'm living where I want to live. My practice is thriving. I love my work again. I have wonderful friends and an excellent therapist who understands food addiction.

When I first started recovery, the changes came slowly. Some of the changes were agonizing. But nearly from the beginning, every step I took brought me to a place much better than the wasteland of my previous existence. Right away, recovery improved my life. And it began a positive process that led in five busy years to the kind of life I always wanted to have.

HAPPINESS AND REAL LIVING

You too can have the life you want. Perhaps you have almost given up hope. Perhaps you've quit dreaming. In a minute I have an assignment for you, but please finish reading this paragraph first. The chapters of this book have been arranged purposefully. If you will read them in order and follow the assignments and suggestions in order, you will give yourself the best possible chance at finding clarity, true happiness, and real living. If you skip around, however, you may miss important building blocks that make later assignments valuable. Later assignments in this book are hard. They require the strength you'll build by doing the earlier assignments.

It is especially tempting to skip to the weight-loss chapter, chapter 15, because when you are in the grip of your eating disorder, you will have the strong idea that all your problems are caused by your weight. I wish I could write that chapter in a code that could only be understood by reading the preceding chapters of the book first.

Take my word for it: If you try losing weight without applying all the other principles in this book, your efforts will fail just like all your diets failed. You have a choice. You can give yourself a real chance at recovery by reading the chapters in order, or this book can gather dust with all of your diet and self-help books—another lost hope.

YOU ARE IMPORTANT

Your life is important. An eating disorder has thwarted it. The disorder has interrupted your thinking, distracted your purposes, stolen many of your hours, and quite possibly, it has also stolen chances, relationships, and opportunities.

I believe with all my heart that you have special, unique contributions only you can give to the world. I believe experiences are waiting for you that are especially for you. I want you to be able to give what you have to offer, and I want you to receive what is there just for you.

This is a world where nothing natural is wasted. Dead trees become food for the next generation of forest. Energy creates matter. Matter becomes energy. Each life gives life to another in both living and dying. In such a world, your life has meaning. You may have lost track of what that meaning is, but it is there for you and you can find it again.

Remember, the assignments in this book are based on the principles explained in each chapter. Read the chapter before doing the assignment. The assignments are important, but understanding the reasons for the assignments is no less important.

FINDING YOUR OWN LIFE

Do you know what you want from life, or has food eclipsed the possibilities? Do you sense your special purpose in this world, or are you so defeated by the bondage to food that you've lost belief in yourself? Struggling against food may have robbed you of the energy to dream. It may have stolen your belief that you deserve to have the things you want.

It's time to reverse the harm done to your self-esteem. We are given wants so we can discover our needs. You deserve to receive everything you need. This beginning exercise is for the purpose of opening a door into your dreams.

1. For five minutes, dream about the life you'd like to be living. Picture the house you'd like, its setting and neighborhood. See the friends you'd like. Picture what you'd like to be doing. Picture your relationships with loved ones. What are they like? How do you want to feel? How does it feel to be you in the life you want?
2. Do one of the following:
   Option 1. Write a description of the future life you want. Be as specific as possible; that is, use words to draw the picture of the life you want.
   Option 2. Make a collage with pictures cut out of magazines that show the future life you want.
   Option 3. Draw your ideal life on paper. Symbolize in some

way your relationships, your work, and your feelings about yourself. Use stick figures, symbols, or pictures for the drawing.

3. Hold your drawing or your description or collage to your heart and say, "This life is mine. This life happens for me. Every step I take brings me further into this life."
4. Repeat step 3 each morning or evening or both for a week. Then put your drawing or description in a place where you will see it daily. Once a day say, "That life is mine."

TEST YOURSELF

Are You a Sugar Addict?

1. Do you think about sugar products frequently during the day?
2. Do visions of certain candies or sweets get stuck in your mind, rarely going away until you obtain the snack and eat it?
3. Are you aware of the location of every sweet thing in your house or kitchen? For example, could you tell me exactly where every package of cookies, every Twinkie, every piece of candy is lurking?
4. If special sweets come into the house, such as a box of candy or homemade cookies, are you haunted by them until they are gone (that is, eaten)?
5. Do you have a very clear awareness about how much of any sweet is left? Do you get angry when you think there's a half-piece of pie left in the fridge and find that someone has snitched some so that only an eighth is left?
6. Do you hide the evidence when you've eaten sweets? Do you wash pans or conceal wrappers so that your mate or children won't know that you've eaten?
7. Do you sometimes try to get everyone out of the house so that you can curl up and eat your special food without anyone knowing?
8. At a party, do you try to disguise your trips to the dessert table? Do you make excuses for the size of your helping?

9. Are you less interested in an activity if no food is involved? For example, if a dear friend were having a party with absolutely no food and an acquaintance were having a party to launch the arrival of a new pastry chef with fresh samples of his desserts, and these parties were at exactly the same time, would you have difficulty deciding which party to attend?
10. If I mention a holiday, is your first thought the food associated with it? Let's try it: Valentine's Day. July Fourth. Easter. Anniversary. Birthday. State fair. Circus.
11. Once you start eating sweets, is it difficult to stop?
12. Do you often break your own rules about when you'll stop? For example: Do you set rules such as, I'll only have two cookies, I'll only eat one bowl, and then break these rules and set new ones, only to break these, too?
13. After you eat all you can (the bag is empty or until you hurt), does your mood change? Do you feel dreamy or out of it? Is your thinking fuzzier?
14. If you'd planned an afternoon of eating and your best friend came to the door, would you try to get rid of her so you could keep eating? Would you feel impatient for her to go? If she called on the phone, would you try to end the conversation quickly? If a housemate came home unexpectedly that afternoon, would you feel angry and cheated?
15. Do sweets make up too high a proportion of your daily food intake?
16. You are at a dinner party and the woman next to you leaves half a piece of pie on her plate. Do your eyes keep straying to that piece of pie until the waiter mercifully takes the damn thing away?

Are You a Refined Carbohydrate Addict?

1. Do you get strong cravings for specific carbohydrates, such as garlic bread or crackers or pasta?
2. Will you go far out of your way to get a specific type of bread, such as scones or homemade breads?
3. At a spaghetti dinner, do you look at the garlic-bread basket and identify a piece that you really want? As they pass the basket, do you watch in suspense to see if anybody else takes

it before the basket gets to you? If somebody takes it, do you feel disappointed? If your husband takes it, do you feel angry?

4. Do you have rituals around bread products? For example, blueberry muffins every Sunday morning, a sausage biscuit on the first morning of vacation?
5. Are refined carbohydrates (bread, pasta, white rice) a substantial proportion of your daily food intake?
6. Faced with a choice between a large scoop of tuna salad on a lettuce leaf or a tuna-salad sandwich, which attracts you more?
7. Is a hamburger without a bun like a face without a smile for you?
8. At a snack table, do you return most often to the crackers or to the celery?

ARE YOU A FAT ADDICT?

1. Is a baked potato just an excuse to carry butter and sour cream? Is bread a good reason for butter?
2. Does whipped cream bring joy to your heart?
3. Is an evening with chips and dip very nearly perfect?
4. When you discover a new potato chip, do you get excited and want to tell all your friends about it?
5. If you are hurtling down the highway at 50 miles per hour and drop a chip in your lap, do you paw around trying to find it, rather than waiting until you stop the car?
6. Is the difference between fried fish and baked fish like the difference between color television and black and white?
7. If you go to a movie and don't get any popcorn (or anything else), do you sit in front of the screen thinking about buttered popcorn more than the picture? Are you astounded that I might consider you'd go to a movie without getting buttered popcorn? If the butter machine is broken, does it sort of ruin the whole outing?

If you answered yes nine times or more in all, you may be addicted to food and eating. A yes to more than half the questions within any one category raises the possibility that you are addicted to that category of food items. If so, you are not at fault.

Very likely a combination of factors contributed to the development of your addiction.

You can change. With time and careful attention, you can have a free and joyful life not controlled by food. This book tells you how to do it.

1

ADDICTION IS AN ILLNESS

SET UP TO FAIL

For years, we have been saying to ourselves and hearing others say to us—both rudely and subtly—that all we have to do is stop eating: "Put down the fork. You'd be so pretty if you lost weight. Your sister eats just one of those."

These messages are demoralizing. Like drops of water on a bar of soap, over time our self-esteem is worn away by them. We have been told we can control our eating, and God knows we've tried. We've not only tried and failed diets countless times, we've abused our bodies with extremes in deprivation or exercise or by eating, say, only bananas for three days.

Rather than being told that we were up against something harder than we alone could fix, we concluded that the fault was in us. Since we thought we were supposed to be able to control it and had failed, we decided we must be weak. We believed we had no self-control.

Thus, we also abused our emotional selves. We told ourselves we were stupid or weak. We abused ourselves when we tried an extreme diet that had no chance of succeeding because it was too foreign to our tastes and schedules. Of course we couldn't maintain such a diet. Of course we failed. Then we nodded our heads and said, "I failed again." *We* took the blame for all our failed attempts.

No one helped us realize we were trying to control something beyond our control.

We are not like normal eaters. We can't tell ourselves to stop eating any more than a person can stop a cold by telling herself to quit sneezing.

When we start a diet that has little chance of succeeding, we set ourselves up to fail. Later I will talk about the impulses and desperation that cause us to send $89.95 to some company that has promised amazing, quick results with its diet plan. But the point here is that continually hoping something will change, trying some extreme measure out of desperation, and failing again are abusive experiences.

I have bad news and good news. The bad news is that change is slow and takes lots of work. Up until now we have been putting our efforts into short-term solutions that barely scratch the surface of the problem. If we really want things to change for us, it takes slogging away for a long, long time, sometimes years.

The good news is that change really is possible. You can go through a process that will truly change your relationship with food. You can have hours, days, even weeks, when you relate to food normally. Instead of being obsessed with food throughout the day, you can live almost casually in relation to food most of the time.

Coming up is an assignment. It will help you become more aware that the cycle of feeling bad about yourself, starting a diet, and failing has brought you abuse. You deserve comfort for having experienced this abuse. Here's an opportunity for you to make a commitment to yourself—that you will treat yourself kindly by learning ways of avoiding similar abuse in the future.

◇

ASSIGNMENT 1.1

Self-Acceptance

1. List ways you've abused yourself, physically with extreme weight control measures, and emotionally with negative self-messages, because of your problem with food.
2. Ask forgiveness from your body for the contortions it's been put through. Assure it that you are learning a new way to treat it that will make it healthier and will also teach you not to abuse it in those ways again.
3. Sit back in a comfortable chair with a teddy bear or pillow. Wrap your arms around yourself and the bear or pillow. Close your eyes. Send yourself warm, loving thoughts. Give yourself some sympathy for how hard it's been to handle this difficult problem all by yourself.

FOOD ADDICTION

Do you understand what an addiction is? An addiction is dependence on a substance or activity to the extent that normal, healthy functioning is impaired. Food addiction is characterized by loss of control over eating, habituation to food, possible physical dependence on food, and negative consequences in any major life function, such as health, work, intimate relationships, friendships, moral and spiritual development, or in relation to the law.

Loss of control over eating can manifest itself in many ways. Loss of control can be over the *types of food chosen*.

A healthy daily food plan includes some protein, some dairy products, plenty of fresh vegetables, some fruit, lots of water, some fiber and grains, and a small amount of certain fats. To eat one food category to the exclusion of others or to eat disproportionately from the food groups is one type of loss of control. For example, many food dependents/addicts eat excessive amounts of sweets and starches. To eat lots of bread and few vegetables or to eat lots of fried foods to the exclusion of fruits and/or vegetables are other ways a person's eating can be unbalanced.

Loss of control can also be seen in eating *excessive quantities* of food. Some food addicts eat healthy, balanced meals, but two or three times the amount the body actually needs.

For most food addicts, it's easier not to eat at all than to stop eating once started. This aspect of food addiction leads to odd food habits, such as not eating all day and then eating from dinner until bedtime. Such a schedule actually promotes out-of-control eating and promotes weight gain. There can be a physical basis for this, and I'll explain that in chapter 2.

Loss of control can mean *difficulty stopping eating* once it's started. Or it can mean that strong urges to eat are difficult to resist. We get a picture in our heads of a certain food and feel driven to obtain it and eat it. The drive is so powerful and yet so nearly unconscious that we may in some ways not even be aware of it, even though it propels us to figure out how to get the food and get it in our mouths.

The drive may be so strong that *we lie or manipulate others* in order to satisfy it. We may lie, even though we are deeply religious or spiritual and fastidiously honest in all other areas of our lives. It's this crossing of our own moral boundaries that is a hallmark of addiction. The urge to eat is so strong we'll defy our own moral standards.

Loss of control may be seen in *eating at inappropriate times or places.* Additional signs of food dependence are, for example, eating many times a day instead of three (or six, in the case of certain medical problems), eating an hour after a normal meal, or eating at work when it's forbidden.

Sneaking food into a situation or setting that is not a normal situation for eating is another warning sign. For example, sneaking a bite from the snack hidden in your desk drawer when you are supposed to be working, or sneaking food into the night table so you can have a bite when your bedmate falls asleep, or sneaking food into the bathroom or shower so that no one catches you finishing off an extra handful of cookies—these are all outside of normal eating patterns.

Yet another instance of loss of control is *taking extreme measures to obtain a particular food,* even possibly risking injury to get it. To risk an accident by veering across three lanes of traffic because the urge for a sweet is so strong you can't waste time driving another half-block and turning at the light, or dipping into your lap for a potato chip while driving 55 miles an hour on the interstate, or getting dressed at 10:00 P.M. to drive through rainy, slick streets to get a sweet—these are all signs that food is in control, not you.

When we do these things, we know in some part of ourselves that this is weird behavior, yet knowing that, we still can't stop ourselves. This is loss of control.

Habituation to food means depending psychologically on food. Examples of psychological dependence are reaching for a sweet when you come home from work as a reward for making it through a day and to make up for spending the day focused on others (similar to the five-o'clock martini), chomping on crisp carbohydrates out of anger because a good friend let you down, or spooning in a frozen sweet because you're lonely and needing comfort. Psychological dependence arises when food is repeatedly used to cope with life.

With certain people, the bond with food is quickly and forcefully established. With many compulsive eaters, this starts very early. Many of my clients can remember extra efforts to get hold of sweets at five years of age. I remember clearly the taste, feel, and consistency of a candy bar I made elaborate efforts to have money for when I was very small.

As Steven Levenkron[1] has pointed out, our first discomfort in life is met with food. After the violent passage through the birth canal, we are given milk. And the most frequently repeated comfort given us as infants is food. The bottle is often used to stop crying regardless of the cause.

With this as a common start, why isn't everyone overdependent on food? I'll discuss this in detail later, but to some small extent, almost everyone is dependent on food for relief of more than hunger. Food is used for many purposes other than nutritional survival. It is used to soften people up socially, to sell houses, to manipulate business sales, to impress a date, as a centerpiece for activities, to stabilize families, to unite a culture. In fact, food is probably used for psychological purposes more than any other activity or substance.

For some of us, however, food is like a lifeline, an essential tool in our emotional survival kit. It takes us away from stress, it numbs our fears and worries, it stops the world and lets us get off. It's a womb, a haven, a cave, an escape, and a refuge.

Eating is an automatic response to feelings—so quickly applied without thought—that breaking this pattern takes tremendous sustained effort. To diminish the power of the bond with food takes a revolution. If food has become a cornerstone, and the cornerstone is to be removed, an equally strong foundation must replace it.

Physical dependence or physical addiction to a substance means the body has altered in some way that makes the absence of the substance painful. This discomfort may be due to a number of factors, but at least three occur with most substance withdrawal.

First, most addictive substances are used to mask pain. The more the substance is relied on, the more we become used to the pain being absent. When the substance is absent, the way in which it mitigated pain is also absent. Without the mask, the pain is, in contrast, worse.

Second, the adjustments the body made to accommodate the presence of the substance may, in the absence of the substance, be painful. With cocaine, for example, the nerve cells have developed extra receptor sites to adjust to the changing concentration of neurotransmitters. This is a physical adjustment resulting from the use of the drug. When the cocaine is withdrawn and the neurotransmitters are no longer held within the synaptic gap, these extra receptor sites hurt. (And it is the presence of these extra sites, which never go away, that make readdiction swift if the person begins using again, no matter how much time he has been drug-free.) These biological changes, and the chemical activities within the brain, will be discussed in more detail in chapter 2.

Third, the body has attempted to learn to operate despite the substance. With alcohol addiction, the body has learned to function as normally as possible despite the presence of a powerful depressant. Since alcohol is a depressant, the body's counteraction must be in the direction of hyperactivity. Add increased heart rate, increased body temperature, and increased brain activity to depressant action, and the person appears normal.

Factors have been averaged. Take away the alcohol, and the hyperactivity is still there. The person is nervous, jumpy, hot, has trouble sleeping, and the vital signs are increased.

So physical addiction occurs when neural functioning and structure are altered as a result of the presence of the chemical. The addictive substance has actually caused an alteration in the organic structure of the body. This physical change makes the presence of the substance imperative.

The signs of physical addiction are increased tolerance, cellular adaptation, and withdrawal symptoms. How is it that one drinker can put away ten strong drinks that would cause another to sink under the table?

Two factors are in operation. The alcoholic's system has adapted metabolically. It has become efficient at processing alcohol. Liver cells have altered in order to do this (at the expense of other important functions).

In addition, the nervous system has learned to operate despite high concentrations of alcohol. When alcohol is withdrawn, the person experiences a host of uncomfortable symptoms that are relieved when alcohol is again ingested. This cycle—discomfort at withdrawal that is relieved by taking the substance—is a strong indicator of physical dependence. It is this cycle that perpetuates use and causes the dependence to become progressively stronger.

It is truly a vicious cycle. Increased use promotes increased cellular change that causes increased discomfort at withdrawal.

When a person is addicted to sugar, refined carbohydrates, and other foods, she reveals the same signs. (Most people who are addicted to sugar are also addicted to refined carbohydrates. Whenever I refer to sugar addicts or sugar addiction, I'm including other food addictions such as refined carbohydrates, corn, and fats.) Similar to the alcoholic who can "hold his liquor," she can eat sugary substances for hours nonstop. (In certain sections of this book, I'll be comparing food addiction with drug and alcohol addiction. For ease and clarity I'll use female pronouns when discussing food addiction and male pronouns when discussing drug addictions. Food addiction seems to afflict females more than males; alcohol and drug addiction, males more than females.)

A normal person may eat a couple of pieces and say, "No more. It's too rich." A sugar addict hears such a statement with awe. We look at those people who don't finish a piece of pie or who leave half a cookie on a plate as if they are not quite normal.

We don't stop eating because we've had enough. We stop when the bag is empty, when our stomachs feel like bursting, when a car turns into the driveway and someone is going to walk in on us. We have been known to finish others' plates (even the plates of strangers in restaurants), go through garbage cans, and shoplift to get sugar. We can eat a half-gallon of ice cream, an entire loaf of bread, and a couple of bags of sugary substances at one time.

Do we have discomfort at withdrawal? You bet. Sugar is, for most of us, a depressant. It tones us down, numbs us, slows us. It masks pain. Take away the sugar, and we are anxious, irritable, angry, restless, and have trouble sleeping. We feel less able to cope. Things seem to be moving too fast and we feel overwhelmed. Does this discomfort go away if we eat sugar? Yes. In its own way, it's as good as a drink.

So, for some people, use of sugar manifests the same signs as more familiar addictive substances. Does it bring about a change in the physical structure of the body? Probably. In chapter 2, I will explain physical addiction in more detail and present the current research and theories suggesting that sugar and other food substances do bring about chemical reactions within some people and that they become dependent on these changes.

If you have strong cravings, if your efforts to control your eating fail repeatedly, if you keep on eating regardless of the consequences for your life, chances are you're addicted to food and maybe addicted to sugar.

In the next assignments, you'll check the extent to which you suffer from these characteristics of food addiction.

ASSIGNMENT 1.2

Making Cravings Conscious

1. For the next twenty-four hours, record the number and length of your cravings for food. Carry a small notebook with you. In it, write the following headings under "cravings":

CRAVINGS

Time	*Length*	*Strength (1 to 10)*	*What Just Happened?*	*Feeling*
An example:				
10:00	5 min.	8	Mom called	Anger/sadness
10:30	6 min.	10	Jim canceled dinner	Disappointment

ASSIGNMENT 1.3

Control Measures

1. List various control measures you've tried. Count the number of diets you've been on.
2. How many rules about food and eating have you set and broken today?

The following illustrates the process of setting rules about food and eating and then breaking those rules, setting new ones, and breaking the new rules.

Rule 1. Before you enter the store, you decide you definitely will not buy a bag of your favorite binge food.

Rule 2. In the store, you find yourself in front of your binge-food section. You decide to buy the bag. (Rule 1 broken.) You make a new rule: I'll only eat three pieces.

Rule 3. You tell yourself you will not open the bag until you get home. You watch the checkout guy to see what sack he puts the bag in. When you get to the car, you rummage through the sack, find the bag, and hold it in your lap as you start the car. You open the bag. (Rule 3 broken.) As you drive out of the parking lot, you eat three pieces. You stop at the light.

Rule 4. You decide to eat just three more pieces. (Rule 2 broken). You eat four pieces. (Rule 4 broken.)

Rules 5 through 11. You keep making new rules and breaking them until the bag is empty.

Rule 12. You feel terrible. To punish youself, you will not eat lunch. You make a rule that you will drive past the drive-thru at the fast-food joint that has good fries and shakes.

Rule 13. You turn into the drive-thru. (Rule 12 broken.) As you wait for your turn to order, you promise yourself you will only order a quarter-pound hamburger. That's good for you and you need to eat something nutritious.

Rule 14. When you order, you order a half-pounder, large fries, a shake, and a cola. (Rule 13 broken.) You tell yourself you will go straight home and not stop anywhere again.

Rule 15. You spy another favorite food store, and so on.

ASSIGNMENT 1.4

The Truth About Consequences

1. List various incentives others have offered you or you've promised yourself if you would change your eating patterns.
2. Cross out the ones that didn't work. How many are left?
3. List various threats of dire consequences if you didn't change. Circle the ones that worked. How many did you circle? Let me tell you something: Failing was not your fault. Food has such a great hold over you only if you are addicted to it.

Can you see that the idea of mind over matter is useless when applied to such a powerful compulsion?

If these assignments are causing you to feel the least bit ashamed or guilty, read chapter 2 immediately.

2

◇

CHEMICAL WARFARE

◇

In this chapter, I'll present the chemistry behind your addiction to food. You may have to push yourself to read about what's happening in your body; some of the information is fairly technical. It is based on results of scientific studies of eating and the effects of food. Every day, new discoveries refine and expand what we know, but enough is now known to demonstrate that an addiction to food has a physical basis.

◇

Let's pretend that most humans feel alert during the day because axeluria pulses through their brains every twenty-two seconds. (I made up axeluria. Don't look for it in stores.)

Let's say you were born with a scanty supply of axeluria, and it trickles through once a minute if you're lucky. You can keep your eyes open, but it's tough going. Other people seem to charge through life and in comparison you feel like you're just shuffling along. You've never known the reason for this, because the relationship between axeluria and alertness is known by only a few scientists who have done important but unheralded studies, and there are no tests for axeluria deficiency, anyway.

Then you discover that if you soak your fingers in quasselmote—a common party activity—you feel brighter. You have more energy. You seem to be more tuned in. Then after a day or two, you wind down. So you soak your fingers some more, and lo and behold, you're recharged again. Before long, you routinely soak your fingers in quasselmote. (I made this up, too.)

Other people engage in social finger-soaking. They get a little charge, they experience about an hour of the need to clean compulsively, but then they become normal again and go about their business.

You gradually soak your fingers more often and use higher concentrations of quasselmote. Your fingers start becoming a little rubbery and you're dropping things, but it's worth it to you because you feel more alert.

Then a terrible thing happens. No matter how much quasselmote you soak in, you're not feeling as alert as you did at the beginning. But if you cut down, because your fingers are really rubbery and your wrists are turning green, you fall asleep.

What has happened? The quasselmote brought about a chemical reaction similar to that caused by axeluria. At first it replaced a function that your body should have been providing. You felt normal alertness.

Then a change occurred. The axeluria tubes in the brain expanded in diameter because of the high quantity of quasselmote in your system. The brain changed in response to the presence of the quasselmote. It began to need the extra quasselmote. Without the quasselmote running through the tubes, they got dry and ached. You had reached the point where you had to keep soaking your fingers to keep the tubes from hurting.

People began to ask why your wrists were green. You wore wide bracelets to cover them up. Even though it had been fashionable at one time to soak fingers at parties, it began falling into disregard because lots of people need their fingers for computers and telephones, and party hosts were driven crazy when all the guests started cleaning compulsively.

You began to feel desperate. You needed quasselmote to function alertly and to keep your tubes from hurting, but your fingers were rubbery, you couldn't count money anymore, the green was getting on your clothes, and people considered it weak to be using quasselmote regularly. Yet every time you quit soaking your fingers, you fell asleep and dreamed that your head was drying in a pottery kiln.

You began to hoard your supply of quasselmote, fearing that you wouldn't have enough. You soaked secretly. You felt more and more ashamed about your need for it. Other people could take it or leave it. But you couldn't leave it. You have a job and three kids. You couldn't afford to sleep a couple of weeks, especially when your head hurt so bad while you were sleeping.

Remember, there's no such thing as axeluria and quasselmote. The addiction process, however, is similar. A person uses a substance that other people may use without having problems. Because the substance replaces or causes an effect that the body normally should provide, it feels very good. The person uses the substance again to repeat the good feeling. Over time, the body makes a physical adjustment as a result of the use of the substance. Then the body needs the substance for two reasons—to promote the original effect sought by using the substance, and to prevent pain in the areas that have been altered.

Addictions to alcohol, narcotics, and cocaine are known to follow this cycle. Nicotine and caffeine very likely do likewise. Without doubt, nicotine and caffeine alter brain functioning. If a permanent physical change occurs with nicotine and caffeine use, it has not yet been identified. But all the symptoms of permanent change are exhibited by long-term users.

Substances vary in how quickly they can cause individuals to become addicted and how many people are susceptible to becoming addicted. Not everyone who drinks alcohol becomes an alcoholic. The development of alcoholism can occur within a few drinks or after years of drinking. On the other hand, nearly everyone who uses crack a few times becomes addicted.

Since not all people who drink coffee and alcohol become addicted and since the addiction process in these cases is usually gradual, we sometimes have trouble realizing that addiction has taken hold. Food addiction exhibits these same slippery characteristics. It happens gradually, and people vary in their susceptibility to food addiction in general and also in their addiction to specific foods.

Remember, addiction results when the use of a substance

alters the body physically in such a way that the absence of the substance causes pain. This chapter explains the alteration brought about by certain foods.

Evidence is mounting that folks who get addicted to certain substances do so because of a chemical function that the substance mimics or, if malfunctioning, seems to temporarily improve, but with negative/addictive side effects.

FOOD ADDICTION—A PREVIEW

What is the process by which some people become addicted to food? Here's the short explanation.

We don't have axeluria tubes in our brains. We do have millions of nerves. Nerves are like spiders with tiny little bodies and long skinny legs of varying number and varying length. The end of one leg does not touch the leg of a neighboring nerve. Instead, small gaps must be crossed before messages can pass from one nerve to the next.

Chemicals are released from one leg into the gap, and this chemical is what stimulates the next nerve to pass on the message. We don't have axeluria in our brains. We do have a variety of chemicals that cause varying reactions.

Two types of brain chemicals are involved in food addiction—*serotonin* and *endorphin*. Both chemicals are released from the ends of nerves. When released, they fill the gap between nerves and stimulate the following nerve. What happens when the next nerve is stimulated depends on where in the brain it's located.

Serotonin promotes relaxation, peacefulness, relief from pain, and a decrease in anxiety. Endorphin gives relief from pain and a sensation of pleasure. Both serotonin- and endorphin-releasing nerves are highly concentrated in the part of the brain that regulates eating, sleeping, aggression, drinking, and sex.

It's possible that people susceptible to alcohol and food addiction have a malfunction in their serotonin functioning. Perhaps an insufficient amount is manufactured or it's not released readily enough. A person with insufficient serotonin is likely to feel stress and pain more acutely than someone with a normal amount.

When refined carbohydrates—sugar products, pasta, alcohol, white bread—are eaten or drunk, serotonin is manufactured and released. If someone is stressed or in pain, serotonin gives relief.

SEROTONIN

There's no such thing as quasselmote, but sugar and certain other foods can promote chemical reactions that make the brain function as it normally should in providing relief from pain and stress.

So if your serotonin level is functioning poorly and your life becomes stressful, you can get some relief from that stress by eating sugar. We all learn pain relief very quickly. When something stops pain, we repeat it. If sugar stops pain for you, you'll eat it again.

You may well have developed a dependence on food through such a process. Without realizing it, you were compensating for a brain malfunction by eating. Food was used as a self-medication.

Will you stop eating? If serotonin reaches certain concentrations, it's supposed to tell you to stop eating. It's suspected that some people have a malfunction in this feedback loop. So these folks can eat a whole loaf of bread without triggering the "stop eating" message.

ENDORPHINS

Endorphins are in a different chemical class from serotonin. Endorphins make us feel good. For some people, eating sweets, starches, and/or fats causes the release of endorphins; thus, for these people, eating certain foods relieves discomfort and feels good.

Certain endorphins also stimulate eating. If you eat sugar and *beta-endorphin* is released, you'll want to eat more sugar. That second helping of sugar will release more beta-endorphin and stimulate more eating—a snowball effect. People susceptible to this process can eat enormous quantities of food. A symptom of this problem is having difficulty stopping eating once you've started.

People who compulsively overeat have been found to have extra beta-endorphin and less than normal amounts of a specific kind of *enkephalin*—another chemical similar to endorphins. Beta-endorphin has been repeatedly identified as a chemical that stimulates eating, especially when it's heavily concentrated in certain areas of the brain.

So here we have a clear cause of irresistible cravings—the presence of a chemical (beta-endorphin) that stimulates the need for a substance (certain foods). What about the other prerequisite of addiction—an alteration in structure as a result of use of the substance? It's been found that when sugar is eaten in high concentrations over time, nerve cells do alter in a way similar to the alteration seen in cocaine addiction (although different nerves are involved).

It's likely that a person becomes a food addict when these two chemical situations are present—a serotonin malfunction and an imbalance in the release of endorphins and enkephalins.

What follows now is a much fuller explanation of the above process. If you're still feeling that your eating problem is your fault, I hope you'll keep reading even though the information is technical and sometimes complicated.

AN UNABRIDGED EXPLANATION OF THE FOOD ADDICTION PROCESS

Here's the uncut, unexpurgated, uncensored version of the above explanation. It contains much more detail about how nerves work, the chemicals involved in food addiction, and how these processes affect your eating.

How Nerves Work

Why do you feel happiness? Why do you feel down? "Well," you might say, "because something happened that made me happy or something went wrong and I'm disappointed."

"Okay," I answer. "You can identify events that increase your happiness. Other events decrease it. But what happens in your body in response to those events that allows you to feel your reaction to them?"

You may pause. You've never needed to know this. Some things feel good to you and you try to repeat those experiences. Other things don't feel good. You try to avoid those experiences. It's been relatively simple up to now. You took the process by which this happened for granted.

Let me describe the internal process to you. You feel virtually everything you feel because of chemicals that are released in your body. You feel well-being when certain chemicals are released. You feel pain if certain other chemicals are released. You feel depressed if certain chemicals are out of balance with others or if certain chemicals are depleted.

"So what?" you tell me. "It works automatically. I have no control over it."

"Aha," I answer, "but you *can* affect how it works."

The truth is, you may have quite an effect on your chemical functioning. Not only that, your chemical functioning may be different from that of other "normal" people. This may be the reason you've had such a struggle with food all your life.

"So what's the use?" you ask. "If my chemical makeup sets me up to gain weight and crave foods, I might as well sit down and eat a cafeteria."

Don't buy the cafeteria yet! You may have been eating to manipulate your chemical functioning. Without knowing it consciously, you may have learned to create certain effects in your brain by eating certain things. You did this for a reason.

So here's what I have to offer you:

- I'll show you how to get the effects you want without using food or any other drug or compulsion.
- I'll help you see how to improve your life so that your brain chemicals make you feel better.
- I'll talk about the reasons that might have gotten you into food in the first place.
- And, joy of joys, by the time we're through with each other, you will know, clearly, beyond a shadow of a doubt, that this weight stuff is not your fault.

Wouldn't it be great to feel okay about yourself, to know for sure that you're not a slob, you're not weak, you're not undisciplined? Imagine knowing that you're a great person with wonderful qualities—who happens to have a chemical problem.

YOU ARE WIRED

Our bodies are not wired the way your house is wired. If your dog bites the light cord in two, the light goes off (and maybe the dog, too). In your house, the wiring is continuous from the outlet to the power lines outside. The wires in our bodies are called *nerves*—but they are not continuous; there are gaps in them.

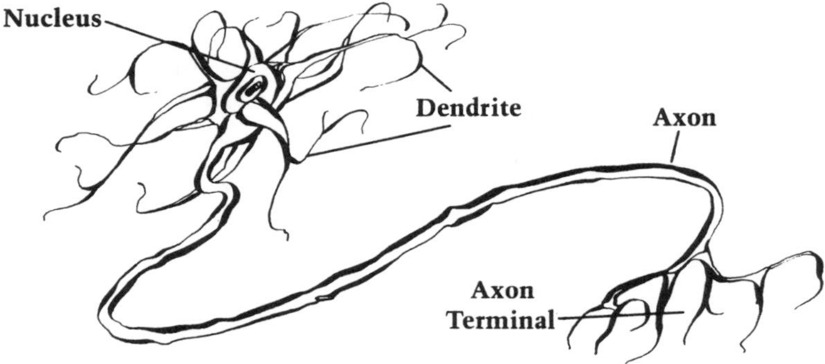

FIGURE 1. Neuron

Figure 1 shows a *neuron* (the smallest unit of a nerve cell). A neuron consists of a *nucleus,* the round middle part, one or more *dendrites,* and an *axon.* Dendrites carry electrical impulses toward the nucleus, and an axon carries the impulse away from the nucleus. The end of an axon widens and is called the *axon terminal.*

Figure 2 shows two neurons. Note that gaps exist between neurons. A gap between neurons is called a *synapse.* Thus, it can be said that we have gaps in our brains. When you step on a tack, for example, the message travels along the neuron until it reaches the end. Then it needs something to ferry the message across the gap to the next neuron (fig. 3). The chemicals that ferry the message across the gap are called *neurotransmitters* (fig.

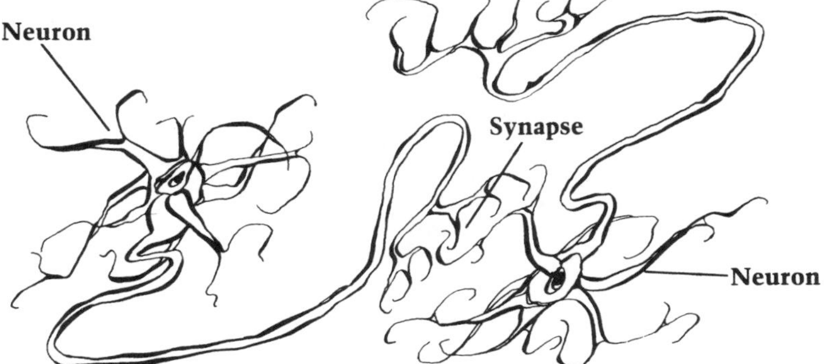

FIGURE 2. Two Neurons

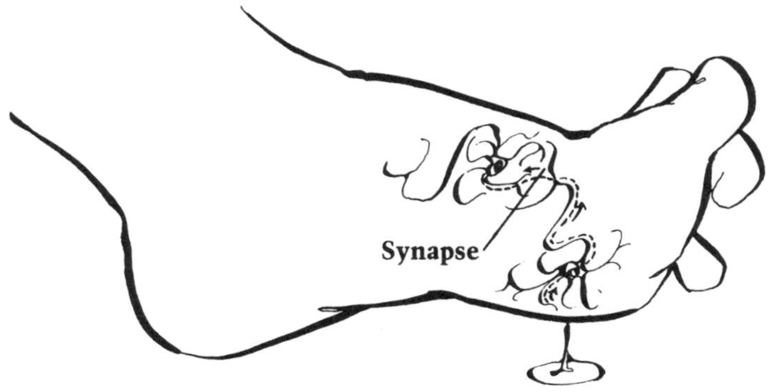

FIGURE 3.

4). This ferrying process repeats over and over again until the brain is alerted that the toe is in distress.

Nerves are one-way streets. Messages travel on them in one direction only. So after the brain catches on, it sends help along other nerves that travel to the mouth and foot (fig. 5).

This whole transaction happens with incredible swiftness considering that an estimated millions of neurons and billions of synapses are involved. Figure 6 shows a close-up of that all-important synaptic gap and what is involved.

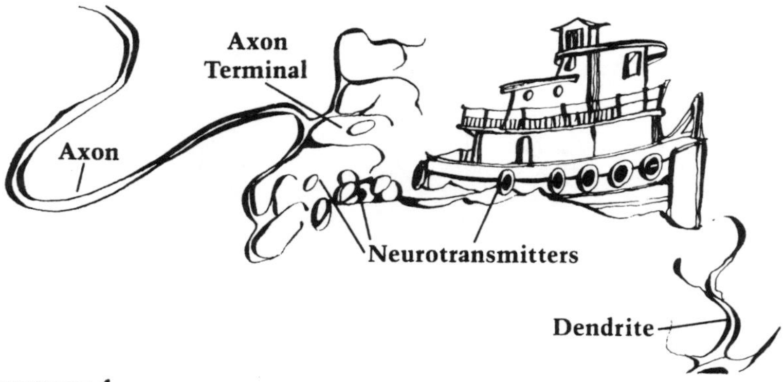

FIGURE 4.

FIGURE 5.

When the electrical message—the *stimulus*—hurtles down the axon, the *vesicles* (holding tanks) where the neurotransmitters are stored release neurotransmitter into the gap. Then the receptors must absorb enough neurotransmitter for the dendrite to be excited.

The entire nerve is covered with a membrane, including the receptors. The neurotransmitter must penetrate that membrane

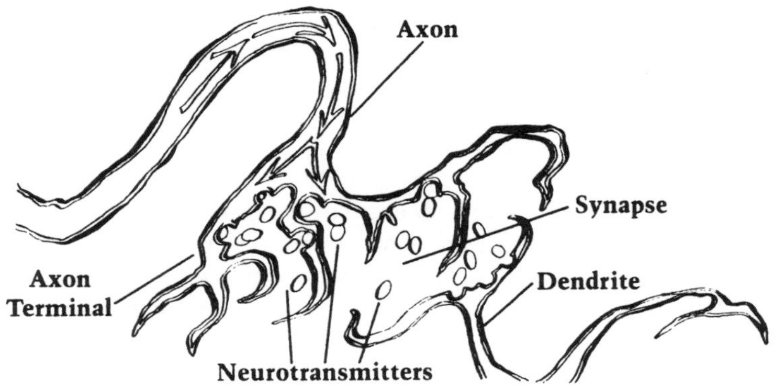

FIGURE 6. **Synaptic Gap**

in order to be absorbed. The neurotransmitter must then be "wiped clean" so that the nerve doesn't keep sending the same message over and over again and so that subsequent messages can get through.

There you have it. The neurotransmitters are essential to this process. Neurotransmitters are being gossiped about quite a lot lately, and for good reason. So far, addiction has been found to involve the synaptic gap and neurotransmitters. That is, in the studies that reveal physical correlates to addiction, the synaptic gap has been found to be the site of involvement.

What are neurotransmitters? They are chemicals that travel from the end of one nerve fiber to stimulate the next one. Neurotransmitters are not created equal. Various chemicals act as neurotransmitters and they all have different effects. Some neurotransmitters are *acetylcholine, norepinephrine, dopamine,* and *serotonin.* These act at specific receptors. Receptors receive neurotransmitters.

RECEPTORS RECEIVE NEUROTRANSMITTERS

At any one axon terminal, only one transmitter is released into the gap and becomes bound to the receptors. The number and sensitivity of receptors can be altered.

Why do we care? Because receptors can be altered by drug use. It's this alteration that brings about lifelong addiction to a substance. So far as is now known, these alterations are never reversed. If similar alterations occur with the use of other addictive drugs (nicotine, opium, alcohol), it may explain why no matter how long a user has been abstinent, if he picks up the drug even thirty years later, readdiction is fast and certain.

The pain of withdrawal is due in part to the fact of this alteration of the body. Thousands of receptor sites have altered to compensate for the use of the drug. They have become used to the drug's presence. Take the drug away, it's missed. The adjustments that have been made are painful in the absence of the drug.

Endorphins and enkephalins are another type of neurotransmitter. These are chemically different than the *monoamines* mentioned above (serotonin, dopamine, acetylcholine, norepinephrine). Endorphin is the body's natural morphine. Drugs such as morphine and opium act at receptor sites that can receive our own internal, self-produced endorphins.

This reminds me of a principle I should insert here. We can only get addicted to substances that mimic what happens in our bodies. No one, for instance, becomes addicted to eating plastic. That's because there's no internal substance that is similar to plastic with a function that plastic could replace. We have no plastic receptors in our brains. Thank goodness.

Let's pretend you are very tiny, about the size of a virus, and you are strolling down a neuron. You climb the knob at the end of the axon, just as serotonin is released. It floods into the cleft and the next nerve gets excited. Now, what do you expect would happen to the host, the person? What will happen to her if the next neuron gets excited?

Depending on which part of the brain that neuron is in, she could feel a little better, feel a little sleepy, feel less like eating. The neurotransmitter serotonin is known to alter mood, decrease appetite, decrease pain, and to facilitate sleep.

The action occurring across the gap depends on many things: the properties of the neighboring neuron, whether it is one that stimulates an action or one that inhibits an action, and where in the brain this particular gap is located. So the stimulation of the next neuron could cause something to happen, such as the release of a hormone that speeds the body up. Or it could cause something to stop happening, like the release of a hormone that relaxes the body.

What, then, makes the action stop? What happens after the next neuron gets the message?

The transmitter is absorbed back into the axon terminal and enzymes come along to sweep up any traces remaining in the gap. This leaves the area free for the next message that comes down the pike. Some other neurotransmitters are also reabsorbed in this way. An exception, acetylcholine, is not. It's destroyed within the gap by enzymes.

ENDORPHINS FEEL GOOD

Magically, now, let's whisk you from a serotonin axon terminal to an enkephalin or endorphin axon terminal. Now we can get very specific about what will happen if an endorphin is released, particularly if we know the region in which the endorphin is released. Endorphins, like opiates, kill pain and give the experience of pleasure. If you eat something and endorphins are released in your eating regulation center, you'll feel good while you're eating.

The *cortex* of the brain is the part at the top of your head. The *cerebral cortex* is where you do your thinking. The more important the function, the deeper in the brain that system is. Systems that regulate survival are the most protected.

The *hypothalamus* is very important because it contains the functions that have to do with long-term survival—eating, sleeping, aggression, drinking, and sex. It's tucked away beneath the cortex and another section toward the center of your head.

This concludes your tour of the nervous system. You have walked to the end of a neuron and observed the release of neurotransmitters, you know that neurotransmitters can either inhibit or excite the neighboring neuron, you know that once the action is completed, the neurotransmitter is either absorbed or wiped out, and you know that the effect of the neurotransmitter depends on which part of the brain it is in.

CHEMICALS THAT FEEL GOOD TO THE BRAIN

If you feel good, then, you can presume that some neurotransmitter is being released somewhere in your brain and is somehow causing that good feeling. So what makes us feel good? What in the world causes endorphins and other feel-good chemicals to be released?

Survival Is a Pleasure

Nature's rule of thumb is this: If an activity is important for the survival of the species, it is pleasurable. Conversely, if an activity is harmful to the survival of the species, it is painful. This makes sense.

Early human beings who found it fun to fall down cliffs and break legs and get huge bruises died off. Early humans who found the drinking of fluids painful dried up in no time at all. The folks who survived enjoyed eating, sleeping, sex, exercise, and got adequate fluids. The ones who didn't like exercise got eaten by whatever toothy carnivores chased them. The survivors avoided injury, sickness, and extremes in weather.

What causes feel-good chemicals to be released? Simple—activities necessary for survival.

It probably was simple during the Stone Age. But we humans like to tamper, and we've tampered with practically everything—not only the atmosphere and dolphins and aging skin and rivers, herons and teeth and gray wolves and flour, but we also tamper with our internal processes. Most of what we've learned to do can either help or hurt, depending on how we use it.

Deliberately or accidentally, we sometimes tamper with the release of our feel-good chemicals, sometimes for very good reasons, sometimes because we have no way of choosing better options for ourselves.

When you eat a meal, you feel pleasure. You probably thought that was because eating is simply inherently pleasurable. No, you have the capacity to feel that pleasure only because chemicals are released in the parts of the brain that moderate and interpret eating. If those chemicals aren't present, you won't feel pleasure with eating—or with drinking, or sex.

ADDICTION

Drug addiction results from tampering with brain chemicals. Alcohol, for example, is a drug that has widespread and immediate effects throughout the brain. It is important for food addicts to look at alcohol addiction for two reasons. First, food addiction and alcohol addiction seem to travel together in families; there may be a chemically similar cause of these problems. Second, food addicts are often at high risk of becoming alcoholic themselves.

So how does alcohol affect the brain? Alcohol depresses the neurons in the brain, primarily by depressing synaptic transmission. There it is again, it affects that all-important gap. Why, then, do people feel good at first when they drink alcoholic beverages? One theory is that the inhibitory centers of the brain are depressed first, so that the drinker experiences a sense of euphoria.

Another theory is that alcohol brings about its effect by altering the membrane of the neuron. According to this theory, at low doses alcohol makes the membrane more permeable and thus more responsive to neurotransmitters (fig. 7). Receiving

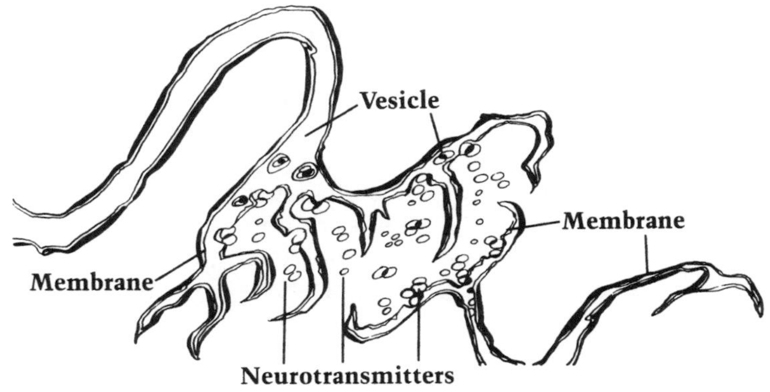

FIGURE 7.

neurons would be more readily excited and a little stimulation would go a long way.

According to this same theory, at high doses the membrane becomes less permeable; ordinary amounts of neurotransmitter therefore no longer stimulate the neighboring neuron. Tolerance, then, or the ability to operate normally despite the presence of alcohol, would mean that the body somehow adjusts to alcohol and overcomes it as much as possible. It could do this by increasing the concentration or amount of neurotransmitter in the gap in order to have a better chance at penetrating the next neuron. Take away the alcohol and then there's too much transmitter and the neighboring neurons are overstimulated.

In fact, the pain of alcohol withdrawal is due to overstimulation. Remove the drug that was acting as a depressant throughout the nervous system and the heart beats too fast, the body temperature rises, the person is jumpy, nervous, irritable, and can't sleep. You see, the brain learned to adjust to the chronic drinking by pumping itself up. It had to do this in order to keep the heart beating and the body temperature up.

Since alcohol depresses, absence of alcohol brings excessive excitability. Tolerance to alcohol is developed very rapidly, so that a hangover is the result of short-term tolerance. A hangover is withdrawal.

Why would anyone get addicted to something in the first place? Who in his right mind would try crack or cocaine, knowing they are rapidly addictive? Why would anyone smoke knowing that most smokers who try to quit experience extreme discomfort for months? Why would someone pick up a drink, especially if he knows that other family members have been defeated by alcohol? Someone whose mind wasn't functioning properly, chemically speaking. Addiction, then, comes about because someone is using drugs to tamper with the brain's chemical functioning. And a person tampers with his brain's functioning because his brain isn't functioning properly.

It's probable that different people have different chemical functioning that predisposes them toward one addiction over another. Which brings us to the subject closer to our hearts—overeating.

FOOD ADDICTION

If a person is fat, why doesn't she just stop eating? You've heard that how many times? You've probably heard that even from doctors and other professionals from whom you expected more understanding.

An overweight person is very likely someone who has been using food to tamper with her brain chemistry. She is tampering with her brain chemistry because something is wrong with it.

So what's wrong with your brain? Recent experimental studies indicate that a malfunction in serotonin functioning may be an important factor in obesity. Serotonin is that neurotransmitter that leads to relaxation and sleep. It decreases anxiety. Serotonin affects mood. It decreases the experience of pain. For some people, inadequate serotonin levels may be causing mild ongoing depression. Carbohydrate intake boosts serotonin release. So people who crave carbohydrates may eat too many of them in an effort to improve their mood or to correct the inadequate chemical levels.[1,2]

Experimental evidence is consistent: Serotonin decreases eating.[3] A feedback loop tells the person, "You've had enough. Quit eating." For some reason, with certain people this feedback loop malfunctions.[4] A person eats a loaf of bread and nothing says, "Stop!"

If you have a disorder in your serotonin functioning, you will experience metabolically caused cravings. You aren't morally weak or undisciplined; your body is screaming to you, "Eat! Eat!"

What causes this? Perhaps you have fewer serotonin neurons than most people. Perhaps this condition was inherited. Serotonin is manufactured at the neuron from tryptophan (which I'll explain below). Perhaps the factory isn't working well or maybe tryptophan isn't getting to the factory in sufficient quantities.[5]

Whatever the cause, chemically caused eating is not your fault. You don't cause it. You're not bad for having this problem. It's a physical abnormality like diabetes.

The problem is chemically based, and you can do something about it. You aren't helpless!

I mentioned earlier that carbohydrates cause an increase in serotonin manufacture. Is that because carbohydrates contain serotonin? No. Serotonin, as I mentioned, is manufactured at the nerve ending. It's made from tryptophan.

Tryptophan is an amino acid. Protein is made of amino acids. When you eat a steak, it's full of different kinds of amino acids. These get separated from each other during digestion and circulate individually in the bloodstream. Amino acids have differing functions throughout the body.

As soon as tryptophan gets to the neuron, serotonin is made and, evidence suggests, is released.[6] The only problem is that tryptophan is often the last fellow into the brain. Here's why.

The brain's no fool. It knows with perfect humility that the rest of the body is nowhere without it. The brain, therefore, protects itself from danger. Since it has the richest blood supply in the body, some chemicals that circulate through the lower body could damage or kill the brain if they entered it. So a barrier surrounds the blood supply entering the brain to screen the chemicals in the bloodstream. It is called the blood-brain barrier.

The blood-brain barrier is very particular about what it permits to pass. Many chemicals are excluded totally, such as serotonin (which answers the question of why, if our serotonin is malfunctioning, we can't take a serotonin pill to compensate).

The chemicals that can go in must be conveyed on carriers. Only so many carriers are available. Not only that, many carriers have exclusive contracts. Some can carry one type of chemical, such as neutral amino acids, and not others, such as basic or acid amino acids.

You eat an egg. It is broken down into amino acids. The neutral amino acids are carried by neutral amino-acid carriers across the barrier, and then the amino acids are reassembled into neurotransmitters, manufactured on the spot.

Carriers transport amino acids across in the proportion present. If the food eaten has many kinds of amino acids and they are greater in concentration than tryptophan, then tryptophan may not make it into the brain. Since most protein foods have a lower concentration of tryptophan than other amino acids, this is most often the case. So if twelve carriers are at the barrier, and you've eaten twelve tyrosine amino acids, eight leucine amino acids, and four tryptophan amino acids, the carriers will not take an equal number of each into the brain. Instead, they'll take six tyrosine, four leucine, and two tryptophan.

We change this situation by consuming carbohydrates. Sugar and starches raise blood sugar. High blood sugar triggers insulin release. Insulin makes other amino acids scamper into the muscles, leaving the tryptophan out, leaving it floating by itself in the bloodstream. With a proportionately higher concentration of tryptophan in the blood, more carriers can load up tryptophan and carry it into the brain.

To get more tryptophan in the brain, eat a tryptophan-rich food, such as turkey or milk, or eat carbohydrates. Guess what food combines tryptophan and sweets? Ice cream, a staple for most overeaters.

Tryptophan has also been shown to reduce moderate pain, both chronic and temporary. A tryptophan-poor diet increases sensitivity to pain. Tryptophan has been shown to augment the pain relief brought about by endorphin release.[7]

If you are an overeater, the following is likely:

1. Your serotonin level is insufficient.
2. This insufficiency may cause you to feel depressed and to be sensitive to pain.
3. You crave carbohydrates to correct the imbalance.
4. Eating carbos, including alcohol and sweets, increases the insulin level in the blood.
5. Insulin causes muscle storage of amino acids that compete with tryptophan for carriers into the brain.
6. Blood levels of tryptophan increase in proportion to competing amino acids.
7. Tryptophan enters the brain.
8. Serotonin is manufactured and released.
9. You feel better. You feel sleepier. Pain is duller.
10. Nothing tells you to stop eating.

ENDORPHINS

What next? Next, endorphins and enkephalins come into play. Remember, endorphins are natural body chemicals similar to morphine. Enkephalins, like endorphins, also give pain relief and a feeling of pleasure, but are of weaker strength than endorphins. Beta-endorphin is well known for stimulating food cravings. *Dynorphin* also increases the craving to eat.

Endorphins feel good. Sugar is suspected of triggering endorphin secretion.[8,9,10] Thus, eating sugar will trigger endorphin release, which will make eating sugar a pleasure. Countless studies show that an increase in beta-endorphin leads to increased eating.

Increased beta-endorphin levels in the part of the brain where eating is regulated have been shown in various studies to increase sugar, starch, and fat intake. Some responses to beta-endorphin are related to dose and context. In animal studies, low amounts of beta-endorphin did not increase intake unless the animals were starving.[11] A high injection of beta-endorphin had no effect unless the animals were stressed.[12] Many other studies have been done, sometimes with conflicting results.

In one interesting human study, beta-endorphin could be separated into two fractions. The first fraction was found to be lower in obese humans than in lean humans, whereas the second fraction was found in obese humans to a significantly higher degree.[13] In another study, obese humans had higher beta-endorphin-to-enkephalin ratios and significantly lower enkephalin activity than the control subjects.[14]

So what does all this mean to those of us struggling with overeating? Not all the votes have been counted, not all the debaters agree on the exact mechanism by which it occurs, but this much is clear. If you overeat, you do so because you are chemically stimulated to overeat.

You're not weak. You aren't stupid. If you have an imbalance of chemicals—too much of some, too little of others—you will eat. While the scientists work out exactly the kinds and doses of chemicals involved, we can do something about it.

Start with these facts. Sugar and starch intake stimulates endorphin secretion. A range of beta-endorphin levels stimulates fat, sugar, and starch eating. (The range of beta-endorphin that causes stimulation probably varies among persons. The foods craved vary among persons.)

A person is probably more vulnerable to this beta-endorphin reaction if she has been fasting, dieting, or under stress. The body may become physically dependent on these physiologically released opiates.[15]

In other words, we may become addicted to our own endorphins and eat to trigger release, because when our endorphins are released, we feel better.

Certain other studies involving endorphins are fairly clear-cut. Among the various types of endorphins, one in particular stands out. Dynorphin is an especially powerful appetite stimulant. Stress triggers dynorphin release. In other words, stress releases a chemical that makes you feel hungry or empty. When you eat in response to this chemically caused hunger, the act of chewing is thought to release another chemical, dopamine, a neurotransmitter that increases comfort level. Here, then, is another chain reaction promoting chemically caused eating. Stress releases dynorphin, dynorphin causes hunger, chewing releases dopamine, and dopamine comforts. Thus, stress was comforted by eating. Many studies demonstrate that mild to moderate stress increases eating. Severe stress usually decreases eating *during the time the stress is severe.* Such stress, however, taxes the body. Severe stress stimulates the sympathetic nervous system, a complex of automatic reactions that are "sympathetic" to your survival when you are threatened. These reactions bring about an increased demand for muscle strength, circulation, and oxygen, and thus nutrients in blood and muscle are used up. When the stress slackens, true physical hunger insures the replacement of spent nutrients.

So the decreased appetite of severe stress is followed with rebound appetite when stress slackens, and this intense craving for food can cause indiscriminate food choices. Sugar, starch, and fat intake can be too great and can trigger beta-endorphin release, which then sets up continued eating past the point of the body's true physical needs.

Thus, we see that mild stress causes the release of dynorphin, which causes an increase in eating, and that severe stress decreases appetite but is followed by a period of rebound hunger when the severity of the stress lessens. The danger of this period for sugar addicts is that they may choose indiscriminately and eat sugar and starch. Poor food choices can retrigger beta-endorphin release and lead to continued bingeing.

Now, how is it that we get addicted to sugar, starch, and fat?

Manipulation of the Endorphin Level

One hypothesis is that a high blood-sugar level increases the sensitivity and number of brain opiate receptors.[16] Studies on animals have shown that glucose does increase the affinity and number of opiate receptors, particularly in the hypothalamus, where eating is regulated.

A creature may be genetically predisposed to have an over-responsiveness to food due to the release of extra endorphins under stress or after fasting. In other words, the secretion of endorphins in a particular stressed animal is insufficient to protect him from the effects of stress. Thus, the ingestion of sugar may be adaptive because the secretion of endorphins provoked by sugar is used as an additional protective mechanism.

What might this mean to you? It could mean that for some reason when you are under stress, the endorphins that would give you relief are not being released. So as you walk around in your stressful life, the discomfort builds and lasts—until you eat something sweet. After eating a sweet, you feel better, because the sweet is able to release the endorphins.

This hypothesis makes intuitive sense to anyone who has struggled with the disorder of overeating. A peculiar quality of the presweet-eating state is the drivenness of it. It's not as if we just casually waltz by the kitchen and, out of perfect freedom to decline, choose to pick up a sweet.

On the contrary, we have no choice, we are driven to get it, driven just as forcefully as any addict who needs a fix. At this point we will lie, manipulate, and cheat. Does that sound rational to you? Of course not. And such an irrational process must have a cause.

The more we discover about how the body works, the more we see that bodies operate as logically as a computer. Our behavior appears irrational only because we don't know every internal step involved. As research and our technical ability progress, I am confident that the day will come when most of these steps are understood. Overeating will be seen as an adaptation to a bodily malfunction. It is an irrational process in the sense that overeating operates without conscious thought, automatically. Fortunately, you need not wait until science finds a solution. You can get relief now, as I'll explain later in this book.

The language of noncompulsive eaters reveals how differently their own process works. They say, "Just forget about it, throw it off, don't let it get to you. Look at me. I just put it out of my mind and went on." People with such good advice are probably being chemically assisted in a way we are not. Their endorphins are probably working just fine. Or they may be one of the millions of Americans addicted to something else that doesn't show as readily as overeating or that is more socially acceptable.

If sweet- or carbohydrate-eating causes an increase in our endorphin levels and/or an increased sensitivity in endorphin receptors, we will quickly learn to eat sweets again to get more relief. Of course, then, sweet- or carbohydrate-eating promotes more eating, and the compulsive eater develops a special sensitivity to carbohydrates.

If sweet-eating causes an increase in the number of endorphin receptors in humans, as it does in animals, it becomes clear why, for a compulsive eater, sugar becomes more and more irresistible. The overeater becomes compelled, even driven to get it, because relief after eating is so immediate. An increase in the number of endorphin receptors would explain why the need for sugar overpowers interest in being with others, why the compulsive eater can eat pounds more sugar than a normal person at a single sitting, why withdrawal is uncomfortable, and why abstinence is so terribly difficult at the beginning.

Scientists may not agree on the specific mechanisms, but clearly something is wrong chemically and/or structurally.

Let's put all this together. Food-addiction-prone people may experience pain more acutely and have lower moods than normal people due to subnormal chemical functioning. Endorphins and serotonin relieve pain. Sugar has an effect on endorphin and serotonin release. Certain endorphins increase eating. Excess sugar can cause an increase in endorphin receptors, a physical alteration similar to the alteration that explains increased tolerance in other drug addictions.

Later, I'll talk about fat and weight loss. For now, I want you to know that just as there's a chemical basis for your need to eat, there's also a chemical basis for the fact that your body stores fat readily and releases it reluctantly.

Congratulations! You've just made it through the most technical, most difficult chapter in this book. You know quite a lot about how the body works. If you are not confused or overwhelmed, skip to the assignments at the end of the chapter. If you are confused, I'm going to explain the physical causes and consequences of overeating in a simpler way and leave out all the ifs and maybes that scientists use to make sure no one thinks they are stepping beyond their research.

YOU WERE BORN

The trouble may already have started if your parents were sensitive to alcohol or sugar, if they suffered from depression, or had problems with blood sugar. If they were overweight or involved in any rigid system such as the military or a strict religious sect, or if they were compulsive workers, compulsive spenders, compulsive sexually, or were perfectionists, the chances are you were born with problems.

You Were Born Sensitive to Pain

Because of insufficient serotonin levels, when you are hurt, you really hurt. If your parents were not skilled at parenting, if they made mistakes with you, it hurt bad.

Sugar and other carbohydrates brought you relief. Carbohydrates affected your endorphin functioning and caused tryptophan to enter your brain cells. Tryptophan manufactured serotonin and it was released. This made you less sensitive to pain, lowered your anxiety, helped you relax, and made you less aware. The increased endorphins stopped emotional and physical pain and gave you pleasure. Stress caused dynorphin release. These various endorphins made you crave more sugar, starch, and/or fat. The rise in endorphins and serotonin improved the effect of each.

Human beings learn pain relief very quickly. If something works to stop our pain, we try it again. Even little beings learn pain relief quickly. If crying brings Mom with warmth and reassurance, we cry again. If eating sugar brings relief and the end of pain, we will eat sugar again.

We ate sugar again. Again it caused the release of endorphins and serotonin. Sugar brought us relief from pain. Sugar also increased our appetites.

We ate more sugar. The more we ate, the better we felt. We did not know we were changing the endorphin receptors in our brains. We did not know we were increasing endorphin receptors. But we may have noticed, as we grew older, that we could eat more sugar than our friends. They would be satisfied with one piece. We weren't satisfied with a bagful.

Gradually, subtly, we became dependent on sugar. We were addicted to our own endorphins and we had to have sugar to get the endorphins to the receptor cells. We became driven to eat sugar. The forms varied. Some of us preferred straight sugar in the form of sweets. Some of us preferred refined starches that, in the body, turn quickly into sugar. Some of us preferred fatty foods. Most of us ate a lot of sweets, starches, and fats.

As the years passed, the addiction became more entrenched. Eating became such a focus for our lives that it became more important than anything else. We began to center our lives around eating. We began to plan what we did in relation to eating.

Oh, yes, by the way, we were gaining weight. We often forgot all about the weight. The important thing was to eat. The weight seemed almost accidental, although we found we could use the weight to hide from others. This would also allow us more time to eat.

All this eating continued to manipulate our brain chemistry as we continued to trigger the release of endorphins and serotonin. We were doing this for two reasons. First, to relieve pain. Second, because we were addicted to the feeling we got when those chemicals were released. They took us away from stress. They made us feel dreamy and out of it.

Originally, long ago, when we started eating to get relief, we had one problem—we felt pain very painfully. Over time, we developed a second problem—addiction to eating. We continued to feel pain very painfully. In addition, we began to need very strongly, with the same force that an alcoholic needs alcohol, the chemicals that eating releases.

We became so driven about eating because of the changes in our brains due to eating high amounts of starches, and because food became the major, sometimes the sole, way of dealing with stress. It was what we knew to turn to, it was dependable, it worked quickly, it never failed, and we could trust it like we could trust nothing else.

Most compulsive eaters are impulsive. You probably want to put this book down right now and stop eating sugar. Most of us hope we can find *the* solution and then this whole mess will be over with. If you quit reading and quit eating sugar, you will still be addicted to eating, you will still feel pain more painfully than others, and it will be only a matter of time before the stresses of life will send you thrashing through your pantry.

The physical addiction is one giant part of the problem, but the problem has other parts too. *Recovery comes about when we pay attention to all the parts together.*

We've just looked at the genetic and physical causes of your eating disorder. In the next chapter, we'll look at the external, environmental causes of your eating disorder. Both are important. Both must be attended to if you are going to get relief from overeating.

ASSIGNMENT 2.1

Disease Inventory: Part I

This exercise has four parts. The first part is given here. The remaining parts appear in following chapters (on pages 75, 102, and 172). I suggest you acquire a notebook that you use just for the inventory. When you have completed all four parts, you will have a comprehensive survey of your relationship with food and the factors that contributed to the development of your disordered eating. I hope you will also see that you contracted this disease due to factors beyond your control. Remember, the most important skill needed for recovery is self-honesty. As you write the inventory, the more honest you are, the more it will give you.

GENOGRAM OF ADDICTION

What evidence is there that you inherited the susceptibility to this addiction? Trace the origin of your disease in your ancestors and role models. Make a genealogy chart of as many ancestors as you or other family members can remember. Next to each name, use the symbols listed below to indicate their involvement in addictive or compulsive behavior. Be alert to clues that point to skeletons in the closet, such as: "He had a small drinking problem," "He died of liver disease," "She had lung cancer," or "He was pretty heavy."

Circle: Female
Dotted line: Death
FA: Food addict
D: Drugs
$: Compulsive spending or shopping
G: Compulsive gambler
CO: Codependent or caretaker
VR: Very religious
Dp: Depressed
ED: Eating disorder

Square: Male
Slashed line: Divorce
A: Alcoholic
S: Compulsive sex
CW: Compulsive worker
N: Nicotine
R: Rigid
I: Chronically ill
Db: Diabetic

3

DEPRIVATION

Let's say chapter 2 has convinced you that you have a chemical problem. So you'll learn about how to fix the chemical problem and you're on your way, right?

No. Not that simple. Attention to chemicals isn't enough. It's important, but if that's all you do, you'll probably fail. Do you need another failure? Give yourself a break for a change. Give yourself all the help you need instead of the minimum.

LESS LASTS

The minimum—a key word. Most of you are probably well-acquainted with having the minimum—of something important. Minimum parenting, minimum attention, minimum boundaries, minimum assistance as children, minimum sanity in the environment, minimum safety, minimum reason to trust, minimum love. If you received minimal emotional support growing up, you are very familiar with deprivation. Deprivation of emotional needs is abusive and harmful. It creates long-standing difficulties in later life and has consequences that reach far into the future. It can influence us daily in almost all of our interactions decades after the original deprivation occurred. Let's look at one example.

A CASE HISTORY

She was a dear baby. Her first experiences with others involved getting her needs met. Her first encounters with pieces of the world, of life, were centered around her needs. When she felt pain, discomfort, cold, or hunger, she could not fix it herself. The length of time it took for someone to respond made an impression on her. The length of time she was hungry or in pain made an impression. Her caretakers were inconsistent. Sometimes she got help right away. Sometimes she was uncomfortable for long periods of time. One of her caretakers, the big female one who helped her most, was distracted. She tended to her brusquely in a slapdash fashion and then disappeared as if she always had a lot of pressing business and could barely afford the interruption the baby was causing. This made an impression.

The baby rarely saw the other big caretaker. When he did do something, he was rough and left something undone, like the diaper not fastened or the blanket off. Later, when the big female caretaker came by, she'd yell at the other one. This made an impression.

The small caretaker was around a lot, but when she would help, she was unsure of herself, giving a sense of incompetence. She did, though, give a feeling of caring. All this made an impression.

Through infancy and childhood, the child continued to depend on others to get her needs met. As her world expanded beyond the safety and limits of the cradle, so did her needs. Gradually, also, she began learning how to meet her own needs, though the ability to meet a need always lagged years behind the development of the need itself. For example, at birth, someone had to get food and bring it to her. As she matured, she gradually learned to feed herself. It took a couple of years for her to learn to get food that was already prepared and set out, more time for her to understand how to get stored food, and longer yet to prepare food.

As an infant, she depended totally on her family for physical and emotional safety. When she learned to walk and explore, she gradually learned how to avoid physical danger. She learned to avoid the hot stove, the busy street, the edge of the bluff. Sometimes she learned these things at the risk of her self-esteem, at the risk of her emotional safety. The time she fell down the embankment, for example, she was scared. That feeling of nothing under her feet was awful. Then her mother jerked her up and yelled at her, "You stupid thing. Didn't you see the edge?"

From this she learned two lessons. She learned to avoid edges and she learned she was expected to know what she didn't know. She was regularly exposed to interactions that threatened her emotional safety.

At birth she was totally dependent for physical contact on the adults around her. If she needed to be held or cuddled, she had no specific way to express it. Not until she could crawl and pull herself up could she move toward people. Real ease in going toward someone had to wait until she could walk. She could communicate the need to be held by lifting her arms to someone, but she would keep doing that only if it worked now and then. (It takes many years, sometimes twenty or thirty years, to say out loud, "I need to be held." A four-year-old will say it only if she's been taught to say it and then has been responded to.)

So she communicated her need for touch by lifting her arms, by crawling up on someone's lap, by grasping Mom around the legs, by sitting as close as possible. She learned about requesting contact from Mom's and Dad's responses. When Dad pushed her away or went away or ignored her outstretched arms, she tried someone else. If Mom pushed her away or went away or ignored her, she tried her sister.

She learned pretty quickly not even to try Dad. If Mom was busy, Mom would say something like, "Go away, damn it, can't you see I'm busy?" The child was picking up lots of lessons from Mom: I'm supposed to watch Mom, read her mood, and figure out whether or not I should approach her. It's not okay to ask for comfort or contact at the wrong time. A lot of things are more important than me. I'm not supposed to need cuddling.

Mom might say, "You stupid kid, you're too old to be held." She might even make a joke out of it and tell her friends at a party ("Do you know what that dumb kid of mine did?"). The child then would learn she had no privacy, that if she made a mistake, lots of people would know and laugh at her. It was the kind of thing that would make her afraid to make mistakes. She would become very vigilant. She would not want to take risks.

Many potential lessons existed in the responses of others. For example, if she snatched her brother's toy and he punched her shoulder and she cried, then Mom picked her up. If the only time Mom picked her up was when her brother hurt her, she'd learn quickly a variety of ways to be hurt by her brother—a small price to pay for being held.

She was deprived—not of the basics for survival; she was fed, clothed, and sheltered (and her parents were quick to point that out when she wanted any more than this). She was deprived of cuddling, safety, acceptance, appropriate structure, safe curiosity, personal power, expression, meaning, and individuality.

To varying extents, they fought against her natural developmental process. For example, initiative is developed between the ages of three-and-a-half and six. She tried to explore her world and her body. She tried to take a toy apart to see how it worked. She had lots of questions. Her mother was too busy for questions. "Go away, can't you see I'm busy?" "You stupid kid, I paid fifteen dollars for that toy." "Where are you putting your hands?" "Shame on you."

The child was caught between the natural forces arising from inside herself and her preoccupied parents. One healthy parent could have made a big difference. One healthy parent could have mediated the stream of negative messages being sent to the child's self-esteem. With two parents unskilled at parenting, she had no way to sift through their negative messages, no way to pick out what was true about her and what was a mistake on their part. So from millions of interactions, she learned who she was. She learned her needs came last, that she should be very vigilant, that she should know everything, that she should not add to the concerns of others, that people would be either too busy for her or entirely absent, that if she made a mistake she was stupid, and that people would laugh at her. She learned a catalogue of lessons about who she was and how she should act.

What she didn't learn could fill a library. She didn't learn she was worthwhile, wanted, or valued. She didn't learn she could take the time of others. She didn't learn to play, explore, take risks, ask questions, or have a dissenting opinion. She didn't learn she could disagree. She didn't learn how to ask for what she wanted. She didn't learn healthy ways to handle conflict, hard feelings, or disappointments. She didn't learn how to communicate feelings. She learned little about healthy grieving. She experienced little intimacy. She did not learn how to be comfortable with her body. She knew survival. She didn't know living.

At seventeen, she launched into the world with a serious deficit in skills. And she did not know she had this deficit. She was pronounced an adult by adults. She was soon into adult situations. She was old enough to have a child. An explorer would be better prepared to cross the Grand Canyon packing a can opener and a piece of string than she was to be an adult, much less a mother. Every day, she suffered from the lessons she had learned and the ones she didn't learn. Every day, low self-esteem cheated her out of joy, peace, and accomplishment. Every day, she was affected by her inability to take her own needs seriously. Not knowing how to communicate feelings made mincemeat out of her relationships. Life was a terrible uphill struggle.

THE OVEREATER'S STORY

Most overeaters have a similar story. The principal players may act somewhat differently, but the consequences are the same. Most overeaters have serious, profound deficits that have led to painful losses and years of suffering. My experience as a therapist has shown me that the lower the self-esteem, the more serious the abuse. Taking a stick to a child is abusive. Screaming to a child that she is stupid for asking that a need be met is also abusive. Not rescuing a child who has been screamed at, not counteracting the actions of a sick parent, is abusive as well.

My clients often defend their parents by saying they weren't beaten. Children have a right to much more than not being beaten. But these clients expect the minimum. If they weren't beaten, their attitude proclaims, it wasn't that bad. If your self-esteem is low, you can count on the fact that you were abused. If it's very low, you were very abused. Remember that to a child, distance, coldness, abandonment, and noninteraction are abusive. The reason doesn't matter to a child. A young child could die if she were abandoned. She knows she's too small to cope with the world.

A child who is kept at a distance, who receives no warmth or assurance, is a child in constant fear of abandonment: If they don't want me, what keeps them with me? What keeps them from walking out and never coming back? Such a child becomes accustomed to fear. The first consequence of poor parenting is that the child learns harmful rather than helpful lessons. The second consequence is that the child becomes accustomed to abuse. Abuse or coldness or meanness becomes familiar. Being treated kindly is unfamiliar. However bad it is, the familiar draws us. The familiar is comfortable even if it's uncomfortable. It seems to fit us. And we know how to respond to it. Our skills match it. We have learned skills to deal with abuse. We don't have skills to deal with kindness.

No wonder women marry men like their mothers or fathers, no wonder we are drawn over and over again into relationships that replicate our childhood experience. It hurts but it's familiar and we know how to behave. It is also an opportunity to work out the unexpressed feelings from childhood. What did you need as a baby, as a child? Take a minute right now and make a list. Then we'll compare yours to mine.

ASSIGNMENT 3.1

Basic Emotional Needs

Let's compare lists. What are some basic needs of a young human?

Physical survival. Oxygen; nourishing, well-balanced meals; fluids; exercise; fresh air; sleep; rest.

Trust. Regular, predictable care.
Affection. Cuddling, holding, loving, respectful physical touch.
Safety. Protection from physical, emotional, and sexual danger.
Boundaries. Actions that preserve identity and sense of self. Appropriate structure that identifies and protects both the adult's territory, jobs, and needs, and the child's territory, jobs, and needs.
Communication. Relatedness through the sharing of thoughts and ideas, explanation, instruction, revealing the inside process of being a person. Support for expression and the development of meaning.
Honesty. Words congruent with actions. Adults taking responsibility for mistakes.
Attention. Listening, watching, and communicating respect and importance by giving time and awareness.
Stimulation. Newness, introduction to differences, support for safe exploration and appropriate creativity.
Tradition. Structure, repetition, security, predictability.
Validation. Confirmation that perceptions, feelings, thoughts, ideas, and wants have a place in the world.
Relationship. A sense of connectedness with others, bonding, intimacy.
Healthy ways to handle feelings.
Personal power, individuality.
Safety and support in working through each developmental task.

I have a few words to say about the last item. As adults, we have a tendency to think our business is more important than whatever business a child is involved in. This is partly an effect of our culture. We place a high value on money and most adult business has something to do with money. It's also an effect of being involved in our own developmental tasks. We all have a tendency to consider our tasks at our own stage of development to be earthshaking and the tasks of other stages less significant. We have a tendency to brush aside children's work, even the work we did as children, as unimportant.

Our developmental thrusts lie behind us like a separate world. When we encounter someone from another developmental stage, it is a meeting as if across a great gap, particularly if the stages are separated by many developmental periods. The outlook, perspective, tasks, and interests of someone in a retirement home are very different from someone wading through middle age. Both are extremely important. Neither is more important.

Each developmental stage is encompassing and absorbing. Some developmental stages clash. Middle-aged parents, busily generating, producing, and creating, often look askance at their greatest creation, their most important product—their teenager—embroiled in the life-and-death struggle of identity development that may manifest tastes, speech, and behaviors horrifying to his or her creators.

Even as adults, our developmental tasks shift. Think about what involved you in your twenties. Compare this to the focus of your thirties. The tasks of a two-year-old learning she is somebody in her own right are as critical and as vitally important as the tasks of a thirty-year-old learning how to contribute to the world or a twenty-five-year-old learning how to be intimate with another human. Indeed, the latter tasks depend on the work done by the two-year-old. So the work of a two-year-old is as vital as the work of a six-year-old and a forty-year-old. It should be validated, supported, and given safe boundaries.

How did our lists compare? Were you expecting less? When you first started out in the world, you knew what you needed. You tried to get it. Something taught you to expect less, to stop trying to get your needs met.

We start life healthy. We start life naturally inclined to communicate our needs. To be sure, our first communications suffer when it comes to the clarity only speech can provide, but we communicate nevertheless. Our communications are integrally connected to our needs. Our needs push out into the open.

The problem arises when our needs conflict with those of our caretakers. A healthy parent can validate both the need and the expression of it. They respond either with the solution to the need or the reason for deferment, making clear that the child is worthwhile even though the need must be put on hold temporarily.

A parent overwhelmed with his or her own personal needs, a parent already fighting her or his own deprivation, an addicted parent, a tuned-out parent, a sick parent, hasn't room for this. An overwhelmed parent becomes even more overwhelmed when presented with the child's needs. So a parent struggling to survive will push away the child's needs in whatever way works. It's not the child's fault, but the child suffers.

Into these deficits many interpretations may fall. A child is an excellent observer but a poor interpreter, because a child's perspective is limited. She has little natural ability to say, "It isn't my fault that they don't hold me. They are busy. I am wonderful. They aren't holding me because their priorities prevent that at this time. But I'm a good, lovable child. I know this is true whether they hold me or not." A child is much more likely to associate the lack of holding with some lack in herself: "They are busy because I'm not lovable enough to get their attention. If I were worth loving, they would hold me."

One attentive adult can thwart such an interpretation by holding the child close and saying, "Daddy loves you. He doesn't know how to express love except by working. You are so lovable. I'm glad you show me when you need to be held," or "I can't hold you long now, because I'm going to work. I love you. After dinner, we'll cuddle, like we did yesterday after I had my resting time." This is one of the essential aspects of good parenting: giving interpretations that preserve the child's identity and developing self-esteem, and honoring the process of asking to get needs met. Teaching the child to verbalize needs without shame is also important.

When a child isn't held enough, she experiences a deficit. It's horrible then if the child is ridiculed, ignored, or hit for asking to be held. It's ghastly if the child asks to be held and is sexually abused. She then learns her needs lead to pain and punishment and will likely aim her wrong interpretation against herself: "If I ask to be held, I am ridiculed. I am wrong to ask for my needs. My needs are wrong. I am wrong to want to be held."

These interpretations can spread so that the child learns to mistrust all her internal messages: "I can't trust my feelings. I felt like I needed affection. If I need affection, I'll be hurt. I'd better not need affection. I better not listen to my feelings. I better not listen to myself. When I listen to myself, I get hurt." Or, in the case of sexual abuse: "If I ask for affection, people I trust touch me in ways that feel wrong and hurt me. When I ask for affection, I am not safe. I am wrong to ask for affection. I better not listen to myself. My needs make people I love hurt me. My needs are wrong. My body is wrong. My body makes me unsafe. I should be ashamed that I want affection."

No untaught child can say, "Mom ridicules me because she hasn't had her needs met either. I am really worthwhile and lovable even though she yells that I'm 'a little brat,' " or, "Dad touches me that way because he has problems. My body is mine and I can choose what happens to it. I'm small and can't get him to stop now, and I can't tell Mom because she's weak and too involved in her own needs to help. But in a few years I'll be bigger and I'll be able to make him stop. I know clearly that this has nothing to do with me. It isn't my fault. I didn't cause this to happen. I'm really worthwhile and good. I know this even though I'm not treated this way." Of course a child cannot supply such an interpretation for herself. We know who we are by the way we are treated. We form our view of the world by the events that happen when we are small.

If we walk around believing our needs are important, that we deserve to find healthy ways to meet them, and that it's okay to ask appropriately to get our needs met, we were taught this by tuned-in, healthy adults. If we live believing we can only expect the minimum, that our needs will probably be passed over, that other people's needs are generally more important, and that we shouldn't ask for what we need, we were taught this by the way we were treated.

These lessons are long-lasting. How we adapt to hurtful and confusing experiences that happen when we are small becomes an invisible part of the way we operate in the world. We become bonded to whatever enables us to survive. As children, we bonded to our parents (because despite whatever harm they did us, we owe them our existence and our physical survival), and we bonded to the techniques we developed to make it through the harm. As adults, it takes lots of work and skilled therapeutic help to perceive the techniques that have become so much a part of us, and to disarm ourselves of them. Because we bonded to our parents and our survival mechanisms simultaneously, it sometimes seems that to divorce our techniques is to reject our parents. Working out this dilemma is another process that takes considerable therapeutic time.

FOOD ADDICTS AND THE MINIMUM

Food addicts are people who have learned to expect the minimum. Our perspective is one of lack and limitation. We expect that there's only so much available, and it will be less than what we need. Long ago we were taught to resign ourselves to getting less. If our needs are consistently unmet, we will adapt but we pay a price; there are consequences. When an emotional need goes unmet, we may try novel approaches. We may try to get it from other people. We may try to persuade ourselves we never really needed it anyway. If it continues to be unmet, does it go away? Let's look at the body. If it gets insufficient oxygen, does it say, "Oh, well, not today. Maybe I can get some oxygen tomorrow"? No, the need for oxygen is not related to the supply. Oxygen is needed whether it is supplied or not.

Affection, trust, safety, and honesty are needed whether they are supplied or not. Emotional needs don't go away. But we can learn to shut them down or to substitute something else for the true need. Food addicts substitute food. Most food addicts—in fact, most people who suffer from eating disorders—have severe, long-term deprivation in regard to their emotional needs, and experience guilt or shame about those needs. Guilt and shame are learned. We learn that our needs are wrong, that we are wrong to have needs, and that we should be content with the minimum. In other words, most food addicts as children were taught to accept deprivation as a way of life.

This lesson was so ingrained that getting enough came to feel wrong or excessive. It's obvious from looking at the list of Basic Emotional Needs on page 53 that as adults we continue to have the same needs. Adults need attention, too. We need someone to listen to us, to uncritically hear us out. We need relationships. We need to connect with others.

But the harm we received as children may interfere with our ability to meet these needs as adults. We need intimate connections with others. But if, as children, we were betrayed, if our trust was broken because adults were so distant, absent, preoccupied, or addicted that our attempts to receive affection or attention were rebuffed, how are we going to trust our friends to act differently?

As food addicts we have some important problems. We have a great deficit made up of unmet needs, but we learned the hard way not to ask for what we need. We developed a system of techniques to get sort of what we needed, indirectly. We adjusted our expectations so that now we expect less than we need. We learned to fill that gap by substituting something to meet the need. Most of the time we substitute food.

You understand by now the physical basis for this. The unmet need, the deprivation, the fear, the shame, are all painful and cause stress. Stress activates dynorphin, which activates the need to chew. You know that happens when a food addict eats refined carbohydrates. The pain goes away momentarily. The need does not. The need is still there and will stay there until it gets attention. Needs are specific. If you need oxygen, water won't do. If you need reassurance, food won't do. After you've eaten, you still need reassurance.

Emotional needs, even some physical needs, have a curious aspect. If they get attention, they are often relieved. For example, if you are afraid of thunder, it helps if someone cares. The thunder is still there, but with caring attention, the fear of thunder can diminish considerably or even go away.

Now can you guess why I advised you to stick with me rather than attempt instant abstinence? Food has rescued you. It hasn't fixed the deficits. If we rip away the bandage, the sore will still be there. If recovery is really going to work for you, we must attend to both problems jointly. We must begin restoring your deficits and attend to your addiction. As we develop ways to counteract the long deprivation you've suffered, we will work on abstinence. Abstinence will give you energy and a clearer mind so that you can be more successful at getting new and old needs met.

THE INEVITABLE FAILURE OF DIETS

It's obvious now why diets have never worked. Any diet that kept you eating sugar also kept alive the chemical triggers for appetite. And diets are systems of food deprivation. No wonder your system recoiled.

We food addicts have a love/hate relationship with control. Many of us have a secret longing for something to come along and control our eating. Time was when we entered a new diet joyfully, not only because our dream of weight loss seemed close to coming true, but because we hoped it would rescue us from the circular agony of hating our bodies, wanting the weight off, and eating anyway. The trouble is that control efforts (diets and rules) never got us off that unmerry-go-round. Food was providing too great a service for us. Food was supplying the nurturing, comfort, escape, and reward that nothing else had.

So you want off the unmerry-go-round. I hope you do. Being controlled by food thoughts, drives to eat, obsessions about the size of your body and wanting to lose weight, and hating yourself, is hell. It can be all-consuming, taking your time, energy, and peace. I promise you this: Unless you follow a system in which you are basically being kind to yourself, your whole self, you'll probably return to the unmerry-go-round. What we do to ourselves when we force ourselves to diet is replicate that childhood experience of physical safety at the expense of our emotional safety.

Remember the girl who was plucked off the embankment and yelled at? She was taught physical safety at the expense of her emotional safety. A diet does much the same. It is an attempt to get on healthier ground physically while ignoring or giving incomplete attention to the feelings food has been fixing. Long-term physical restriction of food will not work. Sooner or later the need for comfort and relief will overpower and even wipe out all memory of the original motives for dieting, and within a very short time the food addict will be whirling around the unmerry-go-round again.

How in the world can one lose weight? If you are addicted to sugar and starches, no food program will be successful so long as you are eating sugar and refined starch. Even a little bit of sugar will trigger your obsession with food and your urge to eat.

Achieving abstinence from sugar is like withdrawing from any other psychoactive drug. Initial withdrawal is extremely uncomfortable and takes a lot of support. Staying abstinent from sugar is another great challenge. We need to make it through both the withdrawal and the dire cravings that accompany it as well as long-term withdrawal. To stay abstinent, we need a very strong, very accessible support system.

Now there's a challenge: using a support system. If we've learned through countless childhood lessons not to ask for help, if our ability to trust has been severely harmed, how do we waltz to the phone and call a stranger and say, "I need to talk because I want to eat?"

OUR SURVIVAL TECHNIQUES

The lessons we learned to protect ourselves from threats in our childhood environment often work against the things we need to do to recover. Our mistaken survival tactics include:

- Always putting others first
- Fixing everybody else in the hope that if they are okay they'll reach back to us
- Not feeling or showing anger or sadness or both
- Looking put-together
- Keeping everyone happy
- Being very responsible
- Not making mistakes
- Not troubling others
- Being brave
- Being invisible
- Keeping our feelings under control at all times

BREAKING THE RULES

These survival tactics are a part of us. They got us through. Extricating ourselves from them can be difficult. Part of the difficulty is that they are subconscious. We developed them so automatically, so young, and so unconsciously that we may be unaware of them. They operate within us as rules that we live by; although unaware of them, we are controlled by them.

Whenever we break a *survival rule* we feel scared and anxious, so scared and anxious that we may eat. The paradox is that to recover, we need to break these rules. Breaking these rules creates such discomfort, however, that we want to cling to the only consistent comfort we know—food.

It takes time to discover and break these rules. And we must be kind with ourselves. If we push ourselves to trample them willy-nilly, we'll want to eat. The penalty for unkindness to ourselves is almost always a drive to eat. Whether we like the idea or not, to recover, we must learn self-kindness. That's different from self-indulgence. I've often heard women say, "I worked too long today, so I treated myself to some food." This is a self-deception. Working too long is an unkindness. It's putting something else first. It's saying the needs of the company are more important than I am. Working too long created a deficit. Food is used to fill the deficit. The real need—to be important enough to rest when tired—is ignored. Food does not fix that need.

Self-kindness would mean quitting before we get so tired or getting comfort from someone for working beyond a limit. Once more, such self-kindness may mean breaking a rule by which we've been living.

Weight loss and recovery are processes with many steps. Weight loss is a later step. Other steps must come first:

- Accepting the fact of your addiction to food
- Building support for recovery
- Using your support system
- Identifying survival tactics that keep you from using or building your support system

- Getting help to break survival rules
- Learning to ask for help
- Making a commitment to use a support team daily
- First abstinence
- Learning to listen to and accept your own feelings
- Learning to identify and meet your needs
- Learning coping skills
- Learning relationship skills
- Second abstinence
- Expanding your ability to get support
- Setting up positive consequences in your life
- Identifying secondary compulsions
- Increasing healthful living
- Body image work
- Working with weight-loss possibilities

ASSIGNMENT 3.2

For the next twenty-four hours, notice yourself. Notice your needs, reactions to others, and messages to yourself. The goal here is for you to become more conscious of your patterns by keeping a log of your feelings and reactions.

Do you have a tendency to take care of others, listen rather than talk about yourself, talk rather than listen, rescue, protect others, or protect yourself? Do you find yourself feeling put upon, used, taken advantage of? Do you feel overwhelmed, small, not enough? Do you feel urges to run and hide, to crawl into a corner away from people? Do you feel confused and torn in two? All of these patterns, deep-rooted though they are, can be altered. Very likely, they stand between you and what you really want from life. But first you must become more conscious of what they are. To achieve such consciousness, record your responses to people. For example:

10:00. Jill asked Rena to go to lunch. I felt left out.
12:00. Went to lunch alone. Felt lonely.

4:00. Noticed Jack and Bonnie leaving the office together. Felt lonely.
5:00. Ellen invited me to go to a movie Friday night. Said no. Don't believe she really wants me to go with her.
9:00. Boss dumped twelve folders on my desk. Expects me to take care of it by 5:00. Feel overloaded and put upon.
11:00. Went to lunch with Ed. He talked the whole time about his marital problems.
3:00. New woman shown around office. She'll be helping reduce Esther's workload. Won't be any help to me at all.
6:00. Still at office trying to finish everything. Everybody else is gone.
8:00. Planning what I'm going to eat when I get home. Can't wait. Supper looks warm, inviting.
10:00. Ate all evening and watched TV. Didn't answer the phone. This is only comfort I've felt all day.

THE ADDICTIVE SYNDROME

If the physical addiction were the only part of the problem, I could tell you how to improve your brain chemistry and we could all go bowling. But if you've observed a recovering alcoholic or drug addict, you know that he must work vigorously to maintain his sobriety.

Why? He's over the worst of alcohol withdrawal in a week (unless he's also used other drugs), he's in better physical shape after a few months, and his body has repaired most of the damage after a couple of years. So why must he keep going to A.A. meetings? Why are sober alcoholics still attending meetings twenty years later? Because anyone who uses a substance to cope with life has learned two deadly principles: avoidance and substitution.

Alcohol, drugs, sugar, and eating are all effective ways to avoid living and feeling. Once we've learned avoidance, we can automatically slip into it again. The next new stress can trigger us into avoidance without our spotting it.

We have also learned substitution. We've learned to substitute a substance for a real need. Any time we eat because we're lonely, we are substituting food for the answer to our loneliness. Food doesn't actually fix the loneliness. It's still there, but food is used as a substitute for a friend. When we eat because we're afraid, we are substituting food for what would help us to be less afraid. When we eat because we worked too hard, we are substituting food for not taking care of ourselves.

Once we've learned to substitute something for a real need, we can confuse ourselves. You're thirsty, you eat. You're tired, you eat. The appropriate response to thirst is to drink; to tiredness, to rest. Food is the wrong answer and eventually we get confused and lose track of the real problem.

Ultimately we build a high pile of problems that haven't been addressed, needs that haven't been met. We become more and more confused about what we need and who we are. When we don't know who we are, we have even less access to what we need and even less chance of getting those needs met. We perpetuate deprivation for ourselves. The longer we go without meeting our needs, the more deprived we are. We feel bad, we feel deprived, our situation feels intolerable, so we eat to numb ourselves.

If we stop compulsive eating without making other changes as well, we'll do something else to numb the feelings, because we've learned that feelings and problems can be avoided by substituting something for the real answer. Drinking, sex, relationships, work, running, bowling, reading, TV, sleeping, controlling people, or coin-collecting can all be done compulsively the same way we approach food. Just as a third language is acquired more rapidly than a second, a second compulsion is acquired more rapidly than the first. Long-time recovering people are very familiar with this.

So if you drop sugar and close this book, the odds are against you. Besides alcoholism, food addicts seem prone to compulsive spending and compulsive relationships. Unless abstinence is approached thoughtfully and carefully, there's a danger of running up bills and charges that can lead to a long bout of financial difficulty and stress, or we can get so high on a new relationship that we feel totally cured. We often lose weight, believe all our dreams are answered, quit therapy, and stop going to recovery support groups. Later, when the relationship inevitably starts falling into the pattern of previous painful relationships, we boomerang. We turn to sugar and eat with renewed desperation. Any compulsion we had before will return with gusto. We end up worse than we were when we started. Now that you are sufficiently warned, I'll mention some other characteristics most of us share.

We are impulsive. We sometimes make important decisions with very little thought or research.

We are black/white thinkers. "If you won't go to the party with me, I want a divorce." "If someone breaks an appointment with me, I'll never trust him again." "When my car breaks down, I want to kill myself." "If I can't do everything on this list, I'm a failure."

We are perfectionists. We expect flawless performances from ourselves in every area of our lives.

We are secretive. We prefer that no one know all about what we're doing. We may cloak this by being too open about other things.

We minimize our eating and its consequences.

We tend to isolate. If we are hurt, we have a tendency to crawl into a corner and lick our wounds by ourselves. If someone steps on our toes, we don't say ouch. We take it, then go away and feel terrible.

We are self-punishing. We work harder and we stay in an uncomfortable situation longer than is good for us. If everyone else in the family takes a break from working, from caring for an elder, from cleaning the house, we push on. We can take it. We think we can handle more than anyone around us.

We are often in a caretaking role. We see the pain of others and reach out. The problem with this is that we often end up caring for others when we need someone to care for us. We tend to give when we need to receive.

We look and act independent; we feel dependent. Our veneer of independence hides long-standing unmet dependency needs. During childhood, a time when we were supposed to be very dependent, many of us had to take care of ourselves before we had enough experience and training to handle it. We were too independent too young. Our parents defaulted. The child inside us is still crying out to be taken care of, to be allowed to fall back into the arms of a reliable caregiver. Deep within many of us is the need to turn life over until we've made up for those tough young years. We tend to look strong to others, especially to those we plan to marry or mate with. Then after marriage or commitment, this need for care often manifests itself as tremendous dependence on the partner. An unspoken struggle with the partner over this need for dependence/independence can be the cause of many marital difficulties.

We tend to react to others with compliance or defiance. We generally have a certain style of reacting based on what worked when we were young. If we survived the family by complying, we tend to be compliant as adults. When we feel safe and trusting in a relationship, however, we may switch to defiance. After so much compliance, we've built up a hefty pile of anger. This anger can come out as a kind of ritual defiance or as subtle rebellion. We may act compliant to someone's face and talk quite defiantly about the person to others. Our actions of compliance or defiance are almost like a reflex. We usually don't think about it. We can respond to ourselves, to our own needs and wishes, from these same extremes. We might be automatically defiant toward an inner need for rest. We might be very compliant toward a craving for shopping. In my case, when I'm exercising or working and my system tells me it's time to stop, my first reaction is defiance. I automatically tell myself I can do a little more.

We operate from these extremes when we haven't been taught to negotiate with others or with ourselves. We automatically say "yes" or "no" if we haven't learned to say, "Just a minute, let's talk about it." Between yes and no are a wide range of possibilities. It is possible to talk it out and work out a compromise that takes care of each person's most important considerations. When we learn this, we can respond to our own urgings the same way, with negotiation, taking into account what's important. So if one part of me wants to rest and another part says, "keep going," I can listen to both parts and decide the wisest course for myself. For example:

> TASKMISTRESS: Push on. If you keep going, you can get this chapter done today.

KINDHEART: You're tired. You can stop in the middle of something.
TASKMISTRESS: If you get this chapter done today, you can get chapter 4 done tomorrow. By the weekend you can feel proud of yourself.
KINDHEART: What does one more day matter? You have plenty of time. If you take care of yourself, you can feel proud that you've been kind to yourself. You'll be less likely to overeat. If you abuse yourself, you'll feel awful.
INTERNAL JUDGE: Kindheart's arguments carry more validity. It is okay to stop in the middle of something. If you feel you must do a little more, I propose that you finish this section and quit. You should then take a break before starting anything else.
TASKMISTRESS: If you stop working on the chapter, you should clean the rugs.
KINDHEART: The rugs can wait till Saturday. You are more important than the rugs. Your need now is to rest.
INTERNAL JUDGE: Your need is more important than your house or your work. I suggest you go out on the back porch, breathe the fresh air, and meditate for five minutes.
AGENT IN CHARGE OF ACTION: I accept the Internal Judge's proposal. I will rest now.

ASSIGNMENT 3.3

Deprivation

If you are dependent on food, chances are food is filling in for important needs that aren't being met. By doing this exercise, you can see what's missing in your life now and what was missing when you were a child.

1. Today's Deprivation
   For ten minutes, write down the ways in which you are deprived in your daily life. What are the rules you make that

keep you from having what you need or from getting your needs met? List these.

2. Past Deprivation
Think about the ways in which you were deprived of important needs as a child. List these.

4

THE GREAT ESCAPE

One plus one makes two. It adds up. Put a person into a painful situation without giving her healthy ways of handling it, then add a physical malfunction that causes her to experience pain more acutely than the average person, and what is the result? An overwhelmed, frightened person who will either want to fight or flee.

Here, I think, is one of the reasons more women than men end up with the disease of overeating—when they are small, they can neither fight nor flee. Trapped little boys have outlets such as sports, fighting, or strenuous physical play to help release fear and anger. Little girls are not culturally supported to fight or express anger. They are taught to be nice and helpful. They are more likely to be required to remain in a difficult situation.

Also, a girl child knows it is not safe for her to flee. She must find escape within the situation. Food will help her do that. If she is frightened or angry, sweet food will release chemicals that soothe her and reduce pain. Food brings her escape. She learns early in life that food will give her a way to avoid feeling so trapped and overwhelmed.

OUR REACTIONS, OUR NEEDS

A friend of mine used to keep his cigarettes in his shirt pocket. He had not smoked for ten years on the evening when he dropped into a convenience store for a carton of milk. A kid came into the store waving a gun. Steve froze while the clerk emptied the cash register and the kid ran out of the store. Then Steve reached into his pocket for a cigarette. It had been ten years since he'd smoked one, but his hand went for the drug that would help him cope with such extreme fear.

When we are overwhelmed, frightened, cornered, confused, miserable, or lonely, our hands may unconsciously reach for solace. The body knows it needs relief and it heads for the relief that has worked before. Only recently has credence been given to the wisdom of the body, the idea that the body is constantly sensing, recording, and reacting to our environment. Long before the conscious mind understands, the body is trying to lead us toward what it senses is positive. If the word *fear* were flashed in front of us so fast we didn't know we'd seen it, our brain would still react almost instantly to the message.

I went camping once with a very dear friend. When it came time to pack the car, for some reason I held back. Though I am usually confident in my packing, I felt as though I wouldn't do it right. I said this to my friend, who remembered that some years before we'd been on a trip and she'd been displeased with the way I'd packed the car. She had been irritated with me. Even today I don't remember that original incident, but my body remembered and held me back from reentering a situation that had earlier caused me discomfort.

Reaching for a sweet may run counter to all our present goals to lose weight, to feel lighter, to wear fun clothes. Yet the body's need to lessen pain may cause the feet to carry the body to the kitchen and cause the hand to put a sweet into the mouth. Nonbingers have great difficulty understanding this part of the process, this nearly automatic, unthinking, unstoppable need for food.

PRIORITIES

Our reactions make sense when we look at our priorities. Survival is more important than appearance; safety is more important than art. If you come through the door at night and hear a suspicious noise at the back of the house, you'll grab that two-hundred-dollar vase if it's the nearest potential weapon. Two hundred dollars is nothing compared to a threat to your safety. Psychologist Abraham Maslow ranked human needs from the most pressing to the more optional. Measured against Maslow's hierarchy of needs, our behavior begins to make sense.

The most critical human needs are for oxygen, water, food, and correct temperature. I clearly remember camping in western Wisconsin without a mosquito net. The night was warm and my sleeping bag hot. But whenever I uncovered my head, little beasties buzzed at me and bit my ears and neck. No matter how much I wanted to avoid those irritating bites, I would automatically emerge from the bag when I got too hot. Try as I might, I couldn't make myself stay protected when my body got too warm. I'd unconsciously fling the bag back, bat madly at the mosquitoes until I cooled off, then burrow back into the oven until the next time I couldn't stand it. My body considered it more important to maintain its correct temperature than to avoid being irritated.

Maslow ranked needs this way, beginning with the most important:

1. Body needs—air, water, food, temperature
2. Safety and protection from harm
3. Status, approval, love, acceptance, belonging
4. Competence, adequacy, security, self-esteem
5. Curiosity, to know and understand
6. Order, structure, system
7. Self-actualization, exploration, newness, values, artistic expression, self-fulfillment, meaning

His hierarchy makes logical sense. If you were holed up in a cave and bears lurked outside, eventually your need for food would drive you from the cave even though your safety would then be threatened. The man who betrays a colleague to land an account has unmet status needs that overrule the need for thinking well of himself.

Since security is a more basic need than self-actualization, no wonder so many women have difficulty leaving the security of a marriage with an abusive alcoholic in order to pursue self-fulfilling activities. Many people leave an unhappy marriage or relationship by falling in love with someone else. The need for love, the need to belong, is stronger than the rule that says one should not get involved with a second person while still tied to the first.

Sure, we can think of exceptions. The artist who lives in a garret on bread crusts sacrifices all of his more fundamental needs for art. We could argue that art is his love, what he wants to belong to, where he finds his self-esteem, but many people who want to be artists abandon the pursuit because the pressure of fundamental needs becomes too great. The exceptions who don't give up only point out how many are unable to sustain defiance of basic needs. Placed against the backdrop of ranked needs, we can see what courage and support it takes to defy a visceral need for a more esoteric one. Generally, in order to make a change in our lives, we have to substitute fulfilling a visceral need with another similar fulfillment.

NEED RANKING AND OVEREATING

Maslow's hierarchy of needs makes very clear the reason most weight-loss programs don't stand a chance. Appearance and artistic dress are less critical needs (unless one thinks her survival is based on her attractiveness) than the need for safety or the relief of pain. You don't decorate the house while the wind is smashing the windows.

I can't remember that I want to be slimmer when I'm hanging on for dear life. If my boss wants me to do the equivalent of climbing the fire escape of the Space Needle, color coordination is not going to be one of my high priorities. A woman who has had no training for adulthood, who is making it up as she goes along, is constantly hanging on for dear life. Sure, I can paddle my kayak through high waves in Puget Sound because I've been trained to do it, but I was not trained to communicate my needs to others. In fact, I was ignored, ridiculed, and endangered when I expressed my needs. I learned many ways to get my needs met—manipulation, subterfuge, meeting others' needs first, ignoring my own needs, and eating. What diet can possibly last when pitted against such compelling forces?

We ate to make up for lack of love, not belonging, feeling incompetent, and to feel nurtured and safe. We ate to make up for the ways we were deprived. What diet, which is just more deprivation, could last? A diet collapses like matchsticks under a sledgehammer when such powerful needs break through.

So food rescued us in two important ways. It provided escape from fear, loneliness, misery, danger, and feeling trapped. It also became a substitute for other needs. Food gave us safety, taking us to a place where we felt warmth and belonging. Food made us secure and fulfilled. There are always new foods and new treats, new concoctions to buy or make, new flavors. Food gave us newness and exploration. We learned to substitute food for many of Maslow's ranked needs. We learned avoidance and substitution.

We confused ourselves quite a bit. Because we were substituting food for other needs, we came to think of food as the solution to those needs. We were lonely, we ate. We were overwhelmed, we ate. We were so bonded to food, we lost sight of the possibility that the cure for loneliness is people, not food. And remember, without relationship skills, we were blocked in our ability to find relief from loneliness by being with others.

A friend isn't a cure for loneliness if we can't be honest with her about what we're feeling, if we can't talk to her when she disappoints us, or if we can't tell her we're angry because she canceled at the last minute. When we can't communicate our preferences, we end up going shopping because she wants to, because we can't say, "I'd like to go to the aquarium today." If these big blocks stand between us and honesty with a friend, we continue to be lonely even when we're with her.

I hope now you're beginning to understand the complexity

of the problem. A diet—any diet—collapses under the pressure of such a far-reaching problem. Can you forgive yourself now for all those failed diets? Can you see that the diet was a solution too small for this problem? You were never at fault. Any diet that keeps you eating sugar, that keeps alive the chemical triggers for appetite, is doomed even if none of the above factors exists (and they do).

Yet another factor is in operation. Many overeaters are tired. We may have an energy deficit. Why is that? One factor may be that our insulin levels make our fat cells reluctant to release fat so that it can be converted to sugar and then burned for energy.

Another factor may be light deprivation. We may be compelled to eat in an effort to get more energy. We are choosing food that should give us energy but doesn't. Others get energy from sugar but we don't, due to the body reactions explained in chapter 2. Even though experimental results aren't yet clear enough to explain exactly what happens in our bodies step by step, enough is known to conclude the following:

- We overeaters have bodies that are chemically delicate.
- Our bodies respond to subtle deficits in minerals, vitamins, light, energy, and needs.
- We are probably eating to correct deficits, but what we eat is not making the correction.
- Eating is an effort to self-medicate. Eating is caused by biological pressure.

There! If you're with me so far, you're ready for solutions.

ASSIGNMENT 4.1

Disease Inventory: Part II

Here is the second part of the disease inventory you started in chapter 2 on page 46. This part is designed to help you become more conscious of the direct and indirect messages you received as a child about food, eating, and weight. Your awarenesses will become more clear by first writing them down and then sharing them with another person or group of people.

IDENTIFYING THE MESSAGE

As a small child, you were taught about food and eating with words (what your parents told you), actions (what your parents showed you), and consequences (how your parents rewarded or punished you).

In your Disease Inventory notebook, write about what you were taught as a small child:

THROUGH WORDS

- What did your parents say about food, sugar, eating, and weight (yours and theirs)?

THROUGH ACTIONS

- What were meals like—warm times of sharing, love, and laughter? Were you tense, pressured, fearful? Were you captive while being disciplined?
- Were meals regular, predictable, and healthy, nutritionally balanced, haphazard, sporadic, at no fixed times, late and unappetizing because you had to "wait for father," of questionable nutritional value?
- How was food a part of family traditions, both daily traditions and holidays, celebrations, and weekends?
- Where and when did you learn about nutritional balance, nutritional content, cooking?
- What mixed messages did you receive as a child? For example, "Eat! It will make you healthy?" "That girl, I keep letting out her clothes!"
- What was the family's attitude toward appearances? Were appearances important no matter what was really happening? Was it more important for the house to be neat for the neighbors than for you to be attended to?

THROUGH CONSEQUENCES

- What were the rewards or punishments for eating the way your family did, or for not eating the way they did?
- How were you rewarded or punished for the way you looked, the way you ate, the way you were the same, the way you were different from the rest of the family?
- Think about your childhood. In what ways did you suffer from the addictiveness or compulsiveness of others? Take plenty of time for this part of your inventory. Be as detailed as you like. Write about experiences you went through as a result of the disease in others.

SHARING YOUR DISCOVERIES

The discoveries you made by writing will be multiplied if you read your inventory to someone who can be warm, accepting, and nonjudgmental. By writing, you've listened to yourself. By reading it, you will experience the connection and warmth of having others hear what you've been through.

If you are in a therapy group, ask permission to read your inventory there. (A good therapy group can concentrate your recovery efforts. Chapter 8 discusses the professional help available.) By reading it in your therapy group, you enable your therapist and group members to spot patterns in the present that relate to patterns from the past.

Option 1. If you are in a therapy group, take this inventory to group and ask for time to read it.

Option 2. If you are in individual therapy, take this to your session and read it.

Option 3. If you are not in therapy, or do not want to read this in a session, do the following:

a. Identify a healthy, loving, supportive friend.
b. Ask if she will listen to you for an hour. Explain that you've been writing about your life and have learned that you will get a lot more out of it if someone can listen with acceptance and caring. If she's willing, set up a time and place where you won't be interrupted by telephones or children and

ask that the information you'll be sharing be kept confidential.

c. At the appointed time, read this entire part of your inventory to her. Allow her to comfort you if you can.

d. Thank her.

ASSIGNMENT 4.2

If you're open to a bit of whimsy, the following test is a lighthearted introduction to the next chapter.

FEELINGS QUIZ

1. Pick the false statement. Food addicts use food to:
   a. Alter feelings
   b. Make up for deprivation
   c. Distract themselves from problems
   d. Take the place of a friend
   e. Avoid doing things they don't want to do
   f. Paint their garages
   g. Feel better
   h. Stop feeling
   i. Put themselves to sleep
   j. Help them forget they don't know how to get something they want

2. Pick the correct statement:
   a. Feelings can be ignored
      (1) For days at a time without penalty
      (2) At great peril
      (3) Because they don't mean anything
      (4) Without consequences in regard to eating behavior
   b. Feelings tell us:
      (1) Lies
      (2) What's going on in other people
      (3) How we are reacting to the world around us and within us

(4) Nothing

3. Mark the true statements:
   a. If we ignore our needs, our eating won't be affected.
   b. Once we are abstinent, a food craving is a sign that we have accidentally eaten some sweetener or that something's wrong.
   c. Feelings have no effect on eating.
   d. We trust easily.
   e. Neglecting ourselves may cause us to eat.
   f. When we feel abandoned, we may find ourselves inhaling food without realizing it.
   g. If we feel something, we're stuck with it. Eating or shopping or sex or drugs are the only ways to make feelings change.
   h. Some feelings are bad or shameful and can never be told. (No one else has felt them.)
4. Fill in the blanks:
   a If I want lifelong peace from food cravings, I must develop the ability to ______ others what I'm feeling.
   b. Many of us who grew up in dysfunctional families missed learning some important skills. We often made up our own rules in order to ______.
   c. Living with joy and freedom means learning to ______ and ______ these self-imposed rules. (Choose one from below.)
      (1) Reinforce and build up
      (2) Publish and teach
      (3) Force our spouse and our children to follow
      (4) Identify and break
   d. We may not realize our survival rules and skills are controlling us in countless small ways nearly all the time. We often need ______ to catch on to this and to change it.
   e. Our self-imposed rules cause us to do things the hard way, to expect too much of ourselves, and to push ourselves too hard, or to quit and not even try. This causes ______, which then may cause illness, injury, compulsive eating, and exhaustion. By breaking free of these rules, we reduce it.
5. When a parent leans on a child for help with adult problems, how is the child affected?

Congratulations, you've completed the test. Even if some questions stumped you, you've learned a lot or reinforced knowledge you already had. The next chapter expands on the thoughts in this quiz.

ANSWERS

1. f
2a. (2)
2b. (3)
3. b, d (most don't, some trust too easily), e, f
4a. Tell
4b. Survive
4c. (4)
4d. Help
4e. Stress
5. Some possible answers follow. You may have thought of consequences I haven't included here: She may become too responsible too young. She may have difficulty playing and having fun. As an adult she may be locked into a caretaking role in her relationships.

5

NATURE'S TELEGRAMS

ABSTINENCE IS NOT ENOUGH

Let's say you follow the program outlined later in chapter 7 and survive withdrawal. You make it all the way to ninety days of abstinence and your brain pathways are slowly changing. Heavens to Betsy, you wouldn't want to lose all this, would you? Perish the thought of a second trip through withdrawal. (Chapter 7 explains abstinence and withdrawal.)

If you're going to make it long-term, like it or not, you'll need to develop an ability you're not used to—paying attention to your needs and your feelings. Let's face it, beyond chemical triggers, the primary reason people overeat is to alter feelings. Either we're eating so we won't feel something or we're eating to feel something else. How did we get so afraid of feelings?

Most of us who grew up in dysfunctional, abandoning, or abusive families were not helped with feelings. Parents modeled not feeling, or controlling or harming others with feelings. Few of us were taught the healthy expression of anger, acceptance of the normal grief process, or words that communicate nuances of feeling. We rarely saw it.

Some of us were threatened or punished for expressing feelings: "You think you're sad? I'll give you something to cry about." "You can't talk to your father like that!" We learned which feelings were acceptable and which ones weren't. Mom may have modeled that it's okay for females to be sad but not to be angry. Dad may have modeled explosive anger while forbidding anyone else to express it.

Feelings are doors into our inner selves. Beyond each door lies intricate and fascinating information about our past and present. If we try to ignore feelings, if we barricade the door to keep it shut, we miss the opportunity to heal the past and we miss important information about what we need now. To keep a door barricaded takes a lot of energy. Many people fear that if they open up to a feeling, it will take them over. A client who has shut out grief may fear that if she starts crying, she'll never stop. A client who has been sitting on a mountain of anger may fear that if she stops containing it, it will erupt like a volcano and harm somebody.

Remember that you always have an escape route from a feeling. As you open up to a feeling, it will swell and grow larger—but any time you become too afraid of it, your system will automatically shut it down. My clients who are opening up to feelings shut them down with statements like "Is this normal?" "What do you call this?" or a question or statement that indicates a leap from feeling to the intellect. Clients close down feelings with a smile, a joke, a concern about the other clients in the room. There are always plenty of escape routes.

The process of opening up to barricaded feelings takes safety and time. When you begin encountering your feelings, be sure you are in a safe place with people you consider safe. A warm, accepting therapist or loving, nonjudgmental friends are usually safe people. Build your trust by taking tiny risks at first. Be sure the location is safe. Check that you have the person's undivided attention. Confirm that you will not be interrupted.

Why do you need to be with another person? Why isn't it enough to do it alone? The feelings must be symbolized with words or pictures. A lot of people say they'll think about it. Why doesn't that work? If we only think about feelings, the symbols are too vague and fleeting for meaning to emerge. If you want to get anywhere with the feeling process, if you want the discoveries that can emerge, you must articulate your experience. Your feelings must be symbolized in either words or pictures, through metaphors or literally by drawing or sculpting. Feelings must be symbolized and felt. Thoughts are in the mind. Feelings involve more than the mind. As feelings are articulated, they are more clearly experienced.

To be in the presence of a good listener has an almost magical effect. Her caring ear can pull pain out of your heart like tweezers pulling out a bee's stinger. With experience, you will develop the ability to go a certain distance alone; keeping a journal and drawing, for example, can be effective ways of symbolizing. But with a caring listener, the process of reaching relief is much faster. Talking draws a picture inside your mind.

When we talk to another person, we are forced to find words that describe the experience. The very process of finding words helps us clarify. The more we talk, the more we define and refine our experience. Talking, unlike writing, is fast enough to keep up with the changing process. After your first sentence, you know more than you did when you started. The act of making the first sentence has moved you along. Articulation actually carries you into and through the process.

FOLLOWING A FEELING

Here's an example of following a feeling from start to finish. A dear friend died. All that she gave me I would no longer get. I'd always have the memories and my love, but I had lost a lot. I found I grieved every loss separately and that once I had opened completely to my grief over a particular loss, it lost its sting.

One of my losses was that this friend had a very tender heart. When she saw something touching, she stopped to absorb it. A vulnerable, open look crossed her face. She was fully living the moment. From her I learned to stop and live the moment. I know I get to carry this gift on through the rest of my life, but I lost sharing this experience in the unique way that I could with her alone.

When I thought about this specific loss, I felt full of pain. It increased in intensity. It filled me. I wanted to talk myself out of it, to offer myself platitudes. I bypassed that escape route and stayed with the loss. It carried me to deeper pain. I saw a big "The End" sign to a significant part of my life. I wanted to remind myself that I would have many other pleasures. I bypassed that escape route and stayed with my sorrow. I walked into it as I would walk through a door. I thought, I can't bear it. It is too great a loss. I summoned my courage and my trust that I could bear it. I bypassed that escape route. I leaned into the pain. I was filled all through myself with powerful grief. It was very strong. I surrendered to it. I did not fight it or struggle. It was incredibly intense. I stayed with it. Suddenly, I was through it. I was in a new place quickly, as fast as spitting a watermelon seed off the porch. I knew suddenly I would be all right. I felt this not as a platitude this time, but as a deep knowing. I was past the worst pain.

I find that when I surrender to the process that thoroughly, I never have to go through that particular wrenching pain again. I may have lesser, milder waves later that are more like faint regret, but these are easily bearable and pass quickly. Once we have been to the other side of this process, all the energy tied up by the feeling itself and by barricading the feeling becomes available to us. Our thoughts are also freed. We have room in ourselves for something good and new.

Remember that as the feelings rise in intensity, escape routes present themselves. You can follow them or bypass them. If you stay with the feelings, it can become incredibly intense. Right before the culmination, I usually fear I'm not going to be able to take it. If I let go to the feeling, if I surrender and stop fighting it, it reaches its most powerful intensity. And if I continue to stay with it, I suddenly scoot through it. I know I'll be okay. I know I'm on the other side.

TELEGRAMS FROM THE INNER SELF

Feelings are also telegrams from our inner selves. They are quick, accurate messages that something in the environment is connecting with something we've been through before. These messages are tied to a wealth of information about our personal histories. Are they right? Can they be wrong? Let's look at this.

Feelings give us access to vast and intricate information. You might say they are like labels on file folders. If we go into the feeling that has presented itself, we discover important information about ourselves. We may discover a fear (another feeling), a forgotten experience, a belief we have about ourselves, or a rule we live by. The process is like a treasure hunt. If we pursue whatever turns up, we'll discover something else. Each new discovery provides access to yet another piece of information.

Is there a bottom to it? Yes and no. Many times the pursuit of meaning takes us to an overall truth, memory, feeling, or rule—a culmination that reflects the present triggering incident. Often we'll sit with this grand discovery for an hour, a day, or a month and see many further applications or connections. Eventually, though, life leads us into a new treasure hunt for a new grand discovery. It's as if we are surrounded by a darkness cut only by a thin trail of light. At the end of the trail is a wide, well-lit cavern in which many patterns are revealed. Eventually we find an opening to another thin, twisting trail through the darkness that leads to yet another warm, well-lit cavern filled with possibilities.

Sometimes the trail is rough and hard. Many give up, but those who gather the courage and support to continue find that over time they are brought to larger spaces where movement is freer and simpler, where the complex is revealed as simple and the simple revealed as complex.

Why should you believe me and try this? How does one follow this trail? And please, you ask, translate.

A DEMONSTRATION

As I write this chapter, I'm aware of a vague hint of anxiety and fear hovering in the bottom of my chest. As I focus on it, it enlarges and pushes against me. It seems to fill my upper body from my throat to my waist. What is this fear about? I open myself to what it has to say to me. I wait and listen to it. Many worries are in this file folder. I look at it. I've scheduled too many clients today! I have set up a schedule that will require too much energy and concentration on too many people for too many hours! I'm angry that I've let myself abuse myself this way. I have so many ideas about feelings and recovery, so much information based on my experience with clients and my own recovery. It's like a gushing waterfall in my head. What if I can't organize it well or communicate it clearly? I might forget something. I might not do it well. I must get this chapter done because I must mail it to my publisher tomorrow! Time and urgency press against me. Now I've looked at all the files in my file folder. If I sit back and stay open to whatever rises to the surface, what happens? Fear grows big in me. What is the fear trying to tell me? It says, "I'm afraid I won't be enough."

How did I get so afraid of not being enough that I would create eight hours of client appointments after six hours of writing? I see now that my fear of not being enough led me to such a ridiculous schedule. I allow myself to drift back in time to the beginning of the fear of "not being enough." I let myself see it.

A picture appears of a little girl (me) in a white dress. Big people are standing around, their heads far above mine like tall trees. I feel lost and alone. If I were "enough," I wouldn't feel lost. Suddenly the picture shifts. I am very, very young. I'm alone. I see myself alone in a house and the adults are all preoccupied with other things. My grandmother is busy with many projects. My grandfather works hard and doesn't deal with babies. My father is gone. My mother is full of need. I am very small, but I must somehow take care of myself because the grownups are either too busy, too needy, or too absent to take care of me. But I can't take care of myself. I am too small.

I am not enough.

The fear is gone. I have tracked down the message it held for me. Now that I've heard the message, the fear has done its job. I realize many things at once. It's not true that I'm not enough. I was enough. But I didn't get the care I needed. I wasn't at fault for not getting the care. That lack had nothing to do with my worthiness.

I feel peace now at having traced the origin of my fear. I have discovered a belief I had about myself. Because of years of recovery and therapy, many understandings lock into place. I realize I was enough, that my experience as a small child led to the development of an innocent belief. That belief has been in me for years and has been the reason I've pushed myself so hard. The discovery of the basis for the fear has caused a relaxing of the tightness, pressure, and tension. I calmly feel I can make a kinder schedule next week, and that today I'll do what I can and it will be enough. My fear is gone.

I could take some shortcuts and do this quickly and in front of you because I've been doing this for a long time—long enough to know that whatever I'm feeling, I'll be safe and that the bottom line will be that I'm good, not bad.

THE PROCESS

Don't expect yourself to do this quickly or easily at first. I shared my process so you could see what it looks like and so I could tell you about the parts of the process and the general direction it usually takes.

First, we have a feeling. It's usually vague, cloudy, and unspecific. If we focus on it, it usually enlarges, deepens, and feels stronger. We may fear we won't be able to take it, but we have a lot of control. We can cut it off and shut it down whenever we are too scared by it. As we focus more, lots of pieces will reveal themselves—other feelings, usually clearer feelings. The sorting-out processes we go through may begin like this:

Fear
Anxiety and anger about schedule
Pressure to finish chapter—enough stamina?
Worry about not communicating clearly

As we allow the pieces of the stew to float around, an idea, fear, survival rule, or belief will emerge.

Fear
Anxiety Anger Pressure Worry
I'm not enough

This belief, fear, or rule will seem like a basic truth and we may have many feelings about it.

> I'm not enough
> Anger   Sadness   Fear of loss   Grief   Fear of failure

Sometimes we have to feel the whole array of feelings before something changes. Sometimes we have to be angry and sad, to cry and shout before the next awareness opens up.

> I'm not enough
> Sadness   Grief   Fear of loss   Anger
> Memory

Very often these feelings lead to an important memory that either demonstrates this belief or was a critical influence in the development of this belief. Whether the incident actually happened as we remember it isn't important. Very early memories might well be a composite of similar experiences. Whether or not the incident was seen this way by others is unimportant. What matters is the way we saw it and what we drew from it. These make up the fabric of our beliefs about ourselves and influence us far more than we realize.

> Memory
> Interpretations   Conclusions
> Who I am and what I can expect

We carry a whole portfolio of beliefs about ourselves and the world based on an array of early incidents. We have held them for so long and had them reinforced so often that they appear to us as truths.

That the truths are not universal, however, can be seen by observing anyone else. Even someone as close as a sister may have an entirely different set of truths—different because they are based on a different array of experiences. She entered the family with her not-yet-finished brain at a different point in the family's history. Tender and unformed, she passed through critical maturational stages in a family that was more or less the same but different in its degree of dysfunction.

What might a portfolio contain? "I'm not enough." "I am not good enough." "People won't listen to me." "People won't give me what I need." "My needs cause trouble."

We might have hundreds of beliefs that seem basic and unshakable. As we grew, we developed survival skills in an attempt to overcome these beliefs. What if you believe you're not enough? Some skills or rules you might develop are:

- I must always push myself to be better.
- I must learn everything I can.
- I must learn what people need from me.
- I must get people to tell me I'm good.
- I must learn to read what people need and provide it so that they'll say I'm enough.

Of course some rules may clash with other rules so a situation can produce confusion and anxiety as we try to work out which rules apply.

Do these rules work? Do they fix the problem? No. Though we may be driven by a rule, we get no lasting relief from obeying it. For example, if you are ruled by the thought, "I must take care of everyone around me," you will not feel peaceful and fulfilled even if you take good care of everyone else.

If I believe I'm not good enough, will I be able to finally get enough reassurance from others or accomplish enough to feel worthwhile? No. You could be president of the United States and still feel inadequate. Reassurance alone is not enough.

Does abstinence fix these beliefs? No. But it allows us to begin feeling and thinking more clearly so we can undergo the process that does bring about relief.

BELIEF RELIEF

So we have this belief about ourselves. As we follow the feeling back to the original belief, what then? Generally four things have to happen in order for a belief to change:

- We must know—be conscious—that we hold the belief.
- We must see what the real truth is.

- We must have the full range of feelings about the causes and consequences of the belief and allow ourselves to grieve the losses we've suffered as a result of the belief and by the loss of the belief itself.
- We must receive care for the pain we've suffered.

As I saw my infant self, I began to understand why I concluded I wasn't enough. I saw I made an incorrect conclusion. The truth is, for a variety of reasons, my adults were unavailable. They slipped in taking full care of me. My unformed, egocentric brain concluded that my own inadequacy caused the problem. But it wasn't true. I was a normal infant, unfinished but not inadequate. I was full of potential, a perfect little infant.

I'm still in the process of handling the harm done many years ago. Here are some of the stages I've been through since I've started healing: For months I lived the idea that I wasn't at fault, that others slipped in their responsibility as caregivers. I had weeks of anger at them for their long-ago mistakes. I had weeks of grief at all the ways I abused myself trying to overcome the wrong belief instilled in me then. As present incidents revealed my various attempts to be enough, I experienced more grief and anger. I sought care for the long years of feeling inadequate and afraid. I was held when I cried. I was listened to when I was angry. I was supported and cherished. This warm, caring attention gradually healed much of the emptiness of my mistaken belief.

Is it gone forever? No. New situations, new pressures, still trigger the old fear, the old belief. But since I've done so much work and received so much care, I can usually find my way back to relief within days and sometimes within minutes.

I've given you this much detail so feelings will be a less-frightening territory. Not all feelings take this much time to discover their source, but most do have important information for you. As you heal the past, feelings become more and more accurate about what you need in the present. They tell you when to rest or when to seek closeness or care. With help and time, you can begin to tell the difference between feelings that push you to follow survival rules and feelings that show you how to be more joyous, free, and healthy.

If feelings are driving you, causing you to isolate yourself, causing you tension and harm to yourself or others, they are probably feelings connected to survival rules and wrong beliefs. They are signals that you need help, care, and attention.

If feelings are helping you make healthy decisions, to take good care of yourself, and to promote healthy relationships, they are appropriate to the present. To discriminate between a feeling carrying accurate information about the present and one carrying unfinished business from the past takes time, help, talking, and the clarity of mind and feeling that comes from abstinence.

THE ACCURACY OF FEELINGS

Back to that original question—are feelings always right? Can they be wrong? A feeling simply summarizes or labels what's in the file folder. It's right about what's in the folder. Fear is accurate in the sense that something in the present is reminiscent of something harmful in the past. That the past experience is being accurately recreated in the present may not be true, however.

When her dad was angry, Jill got hit. If I am angry, will I hit Jill? Jill may fear my anger based on her past hurt. Her fear reflects her past hurt accurately. Her past experience causes her to believe that anger causes hurt. Her belief that anger causes hurt does not, however, have to be true. I won't hit her if I'm angry. Is her fear wrong? No. Her fear is accurate about her past experience. Her past experience was hurtful. Nonetheless, her interpretation and conclusion from the past do not apply to all situations. We have a tendency to interpret the present as we did the past. When we do this, we may miss out on good that's available to us.

We can maintain our abstinence to the extent that we work with our feelings. We must become open to our feelings for two reasons—they reveal unfinished business from the past that affects us in the present and they inform us about our needs. If we aren't operating on information coming from our own insides, we'll have to accept information from someone else. If we aren't listening to our own signals about how to make it through the day, we will have to use someone else's plan. This can make us dependent on someone else and can lead us in a direction we don't want to go.

Recovery keeps us busy. To promote recovery, we must do the following:

- *Take care of unfinished business as it surfaces.* Fortunately, usually only little bits get revealed at a time. This means giving feelings some space in which to surface, then talking about what you're going through, working through past hurt, anger, and grief, and receiving care.
- *Expose your basic beliefs and fears about yourself and the rules you developed to survive.*
- *Stop taking the rap.* Take a look at who participated in the development of the belief.
- *Protect yourself from people who reinforce that belief.* Does Ted give you the message you're not enough? Don't expose yourself to Ted.
- *Expose yourself to people who believe in you and want the best for you.* Does Jan give you the message you're worthwhile? Take a small risk of being more open with Jan.
- *Identify which feelings it wasn't safe for you to have.* Get help learning how to have these riskier feelings. (Sad people often are afraid to be angry; angry people are often afraid to be sad.) A therapy group is a safe place to experiment with the expression of new feelings.
- *Decrease any further experiences of deprivation, abandonment, or abuse.* Neglecting your own needs is abuse and deprivation. Not only is it a setup to eat, but when you do this, you abandon yourself, furthering the injury you've experienced. Rest when you're tired. Sleep when you're sleepy. Drink water when you're thirsty. Be with someone kind and warm when you're lonely. Play some, work some, walk some. Forget about dieting. Your lifelong goal, one day at a time, is to protect your abstinence.
- *Find safe places to begin breaking survival rules.* A major cause of stress is observing all your carefully developed survival rules. Stress causes the release of dynorphin and dynorphin causes the need to eat. Reduce those old confining rules and your stress level will drop. (Admittedly, when you first break rules,

stress goes up, but this is temporary and will decrease as you get better at it.)

- *Hang around healthy people.* Most of us had very poor models. We missed great chunks of information about how to be human. Identify healthy people, watch them, notice how they handle things.
- *Learn relationship skills.* Find groups that will teach you:
  To ask for what you want
  To tell someone she disappointed you
  To express anger, hurt, sadness, and fear
  To reveal expectations
  To resolve conflict
  To make decisions as a group
  To interpret your behavior
  To listen to feedback
  To share yourself with others
  To ask for help
  To tell your secrets
- *Learn coping skills.* Find a group that will teach you how to be safe when you're very angry or very sad, how to listen to your needs, how to meet your needs, and how to recognize when you're really stressed and what to do about it.

ASSIGNMENT 5.1

Developing a Strong Support System

The most important tool for altering your relationship with food is a strong support system you feel comfortable using. Many who struggle with this disease have difficulty turning to others for help. The following assignment begins a series of exercises to help guide you in gradually building warm support for yourself and increasing your ability to use it:

1. Make a list of the people you know who seem emotionally healthy or who seem to be involved in a process to increase

their emotional health (for example, therapy, a recovery program, a support group).

2. Make a list of those people who give you subtle or obvious messages that you aren't worthwhile. Include people who reinforce beliefs that you aren't good enough. Include people who try to talk you out of taking risks that are good for you, people who seem to take more from you than they give, people who put you down, and people who discourage you from having positive experiences.
3. Call a person on your healthy list. Ask if she can talk for ten minutes. She might say no. Healthy people can take care of themselves and set limits to do so. A healthy person is more likely to say no than an unhealthy one, who might suffer through a conversation and then resent you for it. If she says no, ask if she'd be willing to talk some other time. If she is willing, find out good times to call.

If she says yes, glance at the clock or set a timer. Tell her you are reading a book that is teaching you to reach out to people, that you are learning to make healthier choices. Tell her you don't expect her to solve anything for you or to come up with any answers. You would just appreciate it if she'd listen while you talk about your reactions to the book. Express the fear you may be feeling about trying some of the suggestions in this book. Talk for about eight minutes. Ask if she has any reaction to what you've said. Check with her about her time. ("I'd like to ask if you've ever struggled with something like that, but I want to be conscious of your time.") If she has the time and wants to talk about her own experience, and if you have time, listen.

At the end, thank her for listening to you and for telling you about herself. After the call, think about the kinds of responses she made and how you felt when she made them. Did you feel encouraged, built up, warmed, clearer, or supported? Then you did indeed talk to a healthy person. She is a good person to have on your healthy list.

Did you feel defeated, discouraged, heavy, sad, hopeless, or lonely? Then this may not be a good person for you to contact while you are taking these risks. Cross her off the list so you aren't tempted to turn to her when you need help.

6

HOW HEALING HAPPENS

If you saw the movie *The Gods Must Be Crazy,* you heard the percussive speech of African Bushmen. If you are a member of a particular tribe of northwest native Canadians, you can say very delicate consonants that most of us can't even hear. Little children in Iceland comprehend their mother's directions.

I have a good ear. Why can't I hear what these people can? All human babies are born with the capacity to speak and understand any human language. So if a baby can do it, why can't I at forty?

By the time we reach our first birthday, our brains have locked into the pattern of our native language (the language or languages we've been exposed to by that time). At eight months, a baby can indicate recognition of very subtle sounds in speech. But by one year, she cannot detect subtle differences among sounds she has not been exposed to.

What happened? Sounds she was exposed to caused certain nerve fibers in her brain to grow in particular directions and to connect with other particular fibers. Sounds she was not exposed to caused certain other nerve fibers to wither because they received no stimulus. Certain other connections, therefore, were not made. Thus was she programmed to receive the language of her culture (and, in effect, barred from distinguishing sounds foreign to her culture).

When elderly rats have led a dull, boring existence, and then some of them are put into an interesting, stimulating environment where they have much to explore, their behavior changes. They lose their sluggishness, they lose their extra weight, their eyes brighten, and they become more active. When these two groups of rats are dissected, the dull rats have holes in their brains, gaps where nerve fibers have withered. The rats who got a new lease on life do not show these brain gaps.

This research suggests that our experiences are recorded by connections between nerve fibers. New synapses are formed and new connections made with each new experience. If an experience is repeated, the connection is confirmed. Through practice, one route becomes a major throughway. Through neglect, another route becomes a country road. Here we have a possible physiological explanation for the effectiveness of habit or compulsion.

This research presents a possibility. If we want to change our lives and try something very different, perhaps our new effort, repeated often enough, will cause a rerouting in our brains and the old throughway to fall into disuse.

My own recovery experience backs this up. With support, I've changed many old patterns. Now the newer patterns are more automatic to me than the old addictive ones. On the other hand, I know the old routes are still there. When I've relapsed, I've been dismayed to discover how quickly the dust could be swept from the old roads, how quickly I could return to them.

I hasten also to distinguish between a purely behavioral approach and the recovery program I'll be suggesting. To attempt to change behavior alone without giving care to the internal, deprived child deprives her further. To force the outside at the expense of the inside sets up an incongruence that feels sick and awful inside. Anything that feels awful to us, even if we don't know what we're feeling, will cause us to eat.

To truly recover from an eating disorder, we must pay attention to our insides. Research does present the hope, however, that if we are steadfast in our efforts, recovery will get easier as the new patterns become confirmed. I have found this to be true for me and many of my clients.

HEALING

Healing happens from the inside out. If you scrape your hand, the scab is the last part to go. To heal from food addiction, we must attend to two important internal processes—our chemical functioning and our feelings. Healing follows these steps:

- We become abstinent from the drug foods that cloud our thinking and that perpetuate cravings and the need to eat.
- By reconnecting with our feelings and needs, we stop neglecting ourselves.
- We get the support needed to break survival rules that limit us from getting our needs met.
- By ceasing to give what we cannot afford to give, we stop abusing ourselves.
- We attend to our insides, no longer sacrificing our inside self for outside impressions, and stop abandoning ourselves.

ABSTINENCE

We respect our chemical limitations by not eating triggering substances. (Step-by-step directions for this are given in chapter 7.) We follow a program that alters our chemical functioning, or more accurately, stops promoting addictive chemical functioning. Eventually we follow a food plan that restores our bodies to natural, healthy functioning.

RECONNECTING WITH FEELINGS AND NEEDS

By gradually reconnecting with our feelings, we stop abandoning ourselves. Our feelings help us understand our own unique perspective on the world, and they reveal unfinished business. Feelings inform us that we need to attend to something, that something important is happening to us.

BREAKING OUR SURVIVAL RULES

Since these rules often keep us from taking good care of ourselves, we must identify them and break them. This process takes time and help. We are often unaware of the rules we're living by, but they control how we relate to people and how we treat ourselves. Sometimes our rules sabotage intimacy and success. Sometimes they keep us in poverty. Sometimes they cause us to lose people very important to us. Without question, the survival rules we developed long ago can cripple our lives.

To break your survival rules, it is important that you talk regularly with a caring, healthy friend or therapist. If you have a rule that says you shouldn't talk to anyone about what's going on, shop for a therapist you feel safe with. She can guide you in working through the reasons for your rule and help you take tiny risks in breaking it.

Recovery challenges many personal survival rules. Often, the actions needed for recovery are exactly the actions prohibited by the survival rules. No wonder people spend so much money and time trying diet remedies and weight-loss programs. If there's even a remote chance that weight loss can happen without an overhaul of our system for dealing with life, of course we'll grab at it.

STOPPING SELF-ABUSE

We food addicts are very giving, generous people. We are more likely to take care of another's needs than our own. *Codependence* is a related disease that many of us share. We are codependent when we put others' needs before our own, or when we base our behavior or feelings on someone else's behavior or feelings to our own detriment. Many of us have suffered sexual abuse or incest. Someone we trusted touched us in a sexual way that felt wrong to us. Our unhealthy homes did not have the safety and protection we needed. Incest is having something taken from you that you can't afford to give. As incest survivors, many of us repeat the experience of giving what we can't afford to give. This is abuse, and this abuse will force us to eat. To recover, we must learn to sense when we've given enough and to stop at that point. This may break one of our survival rules. Kind people can help us stop this abuse and can teach us how to provide safety for ourselves.

Halting Abandonment

When Dad was drinking, we were abandoned. When Mom was codependent with Dad, we were abandoned. Any time our parents were involved in addictive or compulsive behaviors, we were abandoned. Whenever we turn to addictive behavior, we abandon ourselves. To shop when we feel sad is abandonment. If we are sad, we need a shoulder and an ear. We need comfort, not new shoes. We are accustomed to sacrificing our insides for our outsides. We work too hard to get recognition at the expense of our tired selves. We force ourselves through diets that make us feel emotionally empty. We give more than we have to offer. We make ourselves nice, cheerful people who are flexible and willing to go along with others, but inside we are crying. With recovery, this gradually stops. We learn to listen to our insides so they aren't sacrificed for appearances. If we said we would go to the concert and we know we are so tired that it would be abusive, we call and say, "I realize it's not good for me to go tonight. I'm too tired."

We change our minds, we revise our plans, we shorten our list of things to do. We get more realistic about the amount of effort we can put into Christmas. We stop spending more than we can afford for gifts. We don't offer to put on a huge dinner party. We stop baking for hours for someone's birthday. Finally, we care more for our own well-being than appearances.

THE FEELING YOU

As hard as abstinence is, it is not the hardest part of recovery. Here's the hardest part: Recovery will challenge you to face the issues you've been hiding from. It will require you to take good care of yourself. It will ask the barely possible—for you to entertain the idea that you are lovable, loved, and wanted.

Ongoing recovery requires attention to all sides of yourself, starting with the physical and emotional. Ultimately your whole self will become involved—your spiritual, historical, moral, and purposeful dimensions. But to keep it as simple as possible, we'll start with your emotional dimension.

In the previous chapter, you saw that your feelings can be a storehouse of information about your present needs, past hurts, expectations, and survival rules. We can manipulate our awareness of these feelings. We can close ourselves off, we can ignore them, we can hurl epithets at them. Doing that imperils us. Cut off from our feelings, we must operate without internal signals about what fits us and what doesn't, what matches who we are and what doesn't.

If we ignore our feelings, we can't clean up our histories. We may choose futures that lead us away from our true selves. We may be forced to adopt someone else's pattern for living. If we ignore our feelings, we lose the road map that tells us how to get where we want to go—to get what we need. By not getting our needs met, we feel more neglected and abused. We make choices that are bad for us and lead us further from our true selves. The stress and tension from this neglect, confusion, and lack of direction force us further into the need for food. The food itself becomes a barrier to feeling. Under the influence of drug food, our feelings are hazy. Our thinking is less clear.

How do we start feeling again? How do we renew acquaintance with ourselves? We talk. We put those feelings into words. We talk to people who can listen to us with kindness and care and without judgment. Stay with me. I know I'm asking a lot.

If you are like most compulsive eaters, you would prefer to recover from this disease without involving anybody else. Very likely you have already struggled by yourself for years, making and breaking rules about eating, trying to restrict your intake, pushing yourself to exercise. Why didn't this work? Because you were too alone. You got this disease in the first place because you were too alone. Continued loneliness only makes it worse.

Do you know any recovering alcoholics? The ones who have recovered by receiving help from others—through treatment or Alcoholics Anonymous—are incredibly wonderful people. Do you know any "dry drunks"? These are folks who have quit drinking by themselves and have changed nothing else and learned nothing new about living. These people are hard to be around and very hard to get close to, the drill sergeants of the straight and narrow. Maybe you can change your relationship to food by yourself, but the odds are against you. If it were going to work, seems like it would have by now, doesn't it?

I know the suggestions in this chapter are very difficult, and that doing them will involve breaking patterns that have kept you "safe" for years. For this reason, the best possible place for you to try these things is in a therapy group for compulsive eaters run by a therapist who is skilled in working with food addicts. Not all therapists are fluent in eating disorders and not all eating-disorders therapists speak the same language, so choosing a therapist right for you may take some shopping. Chapter 8 talks about how eating-disorders therapists are certified and how you can find out which ones are in your area and what to look for.

To recover forever, we have to learn to talk to others about what we feel, do, want, need, and care about. We have to begin exposing secrets. I've found that everything I thought was too awful to tell had been done or thought of by the people who listened to me. In nine years of recovery, I've not been responded to with shock or dismay one single time.

ASSIGNMENT 6.1

In the last chapter, you began the difficult task of building a support system. This assignment builds on the work you did there by giving you practice in asking someone to listen to you.

1. Think of someone who truly supports you and who wants the best for you. This should be someone who is warm, caring, and thoughtful, someone who will give you some time. Someone you listed on your healthy list from the last assignment is a good candidate. (This should not be someone who is sharp with you, judgmental, critical, cold, hurried, or angry.)
2. Call and ask if she has ten minutes to talk on the phone, that you have something you'd like to talk about. Ask if she would

mind listening. Say that you don't expect her to solve anything for you, that what you mainly need is for her to listen. If she doesn't have time, thank her and hang up. Think of someone else to call.

If she has time, notice the time on the clock, then talk about anything that's going on with you. Talk about the ideas you've gotten from reading this book, about some way you were disappointed today, or something you've been concerned about.

Glance at the clock now and then. When eight minutes are up, thank her for listening and ask if she would like to say anything. If she has something to share, and you have the time, listen. You need not give advice or solve her problems. If the time appears to be going beyond the ten minutes allotted, ask if she'd like to talk longer. If you have a time limit, tell her what it is. It's fine to explain at the beginning of the conversation that you are doing an exercise to help you learn to tell people about yourself. When the time limit is reached, close the conversation and hang up.

3. Write about how it felt to do this. What rules did you break? How do you feel now?

ASSIGNMENT 6.2

Disease Inventory: Part III

It's time to look more closely at your own food addiction in this third part of the Disease Inventory begun on page 46. The following assignment is one of the hardest in this book. A giant barrier to recovery is denying to ourselves the extent of our involvement with food, but if you will persist in writing your inventory as honestly and courageously as you can and share it with another person or persons, you'll have a chance to get a true picture of your disease.

1. Write the inventory using the guide at the end of this introduction. Three approaches to writing are as follows:

- Set aside an entire day. Go to the library; rent a cabin in a nearby park for a day; go to a beautiful, safe spot in the country and take a picnic lunch; rent a room by a lake, the ocean, a river, in a forest for a day; or go to a convent that allows visitors on retreat. Write for a while, take a break, walk, then write some more.
- Set aside three hours a week, four weeks in a row, in which you will not be interrupted. Go to the library or unplug the telephone or drive to a safe park with your notebook, some water, and reflective music. Each week do one section of the inventory.
- Write a little bit each day, and keep writing daily until you've completed the inventory.

2. Read the inventory. The discoveries you make by writing will be multiplied if you read your inventory to someone who can be warm, accepting, and nonjudgmental. By writing, you've listened to yourself. By reading it, you will experience the connection and warmth of having others hear what you've been through. By reading it in your therapy group, your therapist and group members will be able to spot patterns in the present that reflect patterns from the past.

If you are in a therapy group, take this inventory to group and ask for time to read it.

If you are in individual therapy, take this to your session and read it.

Identify a healthy, loving, supportive friend. Ask if she'd be willing to listen to you for a couple of hours. Explain that you've been writing about your life and have learned that you will get a lot more out of it if someone can listen with acceptance and caring. If she's willing, set up a time and place where you won't be interrupted by telephones or children and ask that she keep what you read confidential. At the appointed time, read all of this part of the completed Disease Inventory. Allow her to comfort you if you can. Thank her.

DISEASE INVENTORY

Starting from your earliest memory of bingeing and/or starving, dieting, and/or purging, chronicle your relationship with food.

The Progression of Powerless Eating

1. When did you first turn to food? Perhaps your reliance on food started at age ten when you came home from school and curled up in front of the TV with a bunch of snacks because no one was there for you to talk to. Perhaps you started skipping breakfast at twelve as a misguided weight-control measure and then began skipping lunch, too—leading either to increased fear of food and decreased eating or to bingeing to make up for the meals you missed.
2. Gradually, over the years, your relationship—your intimacy—with food progressed. Chronicle this progression.
3. Include, if relevant, the progression of addiction to sugar and/or alcohol.
4. What impact has the addiction and compulsion had on all parts of your life in the last five years?
5. Be very specific and honest about your present pattern of bingeing and/or purging and/or starving. How much and how often do you binge? What is your volume of food? How frequently do you purge? How often do you starve yourself?

Control Efforts

1. List attempts to control eating—starving, dieting, purging, laxatives, diet pills, prescription drugs, coffee, smoking.
2. Mark the control efforts that failed.

Unmanageability

1. Unmanageability is a part of this disease. Anyone with an addiction finds that her life gets frayed around the edges. What evidence of unmanageability exists in your life? (It is common for addicts not to realize that manageability is related to the addiction. Addicts initially think life is naturally unmanageable, and that they use food to comfort themselves or help them deal with this unmanageability. In fact, it's the other way around. Addiction makes life unmanageable.)
2. List evidence of unmanageability in:
   a. Emotional state—mood swings, depression, self-esteem.
   b. Relationships, social life, sexual relationships.
   c. Work. Have you been late or missed work due to a sugar low or due to drinking? Have you attacked coworkers

because of sugar anger? Have you sabotaged your own success by not having a clear head when needed or by eating instead of studying or reading or learning?

Adverse Physical Consequences

1. Have you ever risked your life or the lives of others by eating or not eating? (For example, driving lightheaded from starving or bingeing; driving after drinking; fumbling for a crumb at 40 miles an hour; driving for hours on insufficient nutrition or in a glut of mind-dulling sugar.)
2. Have you damaged your body as a result of your addiction? (For example, tooth problems, loss of enamel from purging, fallen arches, inadequate exercise, blood-sugar difficulties, high cholesterol or blood pressure from an excess of fat in your diet, malnutrition from inadequate vegetables or whole grains.)
3. Include food blackouts. How many times have you found yourself with an empty bowl or bag in your lap and no clear memory of a decision to eat? How many times have you stood in front of the open refrigerator without knowing that you were going to walk there? When did you first start having food blackouts? Have these progressed?

Adverse Social Consequences

1. What harm has been done to your relationships? (For example, strained relationships from sugar anger, isolating, mood swings caused by sugar or starving, being undependable, changing appointments or plans with others because of sugar tiredness or lack of interest.)
2. How has your disease affected others? How have the people around you had to adapt because of your disease? In what ways have you abused others—your spouse, partner, children—because of the influence of this disease?

Adverse Financial Consequences

1. Include adverse financial consequences. How has the addiction kept you poor? How has it deprived you of having money for other things you want to do? Include crazy thinking about money so you could spend it on food. (For exam-

ple, breaking your neck to save thirty cents on toilet paper and then treating yourself for your shopping efforts by "taking yourself out"; spending more than is reasonable for meals; rewarding yourself by eating at a more expensive restaurant than you can really afford or by eating out so often that you deprive yourself of money for other activities; spending money on food that you could have used for therapy or recovery; spending extra money on food each week and then telling yourself you don't have enough money to take sensible care of yourself—for example, putting off seeing the doctor or dentist because of the cost when you are spending the equivalent amount on restaurants; not counting the money you spend on food or restaurants because that's a "necessity"—all addicts consider their drug a necessity.)

Adverse Moral Consequences

1. Has the disease made you violate your values? (For example, lying about eating; stealing, hiding, or concealing food; concealing bingeing, purging, or starving.) How is your self-respect doing? Have you lost any because of the effects of this disease?
2. Have you manipulated others so you could satisfy a craving? (For example, getting people out of the house so you could be alone with food; getting everyone to go to a certain restaurant; manipulating toward a specific activity because of the food associated with it; controlling food portions so that you get the most or there will be some left over that you'll eat later secretly.)
3. Include confused priorities—how is food the center of your life? Has it been the center of any of your relationships? What evidence is there that eating has been more important than relating? (For example: You're with a friend; she's talking. You pretend to be listening but you're actually thinking about food and eating. Your body is present but your thoughts and focus aren't on the relationship or the interaction.)

Adverse Spiritual Consequences

1. Include evidence of how eating has been more important than your spiritual development, more important than your

relationships, more important than your health, more important than your peace of mind.

2. How has this disease affected your choices, your decisions, the opportunities you've missed or aborted?

7

ACHIEVING ABSTINENCE

Caution, Anorexics: *This book is not for anorexics. This chapter in particular is not for anorexics. If you are of normal or less than normal weight and relentlessly pursue thinness, do not follow the suggestions contained in this chapter. Talk to your doctor or an eating-disorders professional to get the plan that is appropriate for you.*

Caution, Diabetics: *See your doctor and plan for your proper insulin level before starting any type of abstinence.*

When you achieve abstinence, you will be on your way to remarkable changes in your life. Your preoccupation with food will decrease. Food cravings will weaken and eventually disappear. For the first time, you will be able to make choices about eating. Instead of being driven to rip a snack package open with your teeth, you'll be able to choose to wait until the next meal. Instead of bloating yourself until your stomach stretches painfully, you'll be able to make healthy food selections.

BRAIN ALLERGY

If you are among those who have a brain allergy to certain foods, you will be astounded at the changes in the way you react to events and people. What is a brain allergy? It's a chemically induced reaction in the brain that manifests in emotional or behavioral changes, some of which can be extreme. Douglas Talbott, M.D., is studying food-induced brain allergies.[1] Certain people seem to react to certain foods with extreme emotional reactions. A person with a brain allergy to sugar products, for example, can have intense periods of rage, depression, hopelessness, paranoia, and isolation after eating something containing sugar. These feelings may cause extreme or inappropriate behavior, such as violence, verbal attacks, or self-harm.

Put simply, for some people, eating a cookie can cause a mild psychotic episode, the severity and duration being dependent on the amount of sugar ingested. For an extremely sensitive person, even one cookie can trigger the reaction.

Of course, you probably do not know if you have a brain allergy. Tests for brain allergies are not yet available. If you do have an allergy to sugar, for example, you'll find out when you become abstinent, because the symptoms caused by sugar will cease. For example, if sugar caused extreme emotional ups and downs, you'll find relief from them. You'll have the normal ups and downs that normal people have but the roller-coaster ride will flatten out. You may have come to accept feeling unstable or discouraged as a part of your personal makeup. What a gift to discover you've been feeling down because of a chemical reaction, a reaction that you can avoid simply by avoiding sugar.

For many of us who do suffer from brain allergies, abstinence gives us a shiny new connection with life. We are no longer whipped around emotionally like dogs on the end of a chain. Cranky, brow-wrinkling feelings go away and a window of freshness opens for us.

Instead of trying to work, love, and raise kids through walls of lethargy or irritation, we can get right next to life. We often don't realize what a struggle it's been until abstinence causes these walls to drop away. After you enjoy the celebration of freedom, give yourself some credit for your great courage to keep on trying under the weight of that old, heavy, invisible handicap. People who don't experience this have no concept of how taxing it is to consistently operate as a normal person while being controlled emotionally. It's like running a ten-kilometer race with lead weights on your wrists and ankles (weights no one else can see) while all the other runners are unfettered, and yet being expected to come in among the first ten. Emotional stability; freedom from food cravings; vibrant participation in life; increased awareness of yourself as a distinct, unique, worthy human being; increased touch with your needs, gifts, and purpose—these are the gifts of abstinence.

THE PLAN

Abstinence is not a diet. Abstinence means eating foods with no harmful chemicals. To be abstinent is to avoid any substance that triggers your addiction. A recovering, sober alcoholic is abstinent from alcohol. A sugar addict, to be sober, becomes abstinent from sugar.

For some of us, sugar is a harmful, addictive drug. We are not going on a diet. We are eliminating a harmful drug. Abstinence must be achieved in stages. If you attempt abstinence from too many food groups at once, it will seem like a diet. One day you will feel too deprived, say "What the hell!" and eat everything in sight. Since you don't want this to happen, read on.

Since sugar is the most potent of the food drugs, I recommend starting with abstinence from sugar. Throughout this book, I've made a distinction between sugar and carbohydrates. Technically, of course, sugar is a carbohydrate. But for food addicts, sugar, because of its concentration and potency, is in a class by itself. I therefore recommend achieving abstinence by avoiding the following substances in this order: sugar, refined carbohydrates (lists follow), and fats (partial abstinence or, if possible, moderation). Timing is very important. The first abstinence should be solid and comfortable before you add your second abstinence. People who ignore timing and try to become abstinent from starches and sugar at the same time usually fail.

Your plan for abstinence must respect the importance of avoiding too large a shock of deprivation. When we food addicts feel deprived, we eat. The following timing respects your body's need to make chemical adjustments and your soul's need to avoid the shock of deprivation.

First Abstinence—Sugar and Alcohol

Why alcohol? Alcohol is made from sugar, many bottled alcoholic drinks contain added sugar, and alcohol is a refined carbohydrate with a particularly potent effect on the body. After one month of sugar and alcohol abstinence, aim gradually toward eating three meals a day with nothing in between, or three meals and a snack with nothing in between. (If you've been diagnosed hypoglycemic and require six small daily meals, aim for nothing in between the six planned small meals.)

Refined Carbohydrate Abstinence

One year after the starting date of sugar abstinence, begin *gradual* refined carbohydrate abstinence. Six months after achieving 95 percent abstinence from all refined carbohydrates, moderate your fat intake. I'll be talking more about these last two items later in the book. Chapter 14 tells how to achieve further abstinence.

If you want lasting relief from all the problems of food addiction, if you want to work toward lasting weight loss, take it gradually and slowly. In big letters, write:

ABSTINENCE IS NOT A DIET.
ABSTINENCE IS AVOIDING A DANGEROUS DRUG.

Why am I so insistent that you separate sugar and carbohydrate abstinence? Because within the class of refined carbohydrates is white flour, and white-flour abstinence is very difficult to achieve. Sugar has invaded many normal foods, but the flour invasion is even more widespread. To avoid white flour often takes planning, foresight, and a redefinition of your normal foods. Flour abstinence is much easier if you are already adept at abstinence. Once you know how to swim, new strokes are easily added. Once you know how to be abstinent, carbohydrate abstinence stops being impossible.

Believe me, sugar abstinence is challenge enough. Also, I think it's important for the two endeavors to be separated in your mind. Then, if you have a slip with carbohydrates later, your mind will treat it as separate from your abstinence from sugar. You'll be less likely to throw up your hands and say, "I'm a failure!" If you do have a slip with carbohydrates, you'll still have your sugar abstinence. You'll still have the strength and pride that come from maintaining a successful abstinence. So, if you seriously want success, wait at least six months or, even better, a year before attempting carbohydrate abstinence.

One exception is this: Although alcohol is technically a refined carbohydrate, sugar is added to most alcohol before bottling. Besides, alcohol is also a particularly potent carbohydrate. If you are sensitive to sugar, you will be sensitive to alcohol. Not only will an alcoholic drink cause intense food and sugar cravings, it will harm your judgment. Even one drink will decrease the courage and clarity needed to maintain abstinence. If you are serious about wanting the gifts of abstinence, avoid all forms of alcohol from the beginning.

At first, it looks like abstinence is giving up something. After a while, you'll see that abstinence is gaining something—choices, energy, and freedom to live your special, personal life.

What if you become abstinent and the food cravings don't disappear? What if you don't feel any difference emotionally? Check these things. The two most common causes of this problem are not using enough support or abstinence that isn't clean enough.

SUGAR

I'm no longer surprised when a friend in recovery tells me she's abstinent from sugar and then eats cranberry sauce or a bowl of ice cream or a cup of hot chocolate, all loaded with sugar. Some clients who have had lingering cravings have eliminated sugar but keep eating honey or fructose-sweetened products. Nutrasweet is a real bugaboo for many sugar addicts. Equal, the sweetener, contains aspartame and corn-syrup solids. Corn syrup in any form is a very concentrated sugar product and triggers most sugar addicts. Thus all the soft drinks and desserts sweetened with Equal have a high potential for causing food cravings.

All concentrated forms of sugar must be avoided if your goal is to gain freedom from cravings. This includes fruit juices such as apple, pear, grape, and orange. One glass of apple juice may be equivalent to three or four apples. You would not ordinarily sit down and eat three apples at one sitting. But robbed of fiber, apple juice allows you to consume the sugar of three apples very quickly without the bulk to tell your stomach it's had enough. Figs, dates, and dried fruits are also very high in sugar. They are just like candy and our bodies react to them as if they were candy.

Sugar-free living involves vigilance. Sugar is added to many processed meats. Ham, sausage, hot dogs, lunch meat, bologna, most bacon, cold cuts, smoked meats, and summer sausage are sweetened, usually with sugar. Canned foods such as peas, corn, creamed corn, baked beans, chili beans, and many soups contain sugar. Most salad dressings, most breads, and most sauce mixes contain sugar. A more complete list is given at the end of this chapter.

If you don't want to be triggered by restaurant food, you'll need to know how such food is prepared. Since waiters and waitresses may not be as informed as I am, I take care in questioning them. Sometimes I ask them to ask the chef what sweeteners have been added. Chinese food, which traditionally has been very healthy, is now often westernized—sugared—to accommodate the sweet-hungry western palate. Recently when I stopped at a Chinese restaurant, I found not a single dish absent of sugar except chow mein, which was loaded with flour noodles.

I recently attended a potluck dinner. The invitation had specified sugar-free dishes only. A woman who had brought a dessert stated firmly that it had no sugar. It tasted sweet to me. I questioned her. It had been sweetened with fructose. We must be constantly aware that as a culture, Americans ingest high quantities of sugar and are accustomed to sweetness. Even friends who have heard us say we are sugar-free will offer us sweets. With friends, I think this is rarely deliberate sabotage but an indication of their unawareness of their own high dependence on sugar.

If we seriously intend to protect our abstinence, we must take total responsibility for what goes into our mouths and double-check offerings even from friends and relatives who know of our commitment. Unfortunately, we can't always trust a package that reads "sugar-free." You'd think the food industry was deliberately trying to mislead us, that they are aware of sugar's addictive properties and capitalize on them. I've seen packages labeled "sugar-free" and found two or three sweeteners on the ingredients label. Desserts labeled sugar-free are especially suspect. Be wary of cereals, too. One popular cereal brand stridently advertised as healthy contains more sugar than most.

So if you've achieved three weeks of abstinence and your cravings haven't diminished, talk to another abstinent person about what you're eating. If you've studied the lists at the end of this chapter and you understand the different forms of sugar, if you've discussed your food with a knowledgeable person and you're sure it's sugar-free, look at the amount of refined carbohydrates in your diet.

CARBOHYDRATES

I've warned you to separate sugar abstinence from refined carbohydrate abstinence, but if strong food cravings are still bothering you after three or four weeks of sugar abstinence, you may be eating too high a proportion of refined carbohydrates. Try substituting whole-grain breads, pasta, and rice for refined products. See if your cravings diminish. But don't get crazy over it. If finding substitutes for, say, pizza or garlic bread seems too complicated, don't worry for now. When you are first abstinent from sugar, you should not attempt carbohydrate abstinence, but you may need to taper intake of refined carbohydrates and substitute whole grains to get relief from food cravings.

Once you are cleanly abstinent from sugar and you've moderated carbohydrate intake, the last great cause of food cravings is emotional deprivation. Let's say you skip along craving-free for several days and suddenly you're hit with a tremendous need to eat. Unless you accidentally ate some form of sugar, something's wrong. Something's bothering you. You need something you're not getting. Some feeling you're afraid of is rumbling inside you. This kind of craving signals a genuine emptiness, but it is not food emptiness. This is a craving from emotional emptiness. You don't have enough of something you need. Get support. This is the point that will make or break your abstinence. If you have a safe, effective support system, you are willing to turn to it, and you do turn to it, you will be surprised. As you talk and get attention and guidance about what you need, the craving will magically disappear. If you don't have a support system or if survival rules keep you from using it, your abstinence will be in jeopardy.

GETTING ABSTINENT

CREATE A SUPPORT SYSTEM

Find four to eight people who genuinely support you in this process. (If this step seems impossible, read chapter 6 again. You must ultimately work up to doing this if you are to have long-term, fairly easy, and serene abstinence.) The more people you can find the better. The very best resources for you are other abstinent folks. These amazing people can be found at Overeaters Anonymous, Bulimics Anonymous, Eating Disorders Anonymous, and Alcoholics Anonymous meetings.

Beware of relying on friends or loved ones active in an addiction but not in recovery, those who will not read chapter 9 of this book; those who may be relying on sugar and starches themselves (but are probably unaware of it); and those who consciously or unconsciously want you to stay drugged with sugar. Some people want you to stay drugged because they:

- Fear a change in you
- Don't want a change in household routine
- Want you to remain content with inequities in the family
- Want you to keep serving starchy meals
- Want you to stay happy waiting on everyone else

- Want you to continue being a binge buddy
- Won't know how to relate to you if your relationship isn't centered around food
- May need you to stay fat (for example, they feel safer if you're less attractive, misery loves company, they need you to continue feeling bad about yourself, or they need you to remain the underdog/scapegoat)
- Don't want others finding you attractive

We have a name for people who either subtly or forcefully try to get us to eat triggering foods. The name is *enabler.* An enabler is a pusher who can sometimes be a very kind, well-meaning person. People may enable out of ignorance, need, fear, mistaken kindness, habit, need for control or power, denial, or malice. Many people feel threatened by change, especially if it requires them to change. Whatever the reason, if we succumb to them, we end up being harmed, whether the enabler intended kindness or malice.

List those friends and relatives who seem truly capable of supporting your recovery. Then list those friends and relatives you suspect cannot, and keep it in a secure place. Chapter 9 contains a letter to your loved ones. When you get to it, ask them to read it. Following the letter is a test each loved one can take to determine how willing he or she is to support you. You may want to make copies of this test for your friends and relatives so they can be very clear with you about their level of willingness.

After the willingness check is a list of ways they can support you. You may want to copy this and give it to them so that they can refer to it. Remember, an abstinent stranger can be more helpful than an addicted friend.

Create a Safe Home

Throw out all sugar and, when you get to that stage, refined starch products. If other family members insist on keeping your poison in the house, put all these items in one cabinet, closet, or box that you never need to get into. Feel free to put a lock on it and give everyone else a key.

Call a family meeting, with the following agenda. (The "I" in what follows is you; the "you" is your family members.)

AGENDA

Announcement: I (you) have discovered that sugar is harming me and messing up my life. To stop this, I will have to take some extreme measures. One day, some of these changes won't be necessary, but for now, you (your family) can think of it this way—I am preparing to detox from a chemical that is as dangerous to me as heroin or cocaine.

House changes: I will be doing the following: Eliminating sugar from the house. (If there is an outcry, calmly describe the locked-cabinet idea.) Substituting healthier foods for what I've been eating: For example, whole-wheat bread for white bread, decaf for caffeinated drinks, fruit for sugar products. Becoming a stickler for three regular meals a day at regular times, even on vacation.

Define abstinence. This is not a diet. I am beginning the difficult process of detoxing from what for me is a harmful drug.

Describe withdrawal. When I begin abstinence, I will probably go through a period of withdrawal. I may become anxious and restless. I may have trouble sleeping. I may have periods of being very angry and very sad. I may have intense cravings to eat sugar and starches, especially from the third through seventh days. I may be eating other foods more. These feelings have little to do with you. Don't be frightened, you aren't causing my distress. This is a sign of the chemical changes occurring in my body.

How I will protect myself and you. I will be unable to participate in any major decisions or changes for the next three weeks. If you know of something coming up, let's deal with it now. Otherwise, I'll be available again in three weeks.

I will be talking to other people who have this addiction. I will be gone some evenings so I can attend support-group meetings and sometimes I will need to talk privately on the phone.

Please let me know the amount of support you are willing to give me by reading and marking this sheet. (Give each family member a copy of "How to Support an Abstaining Food Addict," below.)

Model effective boundaries. I'd appreciate your comments, feelings, and reactions. (If someone tries a guilt trip or "what about my needs?" statement, hear them out but stress that this is something you must do for yourself and that you are confident everyone in the family will benefit eventually because when one person gets healthier, the whole family has a chance to become healthier. If the whining continues, say that you feel confident that they will find the strength to work this out but that you will be following your recovery plan no matter what. Then close the meeting.)

Withdrawal preparation. Prepare intense support for the first ten days. Call your supporters and arrange definite calling times for each day. Ideally, you should be talking to someone each morning and evening. Commit to definite dates and times for each support person and clarify who's calling whom. (Minimum support is talking to one person each evening of the ten days.) Give each supporter a copy of the following guidelines, "How to Support an Abstaining Food Addict" (the same information you passed out at the family meeting).

HOW TO SUPPORT AN ABSTAINING FOOD ADDICT

1. Listen to her. Without the presence of the sedating foods, she/he will be experiencing mood swings, painful feelings, and raw reality. Listen to her experience.
2. Refrain from solving her problems or giving advice. Right now, she needs to let it out more than to solve it. If she demands frantically that she must solve a problem, remind her she is detoxing and she can get to it in three weeks.
3. Discourage her from making any big decisions or changes at this time. Withdrawing people are not fully sane.
4. When she talks about feeling restless or fearful, remind her that this is part of withdrawal and will pass.
5. Be alert to disguised cravings in the form of statements like the following:

"I'm not really addicted to sugar."
(You thought so when you decided to detox.)
"My office is having a dessert party. I'm expected to go."
(This sounds like a setup to eat sugar. How far are you willing to go to get your life back?)
"Harry and I have a tradition of having a frozen dessert (sugar product) in the evening."
(Can your relationship survive a change in tradition?)

6. Be alert to switched compulsions such as compulsive spending, working, sex, religion, or television-watching.
7. Remember that alcohol is a refined carbohydrate.
8. Encourage attendance at support-group meetings.
9. Encourage telephone conversations with lots of people.
10. Remind her to take good care of herself: three meals a day, plenty of rest, quiet and alone time.
11. Only give and listen as much as you're willing.
12. Take care of yourself as well.

KNOW THE ENEMY

Learn what sugar is. The following are forms of sugar:

- Beet sugar
- Brown sugar
- Cane sugar
- Corn-syrup solids
- Dextrose
- Food products ending in *ose* except cellulose
- Fructose
- Glucose
- Honey
- Lactose
- Malto-dextrin
- Mannitol and sorbitol are alcohols that convert to sugar in the stomach
- Maple sugar or syrup
- Molasses
- Rice sugar
- Sucrose
- Turbinado sugar

LEARN WHAT SUBSTANCES CONTAIN SUGAR

Alcohol
- Alcoholic beverages

Artificial Sweeteners
- Equal
- Sugar Twin
- Sweet-'n'-Low

Breads and Pasta
- Most breads
- Most cereals
- Most crackers
- Some fried batters

Dairy
- Flavored milk
- Most toffuti, frozen yogurt
- Most yogurts
- Much processed cheese, most pimento cheese
- Sugar-free cocoa mixes

Desserts
- Desserts with obvious sugar, candies, etc.
- Most sugar-free frozen desserts
- Most toffuti, frozen yogurt

Fruits
- Most canned fruits and juices

Meals
- Dinner mixes
- Frozen dinners

Meats
- Most bacon
- Most cold cuts, bologna, processed meats
- Most cured and smoked meat and fish
- Most sausage, ham, hot dogs

Medicines
- Most cough drops, cough syrups, and liquid cold medicines

Seasonings and Sauces
- Ketchup
- Most barbecue sauces
- Most marinades
- Most salad dressings
- Most spaghetti sauces
- Sauces and sauce mixes
- Some salt
- Sweet-and-sour sauce
- Teriyaki

Snacks
- Most crackers
- Some fried batters
- Some potato chips

Soups
- Most bouillon
- Most canned chicken and beef broth
- Most cream soups

Vegetables
- Most canned corn, peas, and round beans

KNOW AND AVOID FOODS WITH A HIGH NATURAL SUGAR CONTENT

- Cider
- Dates
- Dried fruits
- Figs
- Fruit juices

KNOW WHAT REFINED CARBOHYDRATES ARE

- Alcohol
- Refined rye flour
- Rice flour (unless it is from brown rice)
- White flour, including unbleached flour
- White or milled rice

Know What Foods Contain Refined Carbohydrates

- Buns and pizza crusts
- Most breads, including many whole-wheat and multigrain breads
- Most bagels
- Most crackers
- Most cream soups
- Most fried batters
- Most gravies
- Most pastas
- Most pizza dough
- Most sauces
- Wheat bread (If a bread is mostly white with occasional brown flecks, it contains mostly white flours.)

Know What You're Eating

1. Read labels. Labels list ingredients from the greatest amount to the least. So a product with a label that reads "Ingredients: Peanuts, oil, salt" contains more peanuts than oil and more oil than salt. Sometimes we compromise by buying a product with sugar low on the list. Beware, though, of different forms of sugar. Add them together to learn the actual sugar content. For example, in a product containing oil, water, onion, corn-syrup solids, sucrose, and dextrose, the sweeteners together might compose more of the product than the first ingredient.

   Let's suppose a food contains the following ingredients in the amount of the units in parentheses: Oil (6), water (5), vinegar (4), corn-syrup solids (3.9), sucrose (3.8), dextrose (3.7). Add the sweeteners together:

$$\begin{array}{r} 3.9 \\ 3.8 \\ \underline{3.7} \\ 11.4 \text{ units} \end{array}$$

The product contains 11.4 units of sweetener, more units than oil, the first ingredient listed.

We can also be fooled by the following: unbleached enriched flour (wheat flour, malted barley flour, iron, niacin, thiamine mononitrate, riboflavin); water; whole-wheat flour; oil (contains one or more of the following: corn oil, sunflower oil, cottonseed oil, peanut oil, partially hydrogenated soybean oil, or partially hydrogenated sunflower oil); high-fructose corn syrup.

Sugar looks like it's low on the list, but it's actually the fifth ingredient. High-fructose corn syrup sounds safe but it's still sugar. You already know that unbleached, enriched flour is refined.

2. Talk to food servers if you are in doubt about a menu item.

3. Don't eat in cafés that are part of a bakery. These homey places usually add extra sugar to sauces and mixtures.

GUIDELINES FOR ABSTINENT EATING

1. Keep in mind the following overall guidelines for abstinent eating:
   - Fresh, natural food
   - Whole-wheat pastas
   - Whole fruits
   - 100-percent whole-wheat bread

   Find a good health-food or natural-food store. There you can usually find sugar-free soups, ketchup, sauces; 100-percent whole-wheat bread without sugar; uncured bacon; 100-percent whole-wheat hamburger and hot-dog buns; whole-wheat pizza doughs; whole-grain pastas; yogurt without sugar; whole-wheat pie crusts; whole-wheat french and sourdough breads; pimento cheese and other cheese products with no sugar; sugar-free barbecue sauce; sea salt; and sugar-free salad dressings. (Since writing this chapter, I've visited several states in the Midwest where I couldn't even find 100-percent whole-wheat bread without sugar. Many restaurants didn't have whole-wheat rolls or breads. I can only hope that as more and more of us demand sugar- and starch-free products, grocers and restaurateurs will take heed.)

Even in a health-food store, we must read labels. Many of them stock sugared products. Beware especially of jams made with sweeteners other than sugar. They are often enough to trigger the chain reaction. The only product I cannot find is unsweetened ice cream. I make this at home.

2. Eat three meals a day.
3. Never skip a meal.
4. Have plenty to eat for supper. Have some kind of protein for breakfast.
5. Don't worry if you're eating more than usual. If you follow the principles in this book, your dependence on and interest in food will decrease.
6. Eat two or three whole fruits every day.
7. Don't worry that you are eating more chips, popcorn, etc., for now. This is not a diet. You are detoxing from a dangerous drug. When you've been abstinent for a month, read this chapter again.
8. Switch to flavored mineral water. Nutrasweet drinks will keep the cravings going.
9. If you must travel, plan ahead:
   a. Some airlines offer several meal selections, such as diabetic meals. When you reserve your ticket, ask what the meals will be and choose an alternative if you wish.
   b. Many airlines also offer mineral water as an alternative to sweetened, caffeinated soft drinks.
   c. In a car, carry protein snacks, fruit, and water in case you can't find a restaurant at your regular mealtime.
10. Switch to decaffeinated drinks. Caffeine causes insulin release, which triggers appetite and fat storage.
11. Don't drink alcoholic beverages. If you have been drinking more than two ounces of alcohol more than two times a week, you have probably developed some alcohol dependence. If so, your withdrawal may be pretty bumpy because you'll be detoxing from two drugs. Go to A.A. meetings as well as OA meetings.
12. Don't fall in love. I know, that's easy for me to say. But it's important. Falling in love is a great distraction from withdrawal and is bound to release carloads of endorphins. Besides, falling in love while detoxing is often a substitute

addiction, a fixation on a person instead of food. It usually ends in a crash that threatens abstinence.

13. Beware of substitute addictions. Food addicts seem particularly vulnerable to shopping, people, and work addictions. Before abstinence starts, give all your credit cards to a trustworthy person. Develop rules about spending; for example:
   a. No charging
   b. No purchase over $50 without talking to a support person
   c. No purchase over $50 without sleeping on it
   d. Carry only the amount you can afford to spend
   e. Avoid shopping centers

14. Plan ahead if you must go to a buffet or party:
   a. Take your telephone numbers with you.
   b. Ask where the telephone is as soon as you walk in.
   c. Stand as far away from the food as possible. Stand with your back to the food.
   d. If someone pushes food at you, say one of the following:

- "I've had enough."
- "It'd make me break out in hives."
- "I'm allergic to that."
- "I'm full."
- "Sugar makes me suicidal."
- "I'm preventing diabetes."
- "If I eat that, I'll become a raving lunatic."
- "You eat it."
- "I prefer to select my own food."

   e. Decide beforehand what your selection will be, go straight to it, get it, and vamoose.
   f. If you start feeling shaky or deprived, call your support person.
   g. If calling doesn't help, leave.

15. For the first three months, minimize your contact with food:
   a. If you must cook, make simple, quick meals.
   b. When you're through eating, stay out of the kitchen.
   c. Do as little food shopping as possible.
   d. Stay out of those giant food stores with bins and big displays, selections, and samples.

   e. Find a friendly little health-food store.
   f. Do hit-and-run shopping. Always make a list at home. Never buy what isn't on the list. Go in, get it, get out.

16. Get plenty of rest. Don't worry if you have trouble sleeping. This is just a further sign of the drug effect sugar had on your body.

    Many people find tryptophan helps them sleep, although as of this writing, tryptophan has been pulled from the shelves pending an investigation. (Tryptophan is an amino acid—a building block of protein—and the precursor to serotonin. It is available at health-food stores. One tablet is usually plenty—500 or 659 milligrams. Three is the limit. Its safe use by pregnant women, however, remains controversial.) Don't take tryptophan if you are taking the antidepressant Prozac or another serotonin blocker.
17. Take a good vitamin and mineral supplement. Health-food stores have good-quality vitamins.
18. Walk at least thirty minutes a day.
19. Be outside some each day.
20. Don't make any major decisions or changes for the first year.
21. Remember, rapid mood changes frequently accompany withdrawal. This will pass.
22. Go to five support meetings a week.

WITHDRAWAL: THE BIG TEN (DAYS)

Withdrawal is a bitch. It passes. Here's what to expect:

- Rushes of anger
- Periods of sadness and melancholy
- Anxiety
- Restlessness
- Trouble sleeping
- Black/white thinking (i.e., in extremes)
- Strong urges to shop, spend, go somewhere
- Not comfortable in own skin
- Feelings of intense vulnerability

- Some very tricky cravings ("I think I'll wander through the kitchen.")
- Amnesia—forgetting completely that you are withdrawing and detoxing
- Loss of insight—not realizing you're in upheaval because you are detoxing

The above symptoms can occur simultaneously or in any order. To help identify what you're experiencing, check the list now and then during your first week of withdrawal. Withdrawal usually follows this pattern:

Day One. No problem. A little startled at the change in pattern. Perhaps a feeling of emptiness because foods previously used to anchor the day are missing.
Day Two. Feeling strange. Something is missing.
Day Three. Subtle, tricky cravings. Anxiety starts building. Amnesia and denial start. Forgetfulness. Rushes of anger.
Day Four. Restless. Uncomfortable. Angry. "I want to buy something."
Day Five. All of the above with increased intensity.
Day Six. All of the above with some periods that don't seem too bad.
Day Seven. Anxiety and restlessness decrease.
Day Eight. Moments of clarity. Discomfort tapering.
Day Nine. Still periods of amnesia, lack of insight, and anger, but tapering.
Day Ten. Getting better.

Withdrawal Survivors

A twenty-one-day period is required to break a habit or lose a craving. After three weeks, abstinence becomes much easier. You have detoxed, but deep repair must still occur throughout your mind and body. Unlike other drug addicts, you must continue to eat (the alcoholic need not drink to live), so you'll need to be especially vigilant.

Continue to follow the guidelines listed in step 5, p. 123. Stay out of the kitchen. Do minimal food preparation. Plan for special situations. Never miss a meal. If a meal is to be delayed an hour past the usual time, have a salad or fruit and protein.

Three weeks is still very early in recovery. Cravings may be startlingly powerful and subtle, especially when provoked by uncomfortable feelings; a flash of shame or anger, for example, could come dressed as a strong craving. You may still experience amnesia and low insight about this process you're in. Most of us still experience this on occasion after years of recovery. Go to four support-group meetings a week and talk to a support person every day. To keep to your abstinence, you must care for your whole self. When you neglect your feelings, you risk losing your abstinence and your level of recovery.

If you don't make it through withdrawal, the reason is simple. You need more support. Read the next chapter, which describes how to expand support. It might help to know that slips are part of recovery. The healing curve for any disease does not go up without interruption. After you've expanded your support system, read this chapter again and implement any actions you slighted.

SUMMARY

Here is a little lighthearted quiz that reviews some of the information contained in this and previous chapters. Play with it if you like.

1. If you're a food and sugar addict, which two major factors will cause you to crave food?
   a. Air and water
   b. Inlaws and asparagus
   c. Labor Day and UFOs
   d. Biochemical triggers and the need to feel different
2. Foods likely to act as chemical triggers are:
   a. Cabbage, mineral water, and nasturtiums
   b. French bread, sugar-free candy, and frozen yogurt
   c. Turkey, cranberries, and homemade ranch dressing
   d. Apples, herb tea, and popcorn

3. Which of the following foods are unlikely to produce chemically triggered cravings?
   a. Equal, ketchup, figs, most bacon
   b. Honey, coffee, fructose-sweetened cookies, fried chicken
   c. Waldorf salad, cheese omelet, baked potato with butter and chives
   d. Store-bought pimento cheese, apple cider, crackers, Weight Watchers desserts
4. Foods that act as chemical appetite triggers do what?
   a. Stimulate a chain reaction involving the k-cells of the upper intestine, insulin release, a deprivation message to the hypothalamus, endorphin functioning, and serotonin release
   b. Cause the famous hyperkeratinase reaction
   c. Provide an unexpected secondary function in the arms race
   d. Feel tremendous shame
5. When food cravings are triggered chemically,
   a. The urge to eat is nearly irresistible
   b. Eating is optional
   c. The urge to pedal a bike furiously is also triggered
   d. One is satisfied by studying pictures of food
   e. It's easy to put all thoughts of eating out of mind
6. As a general rule, the more foods are refined, the more likely they are to
   a. Go to the opera
   b. Trigger eating
   c. Decrease eating
   d. Wear fancy clothes
7. If you are going to be abstinent from triggering foods, you must
   a. Ignore food labels
   b. Keep it a secret from everyone
   c. Read all food labels and question food servers about the content of restaurant food. (Remember, labels on food items list the ingredients from the greatest amount to the least.)
   d. Trust restaurants to give you what's best for you

8. Which of the following contain the fewest refined carbohydrates?
   a. Water, oil, garlic, sugar, salt
   b. Mannitol, sorbitol, chocolate liquor, PDH, SFT
   c. Oil, chives, cheese, sucrose, dextrose, corn-syrup solids, malto-dextrin
   d. Whole-wheat flour, brown rice, cellulose, salt, molasses
9. Which statement is false?
   a. When you are first abstinent, your withdrawal is similar to that from alcohol and other drugs and is characterized by anxiety, mood swings, and restlessness.
   b. Abstinence is like a diet.
   c. In the long run, abstinence means increased energy, increased evenness of mood, more openness to yourself and to living, and an end to food obsession.
   d. Your best chance to maintain long-term abstinence is to find other abstinent people and talk to them every day.

Answers: 1. d; 2. b; 3. c; 4. a; 5. a; 6. b; 7. c; 8. d; 9. b.

8

HELP!

Few of us recover from this disease alone. Overeating is in part a relationship disease, triggered and worsened by disordered relationships. Recovery is difficult because it requires us to face and deal with our relationship issues. We don't like to ask for help, we find it hard to express our needs and wants, we have difficulty taking a stand on our own behalf. We are more accustomed to keeping the peace, hiding our feelings, and going along with what everyone else wants. Yet we need deeply. We often get into relationships that we pour everything into. We try to look independent, yet we become deeply dependent on a lover or best friend who inevitably lets us down. We are then plunged into hopelessness and despair—despair at the depth of our need and hopelessness at having it filled.

If we haven't been too abused and neglected, we can get a good start with a Twelve Step program such as Overeaters Anonymous (OA), Eating Disorders Anonymous (EDA), or Bulimics Anonymous (BA). Twelve Step programs, which ask only for a small donation at each meeting, offer a sound structure for recovery. By using all the tools they recommend, especially attending meetings and working with a sponsor, you can make them work for you. The difficulty is that it's up to you to build the structure and to use it. If you want to fade away and crawl back into food, you can do so with little resistance. It's easy to disappear.

The paradox most of us wrestle with is that we need help to recover, yet we have difficulty asking for help. Or we can ask one out of ten times but the other nine times we suffer. Or we can ask for a little of what we need but leave out most of it. Or we *can* ask, but then have trouble accepting it. Many of us can get out of this cycle only with professional help. A person trying to recover from compulsive eating or food addiction needs a warm, consistent, reliable human in her life. We need someone to teach and encourage us to get what we need. We need someone to help us work through the fears and hurts that keep us from getting our needs met.

Group therapy seems the most effective ongoing vehicle for recovery from food addiction and compulsive eating, more effective than individual therapy unless particular issues block a person's ability to use the group. Group members can support each other. The work of other group members can model different phases of recovery and stimulate awareness of personal issues. Group interaction can provide a laboratory and training ground to practice new and healthier interpersonal skills.

THE THERAPEUTIC PROCESS

A therapy group for overeaters is a place to learn about the disease, learn the elements needed for recovery, and get solid support in revising one's life bit by bit to include what is needed for recovery. This stage—the group's first item of business—is an exhilarating one. For the first time, the probability of change seems real.

The second stage may be a slump. The relationship issues that have troubled you all your life pop up over and over, usually with a member of your group. She may let you down, she may irritate you, she may infuriate you. Maybe your therapist is the culprit. Perhaps she disappoints you. A chance word or look seems very significant. Her authority begins to chafe you. At this point, you may feel depressed. What if the hopes of stage one were all just dreams?

Many people leave therapy at this point and so cheat themselves of working through to a freedom they may never otherwise know. At this stage, you are very vulnerable to pressure from loved ones to leave the group.

Let's face it, the people closest to us are going to be frightened by our recovery. We are all afraid of change. For you to be able to state your needs and feelings, for you to know you are worthwhile, will shake up all your relationships. It doesn't do much good to reassure our loved ones that in the long run, things will be better for them too. Unless they work on their issues, chances are they will both subtly and rudely interfere with our recovery. They will enable the disease. When we hit stage two in the group, when we come home from group angry or discouraged, we are likely to hear, "Why do you stay with that group (or that therapist)? Why make yourself miserable?" They may encourage us to quit and reward us for doing so.

When you reach stage two, the most important thing is to show up for therapy. When you can, talk about what you're going through. A good therapist can coach you about confronting a group member; she can help both of you work through the issue with your self-esteem intact and steer you both away from being abusive.

If your issue is with your therapist, a good therapist knows how to hear your feelings. Also, irritating but necessary, she can help you get to the issue she triggered. The important thing is to talk it out. Often the encounter is more important than the issue involved. That she listens, cares, works with you, and gives you room to express youself can be very healing even if the issue goes unresolved.

Sometimes an issue with the therapist or a group member feels very familiar, similar to something you experienced as a child. This phenomenon has many names, the original being *transference.* We can often get in touch with this by asking ourselves: What does this feeling remind me of? What occurred earlier in my life that seems similar to this? Working through transference in therapy is critical. Transference frequently occurs in intimate relationships. When it happens in therapy, you get a chance to resolve it with the help of an expert.

Eating-disorder therapists are certified nationally by the International Association of Eating Disorders Professionals. The two categories of certification are Certified Eating Disorders Counselor (CEDC) and Certified Eating Disorders Therapist (CEDT). To qualify for either category, a person must demonstrate knowledge, education, and experience. A CEDC has documented 2,000 hours of work with people with eating disorders. A CEDT has documented 4,000 hours.

All therapists are not created equal. Even among certified professionals, therapists approach recovery differently. Some take a behavioral approach; others a psychoanalytic, systems, or addictions approach. They have backgrounds in mental health, social work, nursing, addictions, psychology, or nutrition. Some are themselves in recovery from eating disorders; others aren't.

Good eating-disorder therapy offers you structure in the form of a recovery plan. The plan in turn offers insight into your propensity for food addiction, the support needed to achieve abstinence, and the experience of being a member of a healthy family. The group should be safe enough to explore tough feelings and issues. The therapist should understand the recovery process well enough to give you a sense of the plan through which she is guiding you. She needs knowledge and skill to help you expose the connection between present and childhood pain and suffering.

THE GROUP

Your therapy group should have very firm boundaries. Your therapist should insist on no sex, no triangulating, and strict confidentiality and anonymity among group members. Your therapist should take a firm stand on the sexual safety of group members and demonstrate, through words and attitude, that her clients are completely safe with her. I am biased toward same-sex groups. Sexual safety is often an issue for women with eating disorders, so I favor groups that are all women or all men led by a therapist of the same sex.

THERAPISTS IN RECOVERY

I am also biased toward therapists in recovery. I find them to be invaluable models for their clients and able to avoid some pitfalls common to therapist-client relationships. That is, a therapist in active recovery is more likely to spot countertransference and thus work through it, less likely to feel superior to or different from her clients, and more likely to notice perfectionism, rigid thinking, and controlling behavior in herself. That she shares the human condition is continually revealed to her.

Therapists not in active recovery may fall prey to their own denial, may be less in touch with their own imperfections, and may be more vulnerable to unconscious entanglement with their clients. In addition, I trust therapists in therapy. I have seen therapists who exude an attitude that they are above the need for therapy. I find this offensive. What does this say about that therapist's attitude toward his or her clients? A therapist afraid of therapy is afraid of contact with his or her inner self. How can the client contact the therapist's inner self if the therapist can't? Much of being a good therapist involves opening up to the client and taking that client's feelings through our own insides, so I wonder how effective a close-minded therapist can be. I believe that therapists out of touch with their own issues fail to see when they are triggered by a client's issues. The therapeutic process, then, becomes very tangled.

CERTIFICATION

We are now inundated with certification processes for therapists. Certifying boards exist for family therapists, addictions therapists, mental health therapists, and so on. We scramble for credentials but I wonder sometimes what the credentials show. I know some superb therapists without master's degrees or any certification. For a certified eating-disorders counselor or therapist in your area, a list of resources is included in the back of this book.

INSURANCE

As a rule, insurance will not cover eating disorders unless one is near death. Most policies, moreover, will not reimburse the insured unless treatment is provided by a Ph.D. psychologist or a psychiatrist, and most insurance companies would rather pay thousands of dollars for a hospital program than hundreds of dollars for an outpatient program.

CHOOSING A THERAPIST

The most important indicator that a therapist is good for you is how you feel when you are with him or her. Do you feel safe? Does she or he seem warm, open, and clear? Does she or he seem accepting of you or do you sense judgment? Does she or he listen well to you? If you don't feel safe anywhere, you may not feel safe even with a safe therapist. Ask what rules or boundaries the therapist keeps. Ask what direction her program takes. If you join her group, observe the other group members. Do they behave as if they feel safe?

It's fine to ask her many questions. Is she comfortable with your questions and your need to explore your own safety? You may ask a question that is not appropriate for her to answer. Can she handle such a question without making you feel wrong? Does she offer another session or two so you can continue exploring whether you can work together? It's good to shop around for a therapist. You might try two or three so you can compare how you feel with each one.

ASSIGNMENT 8.1

1. List the qualities you want in a therapist. Think about whether you want a male or female therapist.
2. Talk to friends in therapy. Ask them about their relationship to their therapist, what it's like, and how they feel about it.
3. Talk to recovering friends in therapy. Find out what their therapeutic process has been like.

9

DEAR BELOVED

You love someone who is addicted to food. You are a husband or wife, partner, lover, friend, mother, father, daughter, sister, son, or brother of a food addict. You may have observed behaviors in your loved one or friend that seem incomprehensible to you. You have said to her (as I mentioned, I use female pronouns because more women than men suffer from this disease) or you have thought, why don't you just quit eating?

Perhaps you have wanted her to lose weight. You may have offered rewards if she would—a new dress, money, a trip. Perhaps you have felt disgusted. Perhaps you have lost respect for her. Her seeming lack of control may be repulsive to you. You don't understand it, you don't like it, and you see it as a weakness that makes you think less of her.

Would you like to understand? I'll describe what it might be like for her on the inside. If you truly want to understand, put down your anger and your judgments for a few minutes. Your anger has a place, your judgments are rich in information for you—I'll talk about that later in this chapter—but if you truly want to understand, you'll have a better chance if you can be open to some new ideas.

THE ADDICTION

What is it like to be addicted to food? It's a nightmare. When she wakes up in the morning, does she anticipate the day with joy? No. She's barely conscious, but her mind is telling her that today she must get control of herself. She must not eat between meals, she must limit her sweet intake, she must eat sensibly, she must lose weight. She's barely conscious, but her thoughts are about not being good enough.

By the way, do you know that you're a good person? Is your worth as a person in any way related to your appearance? If you are a man, this may be a startling notion. As a man, your sense of worth probably depends more on what you do than on how you look.

Many women don't know such peace. An attractive woman of normal weight may often wonder if her appearance is good enough. Women often compare themselves with other women and find themselves lacking. If you are a woman, you know what it's like to feel that your worth as a person is connected to your attractiveness. If you are a man, you may be spared this terrible, draining, ongoing battle. (As women get further into recovery, they get more and more relief from this.)

Women of any size battle with the idea that their appearance reflects their worth. Imagine then what it's like for an overweight woman. She feels that her size proves she is worth less. (And you, secretly, have a similar opinion, don't you? You think a little less of her because of her size.)

Imagine how hard it is to walk around feeling that everyone might, simply on the basis of appearance, judge you less worthy. Imagine how hard it is to overcome that judgment. It would be as bad as having to wear a patch on your arm announcing your religion or your sexual orientation if either were discriminated against. It would be like having a skin color or facial characteristic different from the majority and considered by some to be inferior. Overweight people, then, belong to an oppressed minority. The discrimination they suffer is as arbitrary as all other forms of discrimination, for weight does not indicate worth any more than skin color or facial characteristics or sexual orientation or religion or favorite toothpaste.

What's in the heart is what matters. Size doesn't matter. Unfortunately, your loved one doesn't know that. She thinks that every time you see her, you judge her as less. She judges herself as less. She may feel inferior because of her size. If she gains a pound, she may despair. If she loses a pound, she may think she's a slightly better person. So every morning she awakens frantic about her predicament. She wants to feel she has worth, and her weight is in the way.

HER DAY

She gets up. She has to get dressed. Getting dressed is a horror for most overweight people. Recently, attractive clothes for overweight women have become available, but just fifteen years ago many women had to resort to smocks in order to be clothed.

No matter how expensive her wardrobe, getting dressed is a painful experience. Getting dressed requires looking in the mirror. Even well-designed clothes can't make a person look 100 pounds lighter. She may try on three or four things and feel terribly frustrated because none of them looks really good. Worse, something may feel tight, leading to despair that her weight is even increasing. What a hopeless feeling that is. If the present extra ten pounds have been impossible to lose, another five pounds will be insuperable. She may have trouble putting on her hose. She may have trouble bending over. She may not be able to tie her shoelaces. She has a handicap. Weight is handicapping her, limiting her movement and flexibility.

Once dressed, she must face breakfast. She may greatly fear breakfast. She fears food. She fears that if she starts eating, she won't be able to stop. She may put off eating for as long as possible because of that fear. Like many with this disease, she may skip breakfast. If she's in recovery, however, she may be trying to eat a sensible breakfast. You may not realize the enormity of this. You may not see the courage it takes for her to approach breakfast. She doesn't tell you how frightened she is because she fears you'll laugh or not understand.

If she's going to work, she must muster her courage. Do you remember what it was like to be taunted as you approached the schoolyard? Maybe you were lucky and no one teased you. The person with extra weight runs a gauntlet every morning. She must get from her car to her office without hearing someone remark on her size. If she rides a bus, she worries that she's taking up too much room. That person wouldn't have to stand if she didn't lap into the next seat. Perhaps someone will even say something about it. In her office or school or wherever she works, she worries that she won't fit in the chair, that there won't be a place where she can sit. Her boss and coworkers may have doubts about her because of her size. She may have to work harder than other workers to prove her value as an employee.

If she's in a job that is appearance-oriented—if she's a hairdresser or a retailer or an eating-disorders therapist—she braces herself for the remark that confirms she is not one of the beautiful people. What is she doing here, anyway?

Lunch is a mixed blessing. It's a break from work. Since food helps her cope with difficulties and she's had a difficult morning, lunch offers relief from the struggle. On the other hand, food is the cause of her problem. She's afraid of eating, too. No matter what she chooses to eat, she fears people are looking at her plate and judging her. Leaving work, she runs the same gauntlet as in the morning, except that she's tired, so a stranger's rude remark cuts deeper. In leaving work, she is fighting perhaps the hardest battle of the day. Leaving is freeing—she is now free to eat—yet confining: Food is calling—loudly. It may call so loudly that she'll surrender to it rather than arrange activities with friends. She may prefer to eat alone and unwatched rather than be with others.

Perhaps today was a diet day. Then the puny scheduled meal seems cold and inadequate. The time before and after dinner may stretch emptily before her. Food calls loudly, more inviting than any other promise of comfort. She feels restless, vulnerable. She is continually tempted with food thoughts and visions. The minutes stretch endlessly. Chances are great that eventually she'll succumb.

THE STRUGGLE

When you're normal, you can hardly imagine the enormous pressure a food craving can have. For a food addict it's irresistible. It's as relentless as gravity or the IRS.

So, this person you love is obsessed with eating and possessed by the struggle most of the time. You see her from the outside, where little of the preoccupation shows. She has learned to operate despite it. She probably doesn't let on for fear of ridicule or fear of not being understood. She may not tell you about the taunts she's endured from strangers or the fear that a chair won't be large enough. And she probably doesn't talk about the struggle of dinner—trying to make herself choose wisely yet being taken over by the food and filling herself until it hurts.

A WAY TO UNDERSTAND

You may still want to say, "Why doesn't she eat less, then? If she'd lose weight, she'd feel better about herself and she wouldn't go through this." Two factors keep her eating. Odds are she is physically addicted to certain foods, that her brain has changed in such a way that powerful cravings to eat are stirred. Chemically caused cravings are quite difficult to resist.

The second factor is that her needs aren't being met. Now wait a minute, I'm not saying you should meet them! It's much more complicated than that. She may not even know what her needs are and in the past may have been abused when she expressed them or tried to meet them herself. Food has been used to fill the deficit. Chapters 1 through 3 explain this in detail and I hope you'll read them. The point is that her need for food is both physical and emotional, and to change this takes years. If you really want to understand, there's probably one way you can relate to her pain.

Do you have any addiction or compulsion? Do you smoke? There's a powerful addiction. How many times have you quit? How many times have you thought about quitting? How many times have you said you need to quit someday? Nicotine is a powerful drug. It's so powerful that you can quit for a year and still want a cigarette now and then. People have been known to start again after five years of abstinence. Do you work compulsively? Do tasks call you? Can you not rest until you complete them? Do you strive for perfection around you?

If you have an addiction or compulsion that you're not honest with yourself about, if you are minimizing its power in your life, you might find her struggle harder to understand. Sometimes we are most critical of others when their behaviors are most like our own. If you find yourself judging her harshly or being unduly critical, how about backing off for an hour to take a hard look at yourself?

If you have no compulsions or addictions, it will be harder for you to relate. I know a few nonaddicted people. Some have great compassion for the addicted but have difficulty understanding. They are not, however, the harshest judges.

I find that many angry, judging loved ones fall into two categories. Either they are not looking at their own problems or they are using the weight to deflect attention from unresolved issues with the loved one.

If you are one of the few people in the United States who has neither an addiction nor a compulsion or who hasn't been damaged by growing up in a dysfunctional home, you get up in the morning and feel good about yourself. Most days you get a lot done. You have rich, lasting, mutually giving relationships. You have freedom of choice. You can choose to eat a little less now and then and it's no big deal. You can skip a meal and not eat twice as much the next meal. If you stay up too late, you go to bed a little earlier tomorrow. You get enough rest. You have rewarding contact with friends on a regular basis. You use time alone well and can work and relax without feeling a lot of pressure. Your mind is your own. You can think about your needs or your plans. You can choose not to think. You have lots of choices.

The food-addicted person envies your choices. Food and eating and dieting preoccupy her. Whatever she does, she must rise above this preoccupation to do it. She's really quite amazing.

Can you imagine patching a life raft while treading water in the middle of the ocean? Life is like that for her all the time.

Recovery relieves her from this preoccupation. Recovery brings her closer and closer to land so that eventually her feet touch bottom and she can hold the raft above the water while she patches it. Eventually, recovery lands her on the beach. She will no longer need her life raft. She can use her feet to walk and her hands for many things. Recovery frees her mind, frees her thoughts, gives her choices and self-esteem. If you support her recovery, you support her life. We are not asking that you take responsibility for her recovery, only that you support her. If you really want to help, keep reading.

SABOTAGE

It's incredible, but some loved ones actually sabotage recovery. Can you imagine offering a cigarette to a man who has made it through four months without one? Think it through. If he takes it, you've contributed to the pollution of his lungs. You share some of the responsibility. Not all, maybe just 10 percent. But do you want even 10 percent?

If you find yourself balking at the idea of supporting her, if you find yourself uninterested in learning how you may be sabotaging her, please consider talking to someone about it. If you don't want to help her, if you don't care that you might be harming her, you probably harbor some anger. Hidden or misdirected anger hurts you as well as her. If you feel very judgmental toward her, you may have been judged quite a bit yourself. You may be operating under a heavy burden, too. This burden can be removed. Your anger can teach you a lot and you can be freed from it. Psychotherapy has come a long way in the last 100 years. A good therapist can help you find a freedom, wholeness, and joy you can barely imagine.

I hope you are at least willing to learn how to keep from sabotaging her. To sabotage her pushes her into deeper water. Most compulsive eaters suffer from inadequate or uninformed parenting. As a child, she very likely interpreted this poor parenting as her fault. She received insufficient, unhealthy love. Unfortunately, this makes her vulnerable to anyone who loves her. She needs love so much that she may sacrifice all else, even put herself in harm's way, to be loved. If she didn't get much healthy love, she can't discriminate between healthy and unhealthy. If you're starved, any food will do. If you're starved for love, any love will do. So you, as her loved one, have more power than may be good for her. You have the power to interrupt her recovery. I hope you love her enough to go to extra lengths to support her recovery. Supporting her recovery gives her life. You'll be surprised, but her recovery can give you new life, too.

COMMITMENT TO SUPPORT

Please show how much support you're willing to give her as she detoxes from sugar and starches. Initial each step you're willing to take.

1. I'll give her a break from any important decisions or changes for the first three weeks of abstinence.
2. I will help rid the house of products containing sugar and refined carbohydrates.
3. I won't throw out junk food but it's okay with me for her to do it.
4. I don't want the house cleansed of sugar and starches, but I am willing to store all sugar and starch in a special cabinet or closet or box and keep it closed and out of her way.
5. I'm willing for us to eat regular meals at regular times.
6. I won't bring sugar or starch items into the house.
7. I'm willing to learn how to read labels so I won't unwittingly buy foods that contain sugar or carbohydrates.
8. I won't try to monitor what she eats. It's not up to me to make her abstinent.
9. I won't offer her food.
10. If I want a snack at night, I'll excuse myself from the room and go to the kitchen to eat it rather than unwittingly remind her of food.

11. If I want to go to a restaurant that has enticing displays of sugar products, I'll go when I'm not with her. I won't suggest such places when we eat as a family.
12. If I want dessert at the end of a meal, I'll wait until she has left the kitchen or restaurant and I'll wash that plate myself (if at home).
13. If we go to a fair or activity with lots of enticing food, I won't expect her to enter the section or area where the food is. If I want to go there, I'll meet her afterwards. I'm willing to bring her an item she can eat if she asks me for it.
14. I'm willing to take abstinent foods to potluck dinners.
15. I understand alcohol is a refined carbohydrate. I won't offer her any alcoholic beverage.
16. If she is acting crazy or angry, I'll stay out of the way and take care of myself. I'll listen for as long as I feel comfortable doing so.
17. If she is sad, I'll listen if I can.
18. I'll support her in calling support persons and going to support meetings.
19. I understand abstinence is not a diet and that recovery is one day at a time; I understand she'll always need to refrain from certain foods.
20. I want her to have a healthier, more serene life.

RECOVERY IS NOT DIETING

Food addicts and their families sometimes lose sight of the difference between recovery and dieting. Dieting is eating directed by a reduced-calorie or distorted food plan with the goal of losing weight. Diets have failed food addicts; the food addict did not fail at dieting. Notice the difference? Food addicts and families usually believe that she was at fault for not making the diet work. On the contrary, the diet failed because it was not big enough for the problem.

Your car functions perfectly but it didn't make it up the hill when the streets were icy. Was it the car that failed or was it, without chains or snow tires, being pushed beyond its capacity? Throwing a diet at a food addict is like using a washcloth to paint the house. It's the wrong tool for the job. So what's the plan? Chapter 6, "How Healing Happens," gives the plan in detail. Basically, the approach is twofold:

1. Eliminate foods that perpetuate food obsession and compulsive eating.
2. With therapy and the help of a support network, develop new behaviors that decrease the need for food as a solution to feeling bad.

How long will this take? Recovery takes the rest of her life. Any addict has a chronic disease. Any addict is vulnerable to relapse. All that stands between a sober alcoholic and his next drunk is one drink. All that stands between a food addict and her next binge is one cookie. We food addicts must live life just a little more carefully than other people. We must be more deliberate in talking about what bothers us, in choosing our meals, in taking care of our needs. Most of the time, the rewards are worth the trouble. Sometimes we wish we could be more carefree.

One day at a time, it's a lifelong process. Each day, our choices determine if we're at risk of eating the wrong things. Each day, our first priority must be recovery. Although weight is one consequence of this disease, it is initially beside the point. To focus on weight and ignore the addiction would be like trying to heal a smoker's cough while the person keeps smoking.

WEIGHT LOSS

So what about weight? Will she lose weight? If she stays with her recovery program and maintains frequent contact with support groups and individuals, she probably will lose weight. I might as well warn you, however, that at certain points during the recovery process she might gain weight. If she sticks to her recovery program, it could take two years or five years or eight years before sustained weight loss is possible.

How could it take so long? Weight loss is possible when two things happen—when she is 90 percent free from needing food for emotional support, and when she is willing to exercise.

Weight loss is possible when she is emotionally free enough to maintain an abstinence that goes little beyond physical sustenance. If she's addicted to sugar, carbohydrates, fat, and salt, that could mean three or four years. If she was abused as a child, she'll need to work that much longer to let go of food as a lifeline.

One key to weight loss is raising one's metabolic rate. Diets—which deprive—lower one's metabolism, one of many reasons why she should never again diet. Exercise is the other key to weight loss. After years of pushing clients to exercise, I've found that the willingness to exercise requires a certain level of recovery. Some people never enjoy exercise. Some people are naturally less active than others. If you are one who loves to exercise and feels great afterwards, you probably have trouble relating to someone who doesn't feel that way.

A perceptive, sensitive food addict who has been abused has a lot of grieving to do. Most people don't feel like moving when they are grieving. Their energy level is low. It is used up coping with heavy, sad feelings. So I have found that certain clients of mine simply can't sustain an exercise program while they're grieving. Gentle walking, yes. Aerobic walking, no. I hope you can see the logic of her taking care of the dependence on food first before attempting weight loss.

She gained weight because she used food to cope with hard feelings, and it led to food addiction. Getting abstinent from the addictive trigger foods and breaking the dependence on food must happen before she can sustain wise choices about eating. Obviously, trying to lose weight without breaking the emotional dependence is doomed to fail.

Once she can attend to weight loss, however, she must do it gently. If she is deprived or abused, food will once again beckon. Recovery must always come first. And if that recovery is threatened, weight-loss efforts must be temporarily abandoned and questioned. Why was it threatening? How was it abusive or depriving? What body feelings surfaced? If she maintains her recovery, she can work through the aspects that triggered painful feelings and redesign her weight-loss program. If she loses her achieved recovery, then the weight-loss program will ultimately fail as well.

Nature doesn't know that our society rewards the thin and punishes the fat. Evolution designed women to store fat more readily than men, to have appetites similar to men, to have lower metabolisms than men, and to store fat as they age. This prehistoric survival insurance, however, is no longer seen for the asset it is.

As you get older and less able to hunt for nuts and berries, your body stores fat as it has been programmed to do. As the days shorten toward winter, your body stores energy in the form of fat and you feel sleepier and less active; fat can then sustain you until spring, when the berries ripen. Nature doesn't know, however, that food is on every corner today no matter how old you are, no matter what time of year it is.

Each of us has a programmed weight limit. Weight loss beyond that limit introduces you to the nether world of anorexia or the yo-yo diet syndrome. When you force your weight beneath your body's natural limits, you trade one problem for another.

SUPPORT

You can support her efforts toward abstinence by following the guidelines listed earlier in this chapter. Adjust your expectations. Some weight loss will eventually be possible. A bikini figure may not. Help yourself grasp the importance of recovery by becoming interested in recovery yourself. Read this book. Go to O-Anon or Al-Anon or Codependents Anonymous meetings. (O-Anon and Al-Anon offer strength, support, and hope to spouses, friends, or relatives of people who suffer from food, alcohol, or drug addiction. Codependents Anonymous helps people learn to stop enabling others and to take care of themselves.)

Find out why weight is important to you. Do you want her to look different to make yourself look better? Does her weight deflect your anger away from some other issue? These are excellent topics to explore in family therapy, individual therapy, and support-group meetings.

ABSTINENCE

Recovery from alcoholism is hard, but at least it's clear. The alcoholic's abstinence is never to drink again. How we food addicts wish for such clarity. What is abstinence for a food addict? Since we must eat again, we are forced into gray areas that drug addicts can avoid. The bottom line is this: Abstinence is refraining from foods that cause an addictive reaction—change of mood, increased craving, increased compulsiveness around food—and refraining from using food as an emotional support. If we are addicted to sugar, that abstinence can be fairly clean. If fat products set us off, we have a more difficult challenge.

Part of the struggle of recovery is working out just where our addictions lie and gradually freeing ourselves from them. This takes time. There's no way to do it perfectly. This is one of the many reasons why you can't monitor her food. As she learns her limits, she can let you know which foods would mean sabotage; in time, however, this list will change. Abstinence from sugar means no sugar, but with refined carbohydrates, for example, abstinence may mean being 90 percent clean. Abstinence can also mean not bingeing, not eating between meals, not eating at night, or not eating more than the body truly needs for physical sustenance. At the start of recovery, abstinence is usually less defined and less strict, becoming more refined over time. I am now willing to be abstinent from many more foods than I was at the beginning. Giving up dependence on food as emotional support is not like slamming a gate. It's more like peeling an artichoke. We give up a little dependence here and a little more there. Over time it takes us to the heart of things.

One last thing—relapse is a part of this addiction. Since there's no way to define perfect abstinence, we all cross the line into compulsive eating now and then. Most of the time, we can read this as a warning, get help, and get back to safety. Sometimes we wander in the wilderness for a while before finding the path back. This is not an occasion for judgment. When this happens, we need more support from recovering people.

The support combination that seems to work best is participation in a therapy group designed specifically for overeaters and food addicts, and attendance at Overeaters Anonymous, Bulimics Anonymous, and Eating Disorders Anonymous meetings. Inpatient, outpatient, or residential treatment programs can give her a boost at the beginning of the recovery process or later, when the issues come rolling out. My own program combines all of the above, depending on the needs of the client.

Although we tend to focus on the needs of the person suffering from the disease, you need attention, too. I highly recommend Codependents Anonymous, Al-Anon, or O-Anon. Any of the three will support you as you support her.

◇

ASSIGNMENT 9.1

1. Look up Al-Anon, O-Anon, or Codependents Anonymous in the phone book.
2. Call each fellowship and ask to be sent a meeting list.
3. Attend three meetings (either three different fellowships or the same one three times).
4. After the second or third meeting, talk to someone whose comments you liked.

10

◇

FAT PREJUDICE

◇

"I love to bike, but I don't want to hear the taunts."

"I'm afraid that if I go walking, people will snicker at me."

"I haven't been in a bathing suit for years."

"I'll go to parties again when I'm thinner."

If you aren't doing something you want to do because you fear you will be taunted about your size, you are experiencing fat prejudice, either your own or someone else's. Many of us who carry extra weight have heard remarks that sting. We have heard "for your own good" comments from people we've trusted. We have been laughed at. We've laughed at ourselves. We don't show the hurt. We act like we agree. We take it. Why? Why do we accept comments that we wouldn't dream of saying to anyone else, loved one or foe?

I propose that we become advocates for ourselves and all extraweighted people. I propose that we stop taking it gracefully and begin to respond in ways that educate those who are unaware.

Last summer was hard for me. In the fall, I was scheduled to give lectures on food addiction to various groups of people, including the medical staff of an eating-disorder unit. For six weeks, I was steeped in the misery of hating my body. I had those crazy thoughts of going on a fasting diet, taking extreme measures to lose weight—the usual frantic, panicky mind-whirl of not being good enough. How could people find me credible since I was carrying fifty extra pounds? They would look at my body and turn off my words. Never mind that I had achieved nearly eight years of abstinence from my mind-altering drug—sugar. Never mind that I was no longer obsessed with food and (usually) dieting, that my life was rich, balanced, and sound. Never mind that I had been 90 percent abstinent from all refined carbohydrates for almost three years. People would look at my body and miss my recovery. They wouldn't see that my eating was normal most of the time. They wouldn't see that I exercised regularly. I had become codependent with the fat prejudice of others and I had succumbed to my own fat prejudice.

THE NATURE OF THE PREJUDICE

What is fat prejudice? It's the assumption that someone is worth less because they weigh more. It's as arbitrary and senseless as all other prejudice. Weight is no more a measure of worth than skin color, racial characteristics, family background, religious affiliation, sexual preference, physical disability, age, or eye color. Fat prejudice, like any other prejudice, is an excuse to hate.

Fat prejudice is deadly because the offenders assume they have the right to slur a person of size. Offenders seem unaware that they are acting with prejudice. I was horrified at a recent shoe commercial that said, "And it wouldn't hurt to stop eating like a pig, either." That statement assumes overeating is piglike and disgusting, that overeating is simple to stop, that it's okay for a national commercial to slur people who overeat, and that an overeater's self-hate is justified. Such an angry, hostile statement could get on the air only because advertisers, product executives, marketing consultants, television-commercial salespeople, and consumers are unaware or tolerant of fat prejudice.

I was horrified to hear similar assumptions expressed by speakers at a national convention of eating-disorders professionals. If therapists have unconscious fat prejudice, God save the client. Any derogatory comment about someone's size is unacceptable. Backhanded compliments ("You'd be so pretty if you lost some weight") and tone of voice can also be subtly demeaning. For years, women of size had to be content with dull, tentlike fashions. Office chairs, booths, and theater seats all send the message that one size is supposed to fit all. Panty hose used to be unavailable to those with proud thighs. The millions of diets available all testify to the fact that we should lose weight. Our culture is steeped in messages that thin is in, despise size. We've come to accept this idea without question. We accept the idea of abusing ourselves with self-hate and crazy diets. We avoid desired activities as if we agree that we are members of an inferior society.

It's time to throw off the oppression of fat prejudice, both your own and others. You have extra size because of a combination of biological and sociological factors. Neither is your fault. You personally caused neither to happen. Had you been born 400 years ago or into certain nonwestern societies, you'd be considered normal. In some societies, you'd be revered. Anyone with prejudice is looking for an excuse to hate. Obviously, such a person is not at peace with her or himself. If anyone ever makes a derogatory comment to you, remember these things:

The person is ignorant.
The person has hate to spare and his comment is not about you, it's about her.
His ignorance is not your problem and not your business.

I like to have a stock of snappy comebacks. I usually say these things to myself. Remember, a person looking for an excuse to hate may also be easily triggered into anger or violence. Keep yourself safe by not challenging such a person. If someone says something to me, I remind myself that I'm wonderful inside and out. If a relative or friend makes a comment, I decide how much I care about the person. If she's worth the trouble, I reeducate her. Sometimes I let such a person fade out of my life. I don't need someone who makes me struggle to believe in myself.

If the person is speaking out of misguided concern for you,

ask if she'd really like to understand your situation. If she would, ask her to read chapters 2, 3, 6, and 9 of this book. Best of luck surrounding yourself with people who affirm you and support your recovery.

Assignment 10.1

1. Make a list of the places or activities you shy away from out of fear of fat prejudice.
2. Star the ones you want very much to go to or do.
3. Of the ones you starred, check the one that seems the least risky.
4. Call a support friend. Ask if she'd be willing to go to this place or do this activity with you. Explain that in the past you've let fear of others' fat prejudice oppress you and you are now reversing that.
5. If you have a therapist or support group, talk about the risk you're planning and talk about your fears. Invite help structuring the activity in a way that is safest for you.
6. On the way to the activity or place, talk freely about your fears. Remember the structure you've decided to follow for maximum safety.
7. Before you enter, focus on the truth—you are a wonderful, rich, interesting person. You deserve joy and freedom. Focus on your goal—to open your life to all the things you want to do and to move about with freedom.
8. Afterward, celebrate your accomplishment. Take in your courage and willingness to risk in order to improve your life. Realize you can empower yourself simply by getting enough support.

11

◇

ANORExIA AND BULIMIA

◇

WANTED—DISEASE VOLUNTEER: Seeking applicants to maintain weight at 15 percent or more below normal minimum while perceiving self as fat. Disease includes loss of menstrual cycle and constant obsession with food, eating, and thinness. Prefer adolescent females. Be prepared to be cold all the time, to have downy hair growth over the body including the face, to have slow heartbeat and body swelling. Muscle wasting will occur. Brain atrophy could occur in 80 percent of selectees. Unknown at this time whether this brain damage is reversible. Sleep may be disturbed. High likelihood of thinning of the skull bone, leading to skull fractures in possibly 15 percent of the cases. Unlikely that more than 18 out of 100 will die. Apply at your local high school.

◇

ANOREXIA

Kara Nelson settled herself into her chair within the circle of women who met weekly to receive therapeutic support for recovery from overeating. She sighed and said, "Did you see that anorexic woman by the bus stop?" Two others nodded their heads. "I wish I had that problem," Kara said.

The group unanimously agreed.

How many times has that statement been echoed by women who suffer from overeating and extra weight? The failure of our society to accept differences is tragically perpetuated in the self-image of the extraweighted and the drivenness of the anorexic.

So is that the whole point of anorexia—to be thin? Yes and no. Often, anorexic behavior is started as a solution to a problem. Then, as with other addictive diseases, it takes on its own life and perpetuates itself. Is anorexia, strictly speaking, an addiction? My answer: an unequivocal maybe.

RETREAT FROM MATURITY

Anorexia typically begins when, in response to the pressures in her life, a child acts on the thought, "My life would be better if I were thinner." She begins to restrict her food. (Ninety-five percent of anorexia sufferers are female. Most begin restricting in adolescence.) Some anorexics are overweight prior to the slide into anorexia.

As the anorexic loses weight and gains attention for the weight loss, she may have her first feelings of success and accomplishment. In an overwhelming world that seems out of control, she finally has a heady feeling of being in control. She has the ultimate control over life and death: She can refuse to eat.

From the outside, we can see that she's not in control at all, that the disease is controlling her, but one of the aspects that makes treatment of anorexia so difficult is that the sufferer's own perceptions of being in control and needing to be thin are incredibly powerful.

It's not unusual for anorexia to begin soon after a step into greater maturity—entering middle school, high school, or college. Anorexia frequently arises as girls enter adolescence. Puberty pushes children into sexual maturity. Anorexia is a retreat from that developmental crisis.

Anorexia makes the body childlike again. Menstruation stops or doesn't start, the body loses its sexual characteristics, and the figure becomes immature. Anorexia is one way to drop out of growing up. It's a way to avoid being a sexual person.

Levenkron[1] maintains that anorexia is a disorder of failed dependence. Dependency needs have not been met, so the child arrests her development. It's a physical way of saying, "I haven't had enough care. I refuse to continue the course of life until I get what I need." If weight loss is severe enough, the child doesn't even have to feed herself. Like an infant, a hospital takes over feeding her.

Interestingly, hospital treatment of anorexia usually includes pushing the child into maturity. Anorexics are presented with reality statements, chronological age-appropriate tasks, and behavioral training that rewards taking responsibility. Anorexic patients manipulate and resist these with the intense and subtle skill of any rebellious teenager.

I wonder what would happen if the child were allowed a few weeks of concentrated childhood, if the child (even if she's 14 or 18) were rocked and cuddled and led gently by the hand. What would happen if the child could draw and play with toys and then gradually and gently be drawn though the developmental stages until her chronological age were reached? I wonder.

ESCAPE FROM FEELING

Anorexics generally have immature social skills and difficulty relating to others. This development may have been thwarted by parents who were controlling and who used the child to meet their own needs. One or both parents may be enmeshed with the child. She has tried hard to please them, has complied with their goals and ideas to the point that she doesn't know what she thinks or wants for herself. She is a perfectionist and judges herself harshly, so regardless of how high her achievement is, she sees herself as falling short.

Anorexia is an engrossing escape from these problems and from any feelings of anger that may be buried beneath them. Anorexia gives her one focus and one goal. All the other challenges of life fade beyond the obsession with being thin.

Nearly all people with an eating disorder want to be thin and believe life would be better if this were true. Nearly all eating-disordered people are preoccupied with weight, food, and eating. The difference with an anorexic is the intensity of this obsession. It is all-encompassing.

She originally saw thinness as a solution to the problems of her life. At first, she restricted food in order to improve life. Gradually this goal changed. Thinness became her life. Life became thinness. The disease took on a life of its own.

We look at this child with twigs for legs who's complaining about the fat on her thighs. She spends hours in front of the mirror measuring her belly. She sees her body in such a distorted way, we find it unbelievable. How can she think she's fat?

She has long lists of "bad foods" and a very short list of acceptable foods. Her intake for a day may be a lettuce leaf and a can of diet pop. Another day she may eat an apple and half a carrot.

Overeaters will hide food and lie about the amount they've eaten. Anorexics will hide their lack of eating and say that they've eaten when they haven't. They'll tell their parents they ate somewhere else so they can skip dinner. Or they may have dinner but nothing else the rest of the day to make up for it. They may move food around on the plate and actually eat very little or use sleight of hand to dispose of food into a napkin or a dog's mouth, a deadly game.

Are they hungry? Some are. Some aren't. In a supermarket I observed a pencil-sized woman staring at a snack display. She picked up a small bag of peanuts, held it, then put it back. She took a bag of crackers. She put it back. She took a candy bar, then put it back. After ten minutes of this painful longing, she went to a cooler, got a diet pop, and left the store.

Overeaters can't tell when they're full. Anorexics can't tell when they're hungry. Experiments have shown they have the same gastric sensations that normal people call hunger, but these are not interpreted as hunger.

STRESS AND HUNGER

So what kind of disease is this? Is it emotional? Is it physical? By now you probably know me well enough to predict that I don't believe humans are so easily dissected.

As with most diseases, anorexia has both physical and psychological components. In chapter 2 you read that mild stress increases appetite due to the release of dynorphin. Severe stress, however, activates the sympathetic nervous system, which depresses appetite. Ordinarily, a period of high stress is followed by rebound appetite, due in part to a need to replenish nutrients depleted by the stress.

In rat studies, certain chemical chain reactions produce continued suppression of appetite, especially associated with certain types of severe stress.[2]

If a rat is stressed and can't escape it, if it's a prisoner of the stress, its appetite is suppressed. It also loses appetite when it is exercised to exhaustion. Interesting, wouldn't you say? If a child feels herself trapped in an enmeshed relationship with her mother or father and has no skills to help her separate, if she's been controlled to the point of having no sense of herself, how can she be on her own? How can she escape? Also, we commonly find that anorexics exercise compulsively.

THE TWO SIDES OF BETA-ENDORPHIN

So what is the chemical chain reaction? Chemically stimulated anorexia can occur through several mechanisms.[3] I'll summarize them for you. In chapter 2 you read that beta-endorphin stimulates appetite and promotes cravings for sweets, fats, and carbohydrates. Anorexia routinely results when beta-endorphin is suppressed or blocked. Beta-endorphin synthesis and release can be blocked by the release of certain hormones from the pituitary (in the brain) and adrenal (above the kidneys) glands. This works especially well in combination with a lack of turnover of norepinephrine in the hypothalamus. The hypothalamus, remember, is where eating is regulated.

Translation? Certain chemicals and hormones released by stress can override the appetite-producing effects of beta-endorphin and dynorphin, and cause decreased appetite. These naturally occurring body chemicals function as opiate blockers.

But wait, let me confuse the issue a bit more. Certain opiate helpers, that is, chemicals that promote opiate activity in the body, can also decrease appetite.[4] When certain opiates are in excess, decreased eating and weight loss result.

Some theorists say that dieting/starving releases brain opiates and produces a high that, in some people, overrides the pain of hunger.[5]

Am I contradicting myself? Didn't I say, in chapter 2, that eating sugar was an attempt to make up for inadequate endorphin functioning?

Let me get myself out of this quagmire. Let's say you arrived from the planet Centauri Alpha Five and I was showing you my neighborhood. We'd walk to the corner and I'd say, "This traffic light causes the cars to stop."

You'd smile and chatter with your companion Centaurians. Then I'd say, "This traffic light causes cars to go."

You might smile politely because Centaurians have very good manners, but you'd be confused. I contradicted myself. How can the very same light cause traffic to both stop and go?

You watch the traffic light yourself. Your eyes don't receive earth colors so to you the whole setup is a pleasant shade of puce.

I try to explain that the light contains both red and green colors and the green color tells cars to go and the red color tells cars to stop. Finally you detect that the top light always make cars stop and the bottom light always makes cars go and we're happy with each other until we come to the light that is sideways with the colors all in a row.

Using color graphics, beta-endorphin has been found to be divided into two fractions.[6] We could say some beta-endorphins are greenish and others reddish. Obese individuals have an excess of greenish endorphins and insufficient reddish ones. Lean individuals have the opposite configuration. Yet we have a long way to go before we understand the exact chemical processes that produce overeating and anorexia. We are like the color-blind Centaurians encountering a light that is sideways.

For example, since a third of anorexics start out overweight, did starving change the balance of endorphins in the brain? Is starving itself a stress that produces a chemical imbalance that perpetuates a stress reaction? I don't know. We're only at the beginning of an understanding of the chemical mechanisms that perpetuate anorexia.

THE OBSESSION

What about psychological dependence? Does the individual become dependent on anorexia? Probably. The obsession with thinness is an effective escape from feelings, other problems, and the process of living.

By the time anorexia becomes entrenched, it seems to have moved itself out of the category of an addictive disease and more closely resembles an obsessional disorder.

What can be done? Throughout this book, I've inserted warnings that the plan contained here is not for anorexics. I'm making a presumption about my readers. I'm assuming you have the capacity to take responsibility for structuring your recovery, the ability to ask for help when a suggestion is too hard to do alone, and you want to change badly enough to push on when old ghosts whisper that you might as well quit. I'm assuming that you are seeking to improve your wellness.

Few anorexics want a change. The self-help book that would interest an anorexic is one that would tell her how to be thinner. My goals are opposite those of an anorexic. I'm promoting wellness, she's wanting thinness.

What can be done? In most cases, recovery from anorexia is not a do-it-yourself project. Anorexia harms thinking ability and recovery from anything requires a clear head. Generally, professional help is advisable.

TREATMENT

If I had my druthers, I'd fix the parents. Since that is frequently not an option, the next alternative is long-term treatment with a specialist in anorexia or long-term inpatient treatment in an eating-disorders unit. Hospitalization allows for refeeding so she can be brought out of a starved state. Plus, a team approach is helpful because she has lots of people to rebel against and a chance of finding one person on the team with whom she can bond.

Steven Levenkron has had good results using a nurturant-authoritative approach to therapy.[7] Anorexia is different enough from compulsive eating and bulimia to need a practitioner who has specific experience and training in anorexia.

Frankly, the success rate with anorexics is very low. Cognitive therapeutic approaches don't begin to heal the lost little girl inside. Besides, an anorexic's thinking ability is not too great. Starving people don't think clearly. In addition, prolonged starving causes brain damage. A rise in a body chemical called cortisol causes brain atrophy similar to Cushing's syndrome.[8] Other brain damage occurs because important chemicals become depleted.

The biggest complication to recovery from anorexia is her own powerful resistance to it. Against her will, she must be fed so she can think, and if the starvation has been severe enough, she may never regain full mental capacity. As with most diseases, the prognosis improves if she is treated early, before her brain and heart tissues are eaten away.

If I saw signs of anorexia in my own child, I would not wait until her life was threatened. I'd take action immediately. I'd put my family into family-systems therapy, myself into personal therapy so my own needs were getting met, I'd get her an appointment with a specialist in anorexia following the nurturant-authoritative approach, and I'd put her under medical supervision so her nutritional needs were being met.

If these programs weren't enough to stop her starving, I'd find an inpatient treatment program that used the nurturant-authoritative model and had a strong family program.

Is this costly? Of course! Will insurance pay for it? Typically, most insurance policies don't cover the anorexic until she's in danger of dying. By this time, brain and heart damage may have already occurred.

It is possible to find good insurance coverage. Anorexia is prevalent enough that if I had a ten-year-old daughter, I'd shop for an insurance company that provided coverage for long-term treatment of anorexia and bulimia in both inpatient and outpatient settings, and that covered long-term individual and family therapy with a free choice of practitioners.

The hard news is that an anorexic, bulimic, or compulsive eater in the family is a screaming sign that the whole family needs help. As with most crises, anorexia can be an opportunity as well as a challenge. It can be the pivot upon which the entire family turns itself toward health and growth.

BULIMIA

"I'd be bulimic myself if I didn't hate to vomit!"

Overeaters sometimes feel so trapped by their bodies that even a disease as destructive as bulimia looks attractive to them. Judge for yourself whether the grass is truly greener.

Bulimics binge and then participate in some extreme measures to counteract the binge. Bulimic binges are similar to overeaters' binges. Large quantities of sweet, high-calorie food can be consumed by an eater who feels out of control and unable to stop the binge. However, the pace is different. A bulimic eats quickly, often gobbling her food. If a bulimic is going to rid herself of it, she's eating against the clock. She has to bring the food back up within a certain time or it will be too digested.

A bulimic may eat quite a bit more food than a compulsive eater during a binge. The food that is chosen has to be easily vomited. Bulimics become skilled at learning the combinations of food that can be vomited smoothly. Some bulimics binge rapidly, vomit once, and it's over. Other bulimics binge and vomit several times in one episode. Bulimics may routinely vomit one or all meals each day.

Most food addicts and overeaters love restaurants. We love to go out to eat. Eating out is an anxiety for bulimics. Beyond the privacy of home, getting rid of food is more of a challenge. Someone could walk in during a purge. She could be caught. A husband or parent might get suspicious if she always disappears after meals. The need to purge her food gives the bulimic another obsession that requires planning, secrecy, and dishonesty.

Does this really sound like fun?

Bulimia has a certain notoriety because of purging. Does a person have to purge to be considered a bulimic? No. One way to be bulimic is to alternate binges with periods of strict dieting, fasting, or vigorous exercise.

Other bulimics use laxatives or diuretics. This is not a very effective weight-loss method. A diuretic simply rids the body of liquid. Laxatives carry digested food out more rapidly but the food value has already been extracted by the body. These are poor weight-loss measures but excellent ways to abuse the body. Fluids and electrolytes get way out of balance and can cause a person to tremble, feel queasy, sick, and weak—effective distractions from life's problems.

So bulimics have this in common with anorexics—a compulsion that includes manipulating the natural processes of the body. Bulimia gives a person something she needs and then takes it away.

For some purging bulimics, the purge is an end in itself. They binge so that they can purge. They become addicted to purging, experiencing euphoria with being emptied.

Bulimics don't stand out like anorexics and compulsive overeaters. Even though, like most disordered eaters, they are very concerned about their body shape and weight, they are usually of normal weight or slightly over- or underweight. Yet in a day they may consume many more calories than a compulsive overeater.

REJECTION OF OUR FEMALENESS

How does bulimia get started? With a diet. Numerous studies show that bingeing follows a period of food deprivation. Does dieting cause bingeing? Perhaps. It unquestionably increases the likelihood of bingeing. Food restriction produces a host of physiological responses—elevated motilin levels, unbalanced insulin levels, pancreatic polypeptide responses—that can cause an exaggerated response to palatable food. It also causes changes in the way a person thinks about food and hunger.[9]

While anorexia is a sign of problems with *entering* adolescence, bulimia is a sign of problems with *leaving* adolescence.[10]

> The anorexic individual appears to stumble on the first steps of transition to adulthood—the development of sexuality and the transfer of energy and interest from the family to peers. The bulimic individual usually negotiates these early phases successfully, often becoming sexually and socially ac-

> tive, but falters later in the establishment of intimacy and authenticity in peer relationships and in the separation from her family. She seems to know the steps but cannot dance.[11]

Why?

One strongly supported theory is that bulimia arises from a severe disturbance in body image.[12] The rise in the incidence of bulimia has been connected with vast changes in role expectations for women and the increasing preference for lean women. The young women of today are seen as the first generation to be raised from birth by mothers who reject their own bodies.

The female form has been synonymous with nurturing and producing, but the roles of mothering and nurturing have fallen on hard times. Motherhood is devalued, femininity has been mocked. Thinness can be a rejection of the roles associated with femaleness, an effort to achieve the more admired consequences of maleness.

BULIMIA AND ABUSE

A shocking percentage of bulimics have been victimized. In a well-conducted study, 66 percent of 172 female purging bulimics interviewed had been physically victimized: 23 percent raped, 29 percent sexually molested, 29 percent physically abused, and 23 percent battered.[13] The study observed that bulimia fulfills certain functions:

1. Bingeing and purging leave one exhausted and relieved. It effectively numbs fear, rage, and pain.
2. Bulimia is a safer way to express anger if the victim is currently in an abusive relationship. (Eating-disordered people are very likely to turn anger against themselves rather than toward the people who have harmed them.)
3. Bulimia replays the pattern of abuse in her life.
4. Victims often feel as if they have little control over what happens to them. Bulimia is a desperate attempt to have control over one's own body.

5. Abuse has violated boundaries. Bulimia could be an attempt to set boundaries.

For some, perhaps, bulimia is a way of acting out the past, when something that was put into the woman's body is rejected and thrown out.

PSYCHOLOGICAL CONSEQUENCES

Like anorexia, bulimia can have severe consequences. Fifty percent of the patients studied at the Max Planck Institute in Munich exhibited symptoms of brain atrophy that may or may not be permanent.[14] Blood studies showed that numerous body chemicals were out of balance. A rise in ketone bodies overnight, for example, showed that the glycogen reserve in the liver was being used up. Fatty tissues may be broken down to provide energy for the body but cannot be used in the brain. The glucose needed by the brain comes from protein and if the person is not eating enough, muscles and vital organs are used to provide energy requirements for the brain. The decrease in amino acids also meant that the brain was not getting the raw materials needed to replenish neurotransmitters. These and other imbalances cause decreased thinking ability.

Edwin Pike described the effect of bulimia on the heart:

> Probably 40% of bulimics have mitral prolapse, caused by malnutrition. If they get malnourished enough, their cardiac volume goes down and their cardiac musculature doesn't have enough energy to work efficiently, so basically the muscle kind of sags. If you have ever seen their chest x-rays, their hearts sort of fall into their chests, literally just hang there. The mitral valve . . . keeps the blood from squirting backward. In the malnourished state, there is a functional mitral prolapse, and you want to get them renourished, so . . . when they stand up, they don't faint.[15]

Do you still think bulimia is a handy way to have your cake and get rid of it too?

What else can happen? Body electrolytes can get out of balance. A drop in potassium levels may produce cardiac arrhythmias that, untreated, can cause death. The body can get severely dehydrated. Tooth enamel erosion is common. The esophagus can tear and the stomach can rupture.

RECOVERY

Can bulimics use this book? The chapters on reducing stress and building support can benefit any human being. The chapters on fat prejudice and the letter to the family might also apply. However, bulimics should approach abstinence gingerly. Bulimics are notorious for having lists of bad foods and good foods, alternating between dieting with the good foods and bingeing on the bad foods. I'd rather see a bulimic build up her protein stores and chemical balance by eating and keeping down three hearty, healthy meals a day. "Get real," you may say. "If she could do that, she wouldn't have a problem."

To follow such a simple dietary plan may require squadrons of support. I recommend a therapy group with a therapist who specializes in bulimia and overeating. Recovery requires attention to all the aspects that contributed to the development of bulimia and structures that promote a decline in the harmful, addictive behaviors. At the same time, she must be regaining physical health. Sometimes the damage is so severe, the body so depleted, or the addiction to purging so powerful that hospitalization is required in order to build up the body's strength and stop the personal violence of purging.

Exercise for a bulimic can be dangerous if she's exercising before nutrients have had a chance to rebuild her heart tissue. If a bulimic is purging, exercise can further complicate the electrolyte imbalance. It's a good idea for a bulimic to have medical supervision before she begins exercising.

Bulimia is such a complicated disease that it's a wonder sufferers have been able to recover by attending Twelve Step meetings such as Bulimics Anonymous, Overeaters Anonymous, and Eating Disorders Anonymous. Of course, alcoholism is no picnic, and millions have become sober through A.A.

Professional guidance can, however, provide a more structured path and speed recovery along known paths. The combination is dynamite—the expertise of an eating-disorders therapist or program and a Twelve Step program.

POSTSCRIPT

If you are one of the many overeaters who envied bulimics and anorexics, I hope you now have another perspective on the matter. Extra weight can be harmful, we all know this. Yet drastic measures to eliminate weight such as starving and purging can cause far greater damage that may not even be fixable.

If you have occasionally starved yourself or purged now and then, perhaps it's now clearer that you were trading one harmful pattern for another. You deserve much more than to travel through a jungle of symptoms. You deserve full recovery from the whole syndrome of deprivation, self-violence, and obsession. Yes, you deserve abundance, support, purpose, health, and fullness.

12

TIMING, CHOICES, AND HITTING BOTTOM

If you came to my office hell-bent to lose thirty pounds immediately, I couldn't help you. Many glossy diet programs exist to help you with that. I can only help when you're ready to look at weight as a symptom, a symptom of your dependence on food.

You are a living, purposeful creation. Your life is important. Perhaps it's important because of what you have to give. Perhaps it's important because of what you are meant to learn. Whatever your particular path, it's your choice how intensely you want to live it. It's your choice how fast you want to travel it. Recovery from food addiction ultimately connects you with your spiritual self. Please do not read "religious" in that. By spiritual, I mean the vibrant life force within you, your basic goodness, worthiness, and power. Within this part of you reside the health, awareness, guidance, strength, and instincts that can enrich your life in ways you may not now be able to imagine. While food is the apple of your eye, however, your contact with this other, spiritual part of you is probably limited or blocked. Recovery is worth the effort for many reasons.

GIFTS OF RECOVERY

Recovery brings you more time and greater freedom of choice. You may not realize how much time is consumed by bingeing and obsessing about food. Recovery lessens fear. Fear of people, fear of failure, fear of success, fear of trusting, fear of intimacy—all are gradually healed. Your ability to risk and to find adventure increases. Any addiction steals freedom of choice. The physical demands overrule values, ideals, goals, and good ideas.

Recovery brings you more energy. You can do more each day when your body is no longer sapped by weighty emotional issues and problems caused by the addiction. Recovery opens doors. As you make friends who are also recovering, you will discover possibilities that may now seem unthinkable. Recovering friends are connectors. You'll be surprised how quickly you find exactly what you need once you've learned to reveal your needs to recovering friends.

Another world exists for you, one of abundance, joy, opportunity, peace, and empowerment. This is not a world available to a select few. It's available to those who put one foot in front of the other, one day at a time, and stay in contact with support groups and the inner self. An essential requirement for entry into this world is self-honesty. (If we are hiding from our own truths, how can we expect to find our unique direction?) The longer we are in recovery, the more honest we can be with ourselves and others. Rawboned honesty gets to be a habit and over time we see that it always leads to a better place.

The exciting, golden joy of recovery is that it clarifies our purpose in life. I know few who have had blinding revelations, but I know many who have been led step by step into communities, work, opportunities, or relationships that have connected with their most basic selves. This is the gift of recovery I most treasure.

Your life is yours. If you wish to be guarded your whole life, you may. If you wish to stay with the food, you may. This is entirely your choice. If anyone judges you for this, it is his or her problem. You are free to choose the direction you want your life to take. You are free to choose recovery. You are free to reject it.

You are free to live your life intensely. You are free to temper the intensity of your life.

CONSEQUENCES

Understand that any choice has consequences. Choosing recovery means some loss. Your relationship with food will change. It will ultimately not be enough. If food is everything to you now, recovery will change that. Although you can retreat to the food cocoon at any time, once you've tasted joy and freedom, it won't work as well, and the freer choices will nag at you.

Many people go through all the stages of grief when they become abstinent. They mourn the loss of sugar. They are angry about being different from unaddicted people. They are depressed. They bargain—a little bit won't hurt. This is normal grief. It will pass.

If you reject recovery, you'll suffer different losses. You may lose the people closest to you. If you are focused on food, you are abandoning your mate and children. Your mate may tire of being abandoned and give up on intimacy with you. Your children may be harmed by your mood swings, by inappropriate or excessive anger, by neglect if binges steal mothering time or energy.

The tendency to isolate yourself may make you decline invitations from friends. The fog and lethargy of overeating may make you forget those meetings you do arrange. The mood swings caused by changing blood-chemical levels may cause you to hold grudges, to imagine slights, or to be excessively or inappropriately angry. Your friends may tire of this and withdraw their loyalty. If you're not in a significant relationship, your food addiction may prevent you from finding a healthy one. The time and energy exacted by bingeing may keep you from activities where you can meet others. Low self-esteem may push you to isolate and rob you of the courage to risk meeting others. Unresolved childhood issues may cause you to be drawn to someone who is harmful for you. Lack of esteem, energy, and ability to risk may cause you to miss job opportunities or have trouble following through on educational opportunities.

Oh, yes, addiction piles up mountains of losses. Sometimes one particular loss is too great. We lose a loved one, we see the pain of our child, and we hit bottom. The pain of staying addicted becomes great enough to risk the pain of recovery. In the early days of recovery from alcoholism, alcoholics lost a lot before hitting bottom. They lost families, jobs, homes, spouses, and their health. As more alcoholics gained recovery, however, and spread the word, others learned from their losses and hit bottom sooner.

You have the option of raising your bottom level and choosing recovery before you lose everything. You can look at the women and men who have gone before you and see which direction you want your life to go. You can see the losses other food addicts have sustained and learn from those without experiencing them yourself.

It is your choice. One choice—to stay with the food—gives you the illusion of safety and warmth. It may protect you from truths about your family and the way you've been harmed by them. This option has built-in losses and consequences. The other choice—recovery—guarantees long, hard work, risks, and the loss of food as your primary friend. It offers you contact with your worthy self and your special life purposes; connections with kind, aware people; and some pretty big challenges.

◇

ASSIGNMENT 12.1

Disease Inventory: Part IV

This assignment is the final part of the Disease Inventory begun on page 46. It is very scary. Before you start working on it, set up support. Call a support person and tell her you plan to do a hard assignment on Saturday morning (or whenever) and that you'd like to meet with her when you finish. Tell her you will also share this assignment in therapy.

1. Write about the following:
   If your food addiction or overeating were to continue unchecked, what would happen? How would your story end? What kind of person would you become? What would your life be like if you followed the old patterns of isolating and avoiding feelings?
   Include losses you might incur—change in friendships, rejection by mate or children, loss of health, loss of job advancements or opportunities, loss of self-esteem, insufficient energy to discover and follow your own life purpose. Include the feelings and problems that bother you now. What would your life be like if these continued to bother you or if they got worse?
2. Read this part of your inventory to a warm support person and at your therapy session.
3. Decide what you want your future to look like. Write a description of the future you want to have. Write a statement of commitment to yourself. Read the description and statement of commitment to at least three support persons and at your therapy session.
4. Get input from your support friends and therapy group about steps you can take to create the future you want. Get help setting priorities so that you have an idea what steps you should take first.
5. Make a list of survival rules that could get in the way of reaching the future you want for yourself.
6. Read this list to a support person and at your therapy session. Discuss options that you and your support persons have that would prevent you from being sabotaged by these rules.
7. State out loud your commitment to yourself every morning for a week.
8. (Optional). Incorporate this affirmation as part of your morning ritual—while dressing, combing your hair—for a much longer time.

13

◇

RELAPSE

◇

Food addicts and compulsive overeaters seem to have more trouble with relapse than other addicts. Food addicts try to do more with less. They have a greater challenge than many other addicts and they try to meet it with less support. A recovering alcoholic knows he'd better stick to meetings to keep his sobriety. Many alcoholics commonly attend support-group meetings every day. Yet alcoholics can be fairly safe from exposure to alcohol. They can stay out of bars, they can stay away from drinkers, they can rid their homes of their drug. Not so for overeaters. We still have to eat. We still sit down with the tiger at least three times a day. Yet overeaters think they're doing a lot if they go to three support-group meetings a week.

If an alcoholic drinks one drink, he stands a good chance of losing everything. If an overeater eats one extra bite, she hasn't so far to fall. She may lose a lot if she has one bite of sugar, but most overeaters don't have the sense of being one bite away from a great abyss, as do most successfully recovering alcoholics.

Our drug is so darned accessible. The slide into oblivion can occur very slowly and subtly. Pushers surround us. With so many factors working against us, no wonder we relapse so frequently. Unfortunately, repeated small relapses and occasional giant ones are doubly harmful. First, we see relapse as yet another sign of our personal weakness. We are accustomed to failing. Here's just another expected failure. The veneer of hope and self-confidence from early recovery peels away and we feel more discouraged than ever before. Second, when those close to us see the slip, they also lose faith or become angry. Having confused abstinence with dieting, they may withdraw their support or become less willing to make changes to accommodate our abstinence needs.

What is relapse, anyway? It's a return to an earlier way of coping.[1] Over the years you became increasingly dependent on food to cope with feeling bad. Recovery stopped this progression. It taught you how to gradually replace eating with more helpful support. But then something came along that felt so bad that it was beyond your level of recovery. Something felt so bad that the skills you'd learned thus far were not up to the urgency or the power of the feeling. You reached for something that had stood the test of time. You reached for food—quick, available, trustworthy food.

What does this tell us? It tells us that your level of support was not equal to your level of stress. Either the stress must be lowered or the level of support raised.

WHAT INCREASES STRESS?

Perfectionism. Expecting flawless performances from yourself in many areas of your life. Expecting yourself to have the "right" feelings and the "right" thoughts most of the time.

Black/White thinking. All or nothing, all-right or all-wrong attitudes; judging yourself or others harshly.

Neglecting physical needs. Getting insufficient rest, fluids, sleep, exercise, nutrients, stimulation, and relaxation.

Neglecting emotional needs. Too much isolation, hiding from feelings, too much work, excessive contact with people with whom you can't be yourself. Being controlled by past issues so that present choices are restricted.

How Are Stresses Lowered?

Reduce your degree of perfectionism. We are human, and by nature imperfect.

Get more in touch with physical needs. Once we know what we need, we can meet our needs. When we are tired, we need rest. When we are thirsty, we need water.

Get more in touch with emotional needs. If we're lonely, we can call a friend. When we need a hug, we can ask for one. If we feel too busy, it's time to take a break, go to a park, draw a picture.

Lessen black/white thinking.

Identify survival rules. Repeal them.

Increase contact with recovering people.

Increase contact with people who truly care about your well-being.

Work through childhood issues that keep you a prisoner.

A therapy group can help you identify unnecessary stresses and can support your actions to reduce them. Chapters 6 and 8 discuss support. If you are relapsing frequently, you are not getting enough support. Increase it. If you're talking to someone once a week, talk twice a week. If you're going to one support-group meeting a week, go twice. If you aren't in therapy, seek out an eating-disorders therapist and find out what groups are available. If you're in a recovery group and you've achieved abstinence, you may need a block of individual sessions to get through an important issue that has surfaced.

YOU ARE NOT A FAILURE.
YOU ARE NOT WEAK.

I cannot emphasize too strongly the power and subtlety of this addiction. You need very powerful support to fight against it!

PROTECTIVE STRUCTURES

Our drug is so available. We require firm structures if we're not to succumb. Regular support must be structured and adhered to regardless of how we feel. A therapy group is very good for this.

It's harder to slip away and disappear. You have to show up every week. You're known and expected.

Establish certain support-group meetings as your weekly commitment to recovery and go to those meetings without fail. Let nothing interrupt your attendance. Find two or three support persons that you routinely talk to at least three times a week. Support is a safety net to catch you if you fall.

Why do I keep emphasizing routine and structure? Because all addicts are vulnerable to *denial*. This means that we can be so stressed and have such a tremendous need for relief that we'll turn to the chemicals that brought us relief before recovery. In desperation we'll go to any length to get relief. A drug addict will steal and lie to get his drug and not consider it stealing or lying. Blinded by his powerful need, he cannot see his behavior for what it is. Likewise, when we are under this spell, we may fail to see how much or what we're eating. Plus, once we've started eating, especially if we eat sugar, our brain chemistry changes and so clouds our thinking.

This addiction is a disease of the mind as well as the body. We may be bingeing and not know it. We may be obsessed about eating or dieting and not know it. As our suffering grows progressively more severe, we may remain oblivious to the extent of our involvement with food. It is this aspect of the disease that puts us at risk for relapse. Since our thinking can be affected without our awareness, we may relapse and not catch on to the danger we're in. Structure and close contact with caring, recovering people who know us lessen the risk of relapse, enabling someone to notice before that happens.

ANATOMY OF A RELAPSE

Sandra's mother left a message on her machine: "Sorry, dear, I realize I overscheduled myself. I won't be able to visit next month after all. I'll call in a couple of weeks and pick out another date."

Sandra turned on the television. What else is new? she thought. So Mom canceled again. So what.

She felt hungry even though she'd had a good dinner. She was going to draw but instead watched television and worked a crossword puzzle. Sandra usually needed to be in bed by eleven but this night stayed up until midnight.

The next morning, it was hard to get up. She forced herself out of bed, had her usual breakfast, and went to work. Work was more stressful than usual. Her coworker Ursula seemed to be screeching in her ear. She's irritating, thought Sandra. She's shallow. She wears the wrong colors.

Sandra's boss breezed by. Ralph can't plan well, she thought. He's disorganized. He can't set clear priorities. Sandra's sponsor, Karen, called her at work. "Sandra, I haven't heard from you for a couple of days. What's been happening with you?"

"Nothing much," Sandra said in a rushed voice. "I'm real busy. Work is driving me crazy. I can't talk."

"Going to the meeting tonight?"

"Maybe. I'll see how it goes."

"Sounds like you're planning to miss it."

"I'm not planning to miss it," Sandra said. "My food's fine. I don't have to worry about my abstinence. I know I'll never eat sugar again."

"I'm worried about how you sound," said Karen. "You're pushing me away."

"I'm fine! I've got to get back to work now."

"Call me tonight."

"I will."

After work, Sandra wandered through the shopping center. She felt good there. It was bright and colorful. She wandered into her favorite store. She'd just see what was new. Right away, two items caught her eye. She went directly to them. She had to have them. She deserved a treat. It was more than she had planned to spend on extra items this week, and she really didn't have the money, but she deserved this. She had worked hard. On the way out of the store, she saw something else. She had to have it. She deserved it.

Sandra thought she should leave the shopping center but then she noticed a new store. It wouldn't hurt just to see what kind of store it was. She saw something she wanted. She grabbed it and bought it. She deliberately didn't think about buying it or its cost or whether it was a good choice for her. She deliberately avoided thinking through what she was doing.

On the way to her car, she checked her watch. She didn't have time to eat and get to the meeting. She had to eat. Her therapist told her she should never miss a meal. She didn't feel like eating at home alone, so she went to a restaurant where she felt comfortable and cozy. She ordered a little more than she ordinarily needed. She deserved it. She'd given a lot of herself today. Afterwards, she checked her watch. If she went to the meeting now, it would be halfway over. There was no point to that. She headed home.

Sandra felt lonely. She took her purchases inside and threw them on the couch. She didn't take them out of the bags. She flipped on the television and searched for a movie. She'd seen the movie twice but it was better than nothing. She watched it and then watched the next one. She felt hungry. During a commercial she ran to the kitchen, got a snack, and ran back. She forgot that she hadn't been eating at night anymore. She got to bed at 1:00 A.M. She forgot to call her sponsor.

Sandra couldn't get up when the alarm went off. By the time she dragged herself from bed, she didn't have time for breakfast. She rushed to work. By lunch, she was famished. Since she hadn't had breakfast, she deserved a bigger lunch. That afternoon she slumped. She felt depressed. She was supposed to call a friend to set up walking together. She didn't feel like being with the friend or walking either. After work, she didn't feel like going to the store to get anything for supper. She didn't feel like cooking. She drove through a pickup lane and got a fast-food dinner. She knew the ingredients of the meal were questionable for her. It wasn't really whole wheat. She ordered twice as much as she would ordinarily get. She had more fried items than she really should have.

Sandra couldn't help it. She was too tired to do anything else. At home, she flipped on a movie. The movie made her feel dreamy. She dreamed about how happy she'd be if the perfect mate walked into her life. The telephone rang. She let it ring.

The next day was Saturday. She got up late. She needed the sleep. She decided to take herself out for breakfast, a real treat. She deserved a treat. Breakfast, as late as it was, meant she missed her meeting. As she left the restaurant, she felt at a loss. Now what would she do? She needed to do laundry. She didn't feel like it. She needed to get some fresh vegetables and fruits so that she could get back to eating in a way that was good for her. She didn't feel like it. Today was when she was supposed to walk with her friend, but since she hadn't called her friend and hadn't answered her own phone, the plans hadn't been finalized.

Sandra felt directionless and confused. She decided to go to a movie. She deserved some time off. Besides, the first show was at a discount. She was still full from breakfast but the popcorn smelled too good to pass up. She found herself staring into the candy case before she realized what she was doing. She reminded herself that she didn't eat sugar. She got a diet cola, even though she knew her body didn't handle Nutrasweet well and she'd been off caffeine for months. After the movie, she ran into her sponsor.

"Sandra, do you have a minute?"

"I'm in a hurry. I have to be somewhere."

"Sandra, I'm worried about you. You haven't called. I haven't seen you at the meetings."

"Karen, I'm fine."

"You're acting like I act when I'm running from something. When I'm doing that, I'm in danger of relapse."

"Karen, back off," said Sandra. "I don't need people who don't have faith in me. How dare you put the idea of relapse into my mind. My abstinence is too important to me. I know I'll never eat sugar again."

"Sugar is only part of the issue, Sandra. You may not eat sugar, but how are you on the inside? You don't seem okay."

"Damn it, leave me alone. I'd be okay if you weren't pushing me so hard. I'm crushed that you don't believe in me. I don't want a sponsor who can't support me. Don't call me, I'll call you." Sandra walked away and didn't look back. She got into her car and went to a food store. She got an item that had "sugar-free" on the label, but she really knew that the substitute sweetener was just as dangerous for her. She ignored her knowledge of that. It was her ex-sponsor's fault that she needed to eat.

She ripped the package open and ate it while she drove. She

hadn't eaten while driving in a long time. Before she got home, she realized she was really hungry. She stopped at a store and bought many food items. She pretended to the clerk that she had a large family she was feeding. None of the items were fresh fruits or vegetables.

She took the food inside and ate for a couple of hours. It wasn't yet dinner time. At dinner, she realized she hadn't really had lunch, just a late breakfast. She decided she needed a substantial dinner. She went out, got dinner, and picked up more food items on the way home. It never occurred to her how much this cost. She had no thought of what the spending was doing to her budget.

The phone rang. She answered it. Her sponsor's voice was soft. "Sandra, I won't bother you after this. I want you to know I've been where you've been. You can get out of this if you'll just accept some help."

"Karen, I told you. I don't need help. I'm doing just fine."

"Just remember, with help you can get out of this."

"Okay, thanks for calling. I'll see you sometime." She hung up. She ate more. She felt disgusted with herself. She hated herself. She was worthless. She felt depressed, hopeless. She felt no power to get control over her life. She felt helpless to stop her downward slide. Nothing had ever worked. Support-group meetings didn't work. Having a sponsor didn't help. Her sponsor didn't really understand her. Therapy didn't work. Nothing really worked. The phone rang.

"Sandra, I didn't see you at the meeting today. Want to go with me tomorrow?"

"Hi, Julie. I went to a different meeting this morning. And tomorrow I have a full day planned."

"Okay, give me a call if you want to do something."

"I will. Bye."

Sandra watched a movie. She felt no belief in herself. She resented Julie. Julie was always so energetic, so pro-recovery. She probably didn't have any real problems. She had lost some weight. Sure, life is easy if you're not hauling around extra pounds.

Sunday was similar to Saturday. Sandra spent a lot of money on food. Her day had no shape to it. On Monday she looked at her checkbook and saw she had no money for therapy. She called and canceled her appointment. She was relieved that she got the answering machine. She just said she realized her funds were low and she'd have to quit therapy for a while. Monday night, Sandra felt desperately alone. She stopped at a store and bought some sugar products. She had little else to lose. She felt so bad, she deserved the small comfort sugar would give her.

It's a sad story. Many men and women follow this gray path into emotional oblivion over and over again. With a strong support group, few go all the way to the bottom. If we use our support structures, we get caught before we fall all the way. Relapse is always a danger to anyone who has an addictive disease. The drug—food, alcohol, laxatives, cocaine—offers quick relief from pressing discomfort. Relapse has its own momentum. If uninterrupted, relapse creates an ever-increasing need for the drug.

Life will always present us with disappointments, extra stresses, and heavy pressures. If we neglect our recovery, they will eventually overwhelm us. Relapse then can capture us and take us for a ride.

A CONSCIOUS REFUSAL TO KNOW OR FEEL

Relapse usually begins when we turn away from self-knowledge. Something happens and we deliberately avoid connecting with our fear, anger, sadness, or hurt about the incident. We turn our heads and pretend not to see. Whenever we turn away from feeling or knowing our own truths, we begin to get cut off from ourselves. It's as though by closing a door on one aspect of ourselves, other doors shut. Joy becomes less joyful. Happiness grays. Enjoyment of natural beauty fades. We are slightly more out of touch with our needs. At the same time, we need more. We are vulnerable to whatever has comforted us in the past and resistant to anything or anyone that threatens that comfort, even if the comfort harms us.

This process is cyclical and self-perpetuating. As we turn away from knowing one thing, we miss knowing other things about ourselves. We miss other feelings, other needs. We miss the sense of inner direction that guides us to make good choices. The further we get from accurate information about our inner selves, the more dependent we become on external, solitary comforts. By being out of touch with our needs, we meet them inappropriately or not at all. An internal deficit arises. We become neglected. This neglect creates its own pain. Then we neglect the pain. With each step away from ourselves, we become more abandoned.

Needs grow fuzzy and less clear. They merge into one gigantic need for comfort. If our drug were available only through certain people or in certain places, we might fall quite far before we reached for it. We might have more time to catch on to the process leading us into oblivion. If we had to get into the car and drive to a bar or a pusher's place, that might be enough to catch our attention. We could say, "If I carry this out, I'll be hooked again."

But our drug is one room away. All the ingredients for our drug are in our homes. We will put food into our bodies sometime within the next eight hours. How easy it is to creep back into the compulsion, one bite at a time.

Simplified, a relapse progresses as follows:

1. Consciously turning away from a thought or a feeling
2. Increasing fuzziness about thoughts, feelings, and needs
3. Decreasing ability to meet needs in a healthy way
4. Unconsciously turning away from thoughts and feelings
5. Statements like "I'll never eat sugar again," "I'll never relapse," or "I'll never do anything to risk another withdrawal."
6. Denial about the danger of relapse; denial about our actions
7. Increased feelings of criticism and judgment of others
8. Increased need for comfort
9. Decreased ability to get comfort in healthy ways
10. Increased need for food as comfort
11. Decreased ability to ask for help
12. Increase in confusion, anxiety, depression, helplessness
13. Increasing isolation, defensiveness
14. Decreased ability to accept help

A food relapse may progress differently for different people. My relapses usually take the following shape:

1. Eating larger portions than I need
2. Feeling hungry even when my belly is full
3. Having more hunger than usual—after meals, earlier than usual before a meal, all day instead of just before meals, in the evening despite a good dinner
4. Feeling more desperate about meals, needing mealtime like I'd need a life raft if I were adrift in the ocean
5. Watching other people's portions, comparing my portion to theirs to see if they got more than I did
6. Eating something in the evening or late at night
7. Wanting to eat something mid-afternoon and only if that something is a carbohydrate (if celery were the only food in the universe, I wouldn't be interested)
8. Eating more fried or oily things
9. Drowning foods in butter
10. Feeling that the food in front of me will never be enough
11. Feeling I could start eating and never stop
12. Mealtimes becoming ragged, less defined, less structured; adding extra meals; eating more carbohydrates than usual
13. Deciding it's okay to have a little bit of a white-flour product
14. Eating more than a little bit of a white-flour product
15. Losing white-flour abstinence
16. Noticing sugared foods even though they haven't been in my life for years
17. Having sugar fantasies, recalling the taste of specific sugar items, being more aware of them in restaurants and other places

Through the grace of my Higher Power and the power of the program, I've not fallen further than this since my second sugar abstinence. When I lost my first sugar abstinence, the following happened:

18. Convincing myself a little sugar wouldn't hurt me
19. Deciding I could control the amount of sugar I ate

20. Walking through the supermarket checkout with a large bag of many old favorites; inhaling the entire bag of sugar foods
21. Full-scale dependence on food

After he quit smoking, Winston Churchill was asked if he would ever smoke again. He answered, "I don't know if I'll ever smoke again. I know I won't ever quit again." Food addicts suffer millions of little slips as they relieve tension with food. Our danger is that one day a slip will drag us into a full-scale relapse. Most of the time, we're lucky enough to be caught before we hit bottom. The danger is that we'll slip through the net and not stop. Once we start falling, our range of positive options shrinks until eating seems to be our only choice. To guard against this, it's vital that we attend regular support meetings. If your boss insists that you work during a regular meeting, attend another one.

Recovery requires an ongoing commitment from you. You must learn and practice new coping skills. Talk to safe people about feelings and concerns. Ask yourself what you need and get it. Fight the desire to isolate by being with healthy people. Get help identifying unnecessary stresses and get support in changing them. Get help noticing survival rules and get support in changing them. Get help with nearly everything. If you want to live a normal life free of the endless obsession with food and weight, you can by continuing in your commitment to recovery.

Remember, we do not consciously choose relapse but find ourselves there at the bottom of a long road posted with warning signs.[2] You've probably heard the saying that a binge is the last symptom of a relapse. Relapse begins long before that binge. It is a process that occurs when recovery is neglected. It's what we don't do that induces relapse. Relapse is a process that can be interrupted at any time.

The process of relapse occurs within us. For example, if someone tells me I look like I've gained weight and I slip into the binge-starve cycle, I can't say she caused my relapse. That I slipped because of what she said means that what she said triggered a fear I have about my worthiness. That I slipped means I chose not to work through the pain it caused. No one causes another to relapse.

◇

ASSIGNMENT 13.1

1. Read the Anatomy of a Relapse again. Underline each choice or decision that could have been a warning sign of relapse. Identify the relapse behavior.
2. Put a star by each decision that took her further into relapse.
3. By each star, list options that would have been healthier choices.

◇

ASSIGNMENT 13.2

1. List some things you would do if you were in relapse. Identify your own relapse progression. Arrange the list of decisions or actions in the order they would usually occur as you slipped further into relapse.
2. Read this list to your sponsor. Discuss actions she could take that would help you become aware of what you're doing.

◇

ASSIGNMENT 13.3

1. Make a list of events that could make you vulnerable to relapse (for example, if your best friend were moving away, if you thought someone didn't care about you any more, if someone you trusted violated that trust, if someone made a comment about your size).
2. Share the list with your therapy group as insurance against any of these events triggering relapse.

14

◇

FURTHER ABSTINENCE

◇

If you have followed my recommendations, you are reading this chapter after six to twelve months of sugar abstinence. Congratulations! What you have already achieved is monumental. You've withdrawn from a substance that for you is a highly addictive, dangerous drug. You've given your brain chemistry time to adjust to this change. You've gained the support you need to stay abstinent. You are a treasure! You may skip the next two paragraphs.

If you have jumped ahead from chapter 7 to this chapter, I can assure you I've kept my word. In this chapter, I explain what to do once you've reached comfortable sugar abstinence. This information is waiting for you when you are ready for it.

If you are reading this book for the first time and have neither started building a support system (chapters 6 and 8) nor been sugar-abstinent for some months or if you are about to read this chapter so you can get abstinent from everything at once, I have some motherly advice. If you try to be abstinent from everything at once, it will be a terrible shock to your body, you will not be able to sustain it, and a really effective plan will become spoiled for you. The drivenness of this disease has grabbed you. Doesn't this feel like the other times you've been desperate to do anything to lose weight? Did it work then? Did you feel any better about yourself? Take some deep breaths, remember that you are worthwhile and acceptable right this very minute, and do the exercises in chapter 6.

REFINED CARBOHYDRATES ABSTINENCE

Why is further abstinence needed? Many people who react to sugar with food cravings, food obsessions, and the overpowering desire to eat react similarly to refined carbohydrates. White flour (milled wheat flour), for example, converts rapidly into simple sugars as soon as it enters the body. Soda crackers convert to sugar in the mouth. Thus the body receives refined carbohydrates as simple, rapidly metabolized sugars. However you react to sugar is probably how you react to simple carbohydrates. If sugar products depress you and rob you of energy, crackers, pasta, and other refined wheat products are likely to do the same. If you felt discomfort withdrawing from sugar, refined carbos probably have a similar hold on your body.

Think about it. Do you crave specific refined carbohydrate products? Does garlic bread ring your chimes? Could you eat an entire loaf of freshly baked, out-of-the-oven bread? Is pasta a palate pleaser? Can a plateful of crackers disappear into your mouth as if they never were? Then you probably react to carbohydrates with the same addictive chemical fervor as sugar.

If you want real peace from being haunted by food, if you want an honest chance at a fuller, more purposeful life, refined carbohydrates abstinence is the next step. This abstinence is very difficult to achieve. Sugar has invaded many foods, but the flour invasion is even more widespread. To avoid white flour takes planning, foresight, and a redefinition of food. Here's a reminder. Refined carbohydrates include:

- White flour, including unbleached flour
- White or milled rice
- Alcohol

- Rice flour (unless it is from brown rice)
- Rye flour (unless it is labeled "whole-grain rye")

This abstinence is more feasible if you reach it category by category. Here's the plan:

1. White-flour abstinence—allow at least ninety days.
2. Add abstinence from all other milled flours and white rice (white-rice flour, milled rye breads)—give yourself at least a month to adjust to this before going to step 3.
3. Examine bodily reaction to corn-flour products.

CONVERTING TO WHOLE-WHEAT EATING

White flour is called flour, wheat flour, and unbleached wheat flour. Bread containing white flour may be labeled "whole-wheat bread," "wheat bread," "seven-grain bread," "health bread," and "brown bread." Dark bread, pumpernickel, and other healthy-sounding breads are made dark not by the wholeness of the grain but by the addition of molasses.

If one had less faith in the food industry, one might suppose that it was deliberately misleading us about these breads. It is true that white-flour products make more money than whole-wheat products. Refining and bleaching white flour inflates the grain; so one loaf of white bread requires only *one-quarter* of the flour needed for one loaf of whole-wheat bread—that's four loaves of white bread to one loaf of whole-wheat bread. (Before you do a mind-trip that says you can eat four slices of white bread instead of one slice of whole-wheat, let me hasten to remind you that the chemical interaction within your body is the crucial factor with food addiction.) A reminder—white flour is contained in the following:

- Buns and pizza crusts
- Many whole wheat and seven-grain breads

And in most of the following:

- Breads

- Buns, bagels
- Crackers
- Cream soups
- Fried batters
- Gravies
- Pastas
- Pizza dough
- Sauces
- Wheat bread

If a bread is mostly white with occasional brown flecks, it contains mostly white flours. Whole-wheat bread free of refined flour is labeled "100% whole-wheat bread." If "100%" is not on the label, read the ingredients to see what else is there. I've seen bread labeled "healthy whole wheat" that listed white flour and unbleached flour as the first two ingredients.

Today, we're blessed with many more options: whole-wheat hamburger and hot-dog buns, wheat-free soups, whole-wheat pizzas, whole-wheat french bread, whole-wheat pastas, whole-wheat cereals, and whole-wheat tortillas. With searching, nearly every beloved flour product can be replaced with a sugar-free, 100-percent whole-wheat product.

Most restaurants are willing to prepare sandwiches and hamburgers with whole-wheat bread. If the bread looks too light to you or if the restaurant has a sweet tooth and you're afraid their bread has sugar in it, take your own bread and substitute it. I try to remember to take my bread with me when I go to a restaurant I'm unsure of. When I travel to Canada or across the United States, it's very important that I take my bread with me. Then I needn't be tempted to accept food that's bad for me because I have no other choice. Remember that those colorful pastas with healthy-sounding names may be mostly white flour. Ask for a list of ingredients. One-hundred-percent whole-wheat pasta is now available in most shapes. Of course, you are already abstinent from alcohol since you are sugar abstinent.

CONVERTING TO OTHER WHOLE GRAINS

Brown rice is the substitute for white rice. Rice-flour breads may be made with flour milled from either white rice or brown rice. Read the label.

Rye bread is usually made from milled rye flour. Read the label to find out. If it says rye flour, it is milled. If it says whole-grain rye flour, it is not refined.

CORN FLOUR

Finally, take a look at corn flour. Do you get draggy after corn chips? Do corn-flour products trigger cravings? If so, you are having a chemical reaction to corn flour and abstinence is the only answer. If corn-flour products do not cause lethargy or any emotional reaction, the following test will tell you whether you need total abstinence or moderation.

Put ten corn chips in a bowl, close the bag, and put the bag away. Go into another room, eat the chips, and stop when the bowl is empty. Now what? Do you need to be chained to the wall to keep from getting more? Can you stay out of the kitchen for the next hour? Does the bag haunt you all afternoon? A positive answer to any of the above means you have difficulty moderating yourself. You can try artificial control—buying only one small bag at a time, only eating this bag when you get home, only eating such products in restaurants, where the portion size is controlled. What happens to you after you've had the product? Does other eating increase? Does your preoccupation with food and eating increase? If you want peace from this, abstinence is the answer.

BINGE ABSTINENCE

If you are successfully abstinent from sugar and mostly abstinent from refined carbohydrates, your relationship with food has changed. Most of the time, you are probably less obsessed, less driven by food than on your best days before recovery. And binges have changed for you—they are fewer and shorter. I remember when I first realized that my new definition of a binge was eating an extra piece of bread or an extra fruit—quite different from the old days when binging meant plowing through whole bags and cartons for two or three hours.

The long-term goal is to eat three healthy, reasonable meals each day with nothing in between. Some people do better with three meals and a planned snack. For some, the snack keeps blood sugar even. For others, any snack is an invitation to keep on eating. Take binge abstinence in steps:

1. Three meals a day and a planned, defined snack. Don't wait until snack time to determine what you'll have. In the morning, plan whether it will be popcorn, a glass of milk, a piece of fruit and a slice of cheese, or a piece of fruit and a glass of milk. Bread or cracker snacks don't seem to work so well. Many find even whole-wheat crackers a difficult snack to stop eating.
2. Three meals a day, nothing in between. An exception to this is when traveling or when a meal will be delayed past your normal eating time. Rather than get too hungry or let blood sugar get too low, have some V-8 juice, some cheese, a piece of fruit, or a glass of milk.
3. Three meals a day, nothing in between, reasonable portion sizes.

BECOMING BINGELESS

If you routinely binge in the afternoon and at night, each binge time must be dealt with separately. Which would be easiest to eliminate? Start there.

Set up lots of support from friends, plan fun activities, and make yourself busy or go to a meeting during that binge time every day for at least one week. Don't substitute something boring like housework or errand-running for a binge time. Who'd want to stop bingeing to mop the floor? The goal is to become abstinent from bingeing and eating *at that time.* The easiest way to avoid a binge is to not eat at all at that time. You may have to plan your mealtime earlier or later to adjust for the difference in intake.

At first, it may feel as if something is missing or as if you've forgotten something—and you will probably feel very hungry. If you must eat, choose a protein, fruit, or V-8 juice.

As with early sugar and carbohydrate abstinence, you will go through withdrawal. This time, however, it will be milder. You may experience anxiety, mild grief, a feeling of emptiness, or mild forgetfulness, and, as is common, you may forget the cause of these symptoms. You may feel worried about yourself and not remember why. If you talk to your sponsor every day, she can remind you that this is withdrawal; these symptoms will pass.

Then one day you forget about eating during that time. Suddenly you have more time. You can get more done. You have more choices.

Once you're comfortably abstinent from bingeing at that time, out of nowhere will come a craving, a desire to eat at that old time. Why? You know the answer now. Something's wrong. You need something you're not getting. You're not feeling something that's nagging at you. Call someone and talk about it. The need to eat will disappear when you discover what you need.

If you're eating three meals a day, nothing in between, you're doing very, very well. Think about your old bingeing days and appreciate the contrast. Be sure you're not eating too little. Be sure you're eating enough so you don't set yourself up to snack or binge out of hunger. Here are some general guidelines:

- Eat some protein in the morning so that you don't set up cravings that day. A breakfast that is totally carbohydrate, though not refined, might still trigger an addictive reaction and consequent food cravings.
- Eat fresh vegetables every day.
- Eat enough at dinner so that you won't need to eat later at night.
- Never skip a meal.
- Have a snack rather than delay a meal too long.
- If the snack is a natural sugar (for example, fruit) have a small amount of protein also.

PROPERLY PROPORTIONED PORTIONS

The next step is to eat portions normal for your age and activity level. I've found this to be very hard to do. If I am in touch with my sponsor and aware of my body, I hardly have to think about it. As I get out of touch with my sponsor and my body, however, my portion sizes become larger and I approach meals like a vacuum cleaner. My willingness to eat normally is dependent on my internal health. If I do the things that keep my recovery going, namely talking and feeling, mealtime is a breeze. But now and then I get irritated at this extra effort required of me, and I stubbornly refuse to call my friends, or I get lazy. My meal sizes grow. For me this is a back-and-forth effort, sometimes a struggle, sometimes ridiculously easy.

When I am in touch with my body and I'm willing to listen to it, it tells me when I've had enough. I can feel its fullness. My sponsor tells me we sigh when we've had enough food. I've found that if I listen for the sigh and put my fork down when I hear it, I soon discover that I'm full and have no need for more. My willingness to go through this is entirely dependent on the state of my recovery.

MODERATING FATS AND OILS

The last major abstinence category is oils and fats. Since certain oils are essential, total abstinence from oil is harmful. Wait at least three or, better, six months after comfortable refined carbohydrate abstinence before fooling with this category.

First, I recommend fat abstinence. This abstinence includes refraining from obvious animal fat or cooking products in animal fat. Cut fat off meat. Broil or grill hamburgers, steaks, and pork chops. Bake or grill chicken. Stir-fry meat that has been trimmed of obvious fat.

Don't panic! This is not a diet. It's a revision of your style of eating. Ideally, you are doing this one-and-a-half years after first achieving sugar abstinence. If this seems overwhelming, you are reading it too soon. Stop reading at the end of this paragraph. Read this part of the chapter again a year from now. Once you have achieved other abstinences, you'll find it easier to add new ones. Over time, because of the many benefits of abstinence, you will be more willing to change how you eat.

If you are still reading, I'm assuming you are not overwhelmed by the idea of expanding your abstinence. You have been sugar abstinent for a year and refined-carbohydrate abstinent for six months and can see the benefits of abstinence—decreased preoccupation with food, clearer thinking, clearer sense of feelings and needs. You have changed the way you eat and have begun to trust that there are other ways to get your needs met besides eating. Fats and oils are high-calorie foods. Although they may trigger addictive chemical reactions in the brain, total abstinence is not healthy. Moreover, their use must be tapered. A sensor at the beginning of the intestine notices how much fat goes by. If fat intake is drastically lowered, you feel deprived. So you must decrease your fat intake gradually enough to fool that sensor. This abstinence, too, must proceed step by step:

1. Eliminate animal fat.
2. Moderate fried foods.
3. Moderate cream.
4. Moderate sour cream.
5. Moderate butter.
6. Moderate mayonnaise.

Animal Fat

Convert your cooking style. Use oils for frying instead of animal fat or lard. Broil, grill, or bake instead of frying. Use herbs or broths for sauces or flavorings instead of fat-based gravies. Stir-frying produces delicious meals. Use a paper towel to blot fat from bacon or a hamburger after broiling. Reduce the amount of bacon you eat. Halve the serving or halve the number of times you eat it. (This is, of course, sugar-free bacon.)

Moderation

Work on one food at a time. Don't change or try substitutions for another until you're comfortable with the first. Play with different kinds of moderation to find what works for you. For example, I was going crazy with butter so I stopped buying it and wouldn't have it in my house. I got used to not using butter and after some weeks of ease without it, bought it again. I could then add a minimum of butter and be happy with it. Some months later, I went crazy with it again. By now, you can diagnose my problem. Something else in my life had gone haywire. That's why food got more important. I stopped buying butter again. I worked on my problem.

I still fluctuate with butter. Here are my choices. I can avoid all this hassle by eliminating butter from my food plan. Or I can only have butter when I'm out. Or I can substitute a healthy oil for butter.

You have the same choices. With each food, you can try temporary total abstinence and then add it to see if you can eat it in moderate, healthy proportions. If you can't, you can try rules, such as not having it in the house and only eating it when out with others. Or you can try substitution and see if that is as satisfying after you get used to it. Try tapering something gradually. If you normally have a big serving, can you serve yourself a bit less? If a certain food haunts you, calls to you, causes cravings and increased eating, abstinence will give you peace.

SUBSTITUTIONS

For	*Try*
Fried foods	Baking, broiling, stir-frying, grilling
Sour cream	Yogurt, blended cottage cheese
Butter	Oils, seasonings
Potato chips	Thin-sliced baked potatoes
Cream	Condensed milk
Mayonnaise	Low-fat, sugar-free mayonnaise

I'm sorry I can't give you a plan with fats and oils as clear-cut as with the previous food categories. I have to work this out individually with each client as she becomes ready. It takes trial and error, observing results and consequences, and trying again. Honest communication with a sponsor or therapist is invaluable at this time.

VIOLENCE OR PEACEFUL COEXISTENCE?

We always thought only brute force could control our eating. Diets have been such attempts at force. It turns out that except for the violence that is withdrawal, our eating responds best to gentle, caring attention rather than harsh words or shame or ridicule.

The mystery to me is that I sometimes avoid getting the care I need even though I know my recovery depends on it. Am I setting myself up to eat or is this the incredible, persistent pull of the disease? Is my fear of trusting and asking for help so deep that overcoming it is sometimes just too much trouble? Whatever the reason, many food addicts and compulsive eaters seem to follow a grand cycle—one week reaching out, talking, and being in touch with our body's every need; the next week, isolating, talking less, and being less tuned in. Rather than beat ourselves up for our very human inconsistency, we can commit to certain support-group meetings and ensure that we get carried back to the phase in which we treat ourselves with the respect we deserve.

LISTENING TO MY BODY

What about those recovery plans and books that say, "Just listen to your body. It'll tell you when, what, and how much to eat"? After eight years of sugar abstinence and nine years of recovery, I can finally hear my body guide me toward good food choices 70 percent of the time. If someone can do this right off the bat, I assume she has no food addictions, is less damaged by her family, and has a disease that has not progressed as far as mine did. Three factors can make it difficult to listen to the body:

1. If we eat trigger foods, the chemical reactions in the brain will tell us to keep eating. This is a false message. We are not truly hungry. Our perception of hunger is chemically induced. When we listen to the body while under the influence of a drug, it will lie to us. Is the smoker making a healthy choice

when his body tells him to light up? No. The chemically induced craving spurs an unhealthy action.

2. Survivors of sexual or other physical abuse may be very out of touch with their bodies. For years I walked around unaware of myself from the neck down. I was all head. I lived in my mind. I couldn't listen to my body because I was dissociated from it. Many abuse survivors are split in this way.
3. Hunger messages may actually be caused by emotional emptiness. The desire to eat is masking the need for another kind of fullness.

Through recovery we gradually work toward being receptive to internal guidance about what and how much to eat. As our abstinence becomes cleaner, we are less confused by misleading chemical signals. As we heal the damage done by incest and violence, we reconnect with our bodies. As we become comfortable getting support, we are able to distinguish emotional emptiness from physical emptiness.

Many times now, my body tells me exactly the right amount to eat. As I serve myself, something says, One more spoonful will be too much. I don't always listen to this voice. My willingness to respond to my internal guidance is entirely dependent on how well I'm taking care of myself. This voice is harder to hear when food is being served to me. Once it's on my plate and I have begun eating, I have more difficulty stopping at the point when I've had enough. If you, like me, have progressed deeply into the disease of overeating or food addiction—if you could be diagnosed as a late-stage, chronic compulsive eater—you, like me, may at times need to substitute structure for internal guidance.

When I take excellent care of myself, I can relax a bit. If I am in tune with my body, I can stretch the rules—rules about three meals a day or mealtimes. I can add a sensible snack, certain that my hunger is physical. But I must remain vigilant. If my self-care slips, denial creeps up on me.

When I am under stress, I batten down the structure. Stress distracts me from my body, so I must rely on my guidelines and support system until it has passed. Striking a balance between relaxed and relapsed takes experience and self-knowledge. Few of us can do it perfectly. Most of us rely heavily on our support persons. We talk frequently enough to notice when stress increases and when our stress level is likely to affect our eating. In fact, an increase in eating is a reliable sign that our stress level has increased.

ASSIGNMENT 14.1

Discuss your level of abstinence with your support person and your therapy group. Accept appropriate feedback about the extent and timing of your abstinence. If you decide to expand your abstinence, discuss this with your support person and therapy group. Set up enough support to successfully survive withdrawal. Continue sufficient support until the new abstinence feels comfortable.

ASSIGNMENT 14.2

Write about the following: How does bingeing benefit you? What safety does it provide? What does it protect you from feeling?

ASSIGNMENT 14.3

Plan an evening meal that has just the right amount of food for you. Commit to your support person that you will eat just that amount and no more. When you've finished the meal, leave the table immediately. In another room, write about how it felt to leave the table before reaching your usual level of physical fullness. Read this to your support person and in therapy.

15

◇

WAIT!

◇

Most clients who come to me do so initially because they are dissatisfied with their weight. A usual consequence of food addiction, weight is a blessing, a curse, and an accident. All addictions have serious consequences, but compulsive overeating is the only addiction with a consequence everyone can see at all times. Since this consequence is what sends people for help, it is a blessing. Unfortunately, like most addicts, we are impulsive, driven, and frantic for quick results. This makes us vulnerable to schemes that promise quick weight loss. Extra weight can be life-threatening; it can impair the health and strength of the body. In some medical circles, however, mild obesity is now considered much less risky than yo-yoing between weight gain and loss.

Extra weight swallows self-esteem. We believe it demonstrates a lack of moral strength, a lack of willpower. And we think everyone else thinks that. So we move through the world in a posture of silent apology. Occasionally we abuse ourselves with crazy diets or exercise. We send $39.95 to the latest diet scam in an effort to rid ourselves of the terrible, subtle torture of believing ourselves inferior. When we fail, however, we don't demand our money back because we did not follow the plan exactly and because deep down we believe the failure is due to our own weakness.

We fear abuse: the taunts; the rude, intrusive comments from ignorant loved ones or strangers; the scapegoating by family members who avoid their own issues by picking on the weighted one. We fear discrimination, that our weight will be the unspoken reason why we lost the job, that we'll be passed over for job opportunities, that they'll be given to the pretty people.

I fall into the same trap. Despite all I know, I wonder sometimes, do potential clients discount me because of my extra pounds? Do they take one look and think, her program couldn't work? Should I parade my old polyester pants, the ones I wore before recovery that are four sizes bigger than I wear now? Should I display the pictures of my female ancestors to show I'm beating the genetic odds, to show I'm lighter than they were?

We fear our weight could make our mates reject us. Fear of potential rejection keeps us from parties or activities where we could meet people to date. If we do go out, we're so sure no one would find us attractive that we act apologetic for even being there. We don't walk or bike or ski because we're afraid of rude remarks. We are fearful of every new setting because we don't know if we'll be able to find a place to sit. We worry: "Will I fit in the booth at the restaurant, or worse, will I get stuck and have difficulty getting out?" "Will I be able to get out of the back seat of the car?" "Will the airplane seat belt go around me or will I have to ask for an extension?" "Will that chair hold me?" Each time we enter a room, we quickly scan it to solve the problem of where to sit. These anxieties can tip the balance—it's easier to stay home than risk embarrassment in an unknown setting.

No wonder the cork pops and we occasionally get crazy over losing weight. I mentioned that the weight is accidental. In a certain sense, this is true. We are usually eating for the drug effect, not for the weight. If eating didn't cause weight gain, we would still overeat, because we are using the food to handle our feelings and the eating process triggers a chemical release that numbs us. So most of us, as we pick up the food item, are not thinking, this will increase my size. Most of us are thinking, I need relief desperately.

The weight, however, can be useful. Many who have been sexually abused feel protected by their weight. It is a screen to hide behind. Weight also fosters isolation, toward which most addicts tend. Weight is one more good reason for staying home and munching rather than braving the unknown, the possible taunts, the tiny chairs.

After years of being heavy, we no longer believe we could be otherwise. Weight informs our self-image. This hurts us, but it also gives us a feeling of being grounded, of being women and men of substance. Paradoxically, however, many people with extra size feel small inside, that their inner selves are small. In groups, we easily become invisible and fade into the wallpaper. We hide behind the fat as behind a curtain. We are tortured by the thought that the extra weight broadcasts our inferiority.

Eventually the disadvantages, the irritations, and the loss of esteem drive the food addict toward some weight-loss scheme or into obsessing about weight loss. These efforts are usually doomed. They plunge us into unsupported, unacknowledged withdrawal. If the diet plan contains sugar, the sugar addict hasn't a prayer. Chemical pressure will defeat the diet in days if not hours.

ANGER

Sometimes we try to lose weight so others will think better of us, but the victory is a hollow one. As much as we want to be accepted, we recoil when acceptance hinges only on our size. Our inner self, the one neglected as a child, the one abandoned by driven dieting, gets angry. Then many of us turn the anger against ourselves. Instead of getting angry at our friends and loved ones for being blind to our inner worth, we blame ourselves. This feels so bad that we eat to relieve it, and the weight goes up.

SUBSTITUTE COMPULSIONS

Some of us handle anger by compulsively shopping, exercising, or working. These compulsions may look more acceptable than eating, but they all have consequences. Credit cards that have hit their limit, for example, may mean a burden as heavy as weight—ahead lie years of interest payments, little spending freedom, and tension that may trigger a binge.

Compulsive work and exercise are socially sanctioned, but any time we are driven to do anything, we are abandoning ourselves. Workaholism hurts our relationships and can cause tension and exhaustion that may send us back to the food. Compulsive exercise may harm our tendons and muscles and may push our bodies past the point of health.

Underneath, the problem remains. We are driven. We are running from important feelings. We are pushing toward an elusive, phantom relief: "If only I do this, I'll feel worthy." We are missing our lives. If injury or exhaustion keeps us from exercising, all that we've been running from will still be inside us. We'll either need the food again or we'll compulsively diet and head toward anorexia.

Those who do lose weight are grieved to discover that their fantasy—"If only I'm thin, everything will work out"—is untrue. Thinness does not guarantee wealth, love, or happily-ever-after futures. Thin people have all the same problems they did before they lost weight. Unless we have a strong, supportive recovery system, we'll handle this disappointment like all other feelings—by eating or by some other compulsion. The grief, the resentment, and the anger can send us to the food, the only friend who's always been there. Or we can get tipped into anorexia, pursuing ever-greater thinness.

If weight loss is to last, it must not be another aspect of the compulsion. For many, dieting has been yet another obsession surrounding food. It has been another way of being driven, of not feeling good enough, of focusing on outside things to avoid the inside. Lasting, healthy weight loss isn't driven. If weight loss is to last, the process must allow one to stay emotionally healthy, sober, and in recovery.

MELTING THE COCOON[1]

So, do we throw out the scales? Is weight loss impossible? I'm not going to lie to you. Once the fat is on our bodies, we face some severe bodily resistance to weight loss. We have a chance, and I'll explain that chance soon, but to some degree, what is possible for us is limited.

Our weight range is set genetically. If we overeat, we can raise the limit, but there's a point beneath which we can't lower it. How were your ancestors built? Were they stocky, broad people? Then it's unlikely you'll ever be wispy and willowy.

Your genes don't know thin is in. They are programmed for your survival. If you have dieted off and on through your life, what you've told your body is that it will be subjected to periodic starvation. It has responded to this crisis by lowering your metabolism. It's ready for you now. So should you starve again, it's prepared to hoard calories—you will live even if the famine lasts a long time.

When one eats a concentrated sugar product, *insulin* is released. Insulin makes the blood-sugar level drop. How does it do this? By speeding up the process by which sugar is converted to fat and stored in fat cells. This can cause you to feel hungry right after you've eaten. High sugar intake causes a sharp rise in blood-sugar level, which triggers insulin release, which spurs fat storage, which lowers blood-sugar level, which causes hunger. The other links in the chain, the release of pleasure-giving brain chemicals, have already been explained in chapter 2.

So how do we get the fat out of the cells and use them as fuel? Therein lies the crux of weight loss. Weight is maintained through chemical interactions. Weight loss occurs through manipulation of these interactions. Insulin not only promotes the conversion of sugar to fat, it promotes the maintenance of fat, causing a chemical resistance to the process of converting fat into energy. Thus, when insulin is circulating through the bloodstream, fat is going to stay in hiding.

As if low metabolism, genetic limitations, and roving insulin weren't enough, we also have *lipoprotein lipase*. This irritating little chemical hovers around fat cells when they are low in capacity and chases drifting fat back into the cells, like a barker shoving folks into the sideshow until the tent is bulging.

Face it, your body doesn't give a hoot about fashion. Your body is into survival. It is well programmed to keep you alive and has numerous tricks to ensure your survival through winter famine, diet-caused famine, and emotional distress.

WHAT'S A BODY TO DO?

If you want to take your weight down to your genetic limit in a healthy, lasting way, five major challenges await you:

1. Abstain from foods that chemically trigger appetite.
2. Decrease dependence on food for emotional support.
3. Increase metabolism.
4. Deal with the safety and protection size has given you, and accept a changing self-image.
5. Eat in a way that promotes level blood sugar and discourages excessive insulin release.

CHEMICAL TRIGGERS

Obviously, weight can't be lost if the body is chemically triggered to keep eating. Triggering foods must be identified and abstained from. Chapter 2 explains the chemical process by which sugar, refined carbohydrates, and fats trigger food addicts to keep eating. Feel-good chemicals are released. We feel sleepy and out of touch. A feedback loop that should tell us to stop eating is defective. We can eat past the point of our stomachs aching, past the point of being nauseated, until the cupboard is bare, or someone is about to catch us. As long as we are chemically triggered, no diet or sensible food plan can work. Not every food addict has this sensitivity to carbohydrates. Also, sensitivities differ. Some people are very sensitive, others less so. Some eating-disorders therapists have done well promoting an eat-what-you-want, listen-to-your-body plan. This plan can work for people who are not chemically sensitive to carbohydrates. But if you are, such a plan is no more effective than telling an alcoholic to listen to his body and stop drinking before he gets drunk. For those of us who are physically addicted to sugar and refined carbohydrates, just a little bit can trigger us all the way back into the full-blown disease. We are just like alcoholics. We are alcoholics of sugar.

Those of us who have achieved abstinence and then eaten sugar again have been amazed at the speed with which all the craziness of the disease resumes. The cloudy thinking, loss of touch with feelings, separateness from others, and unmanageability of living are back so fast it's like being sucked into a vacuum. The clarity, energy, and purpose we enjoyed just a day before seems remote and out of reach. In our denial, we may say, "This won't last. I've only been here a day. I can get out of this easily." But climbing back out of a relapse is as hard, sometimes harder, the second or fourth time than it was the first time. Back we go through withdrawal, hopelessness, anxiety, and anger.

This is why I find the eat-what-you-want philosophy, whose promoters verge on evangelistic in their zeal, so dangerous. Our bodies are very different from one another. Naturally this difference includes variations in chemical functioning.

Then what's the plan for abstinence? Withdraw from chemical triggers, one category at a time. Don't try to do it all at once or it will seem like a diet. You'll feel deprived, and you'll relapse. Read chapter 7, do the exercises, set up support, and withdraw from sugar first, since that is the most potent chemical stimulant. Chapter 7 describes withdrawal and what you can expect.

Remember that when you eliminate sugar, you eliminate your anesthetic. All your anger, grief, disappointment—all the feelings sugar was cloaking—will come out of hiding. Learning to accept help with these feelings is part of recovery from this disease. Chapter 8 describes the help available.

After three weeks, the worst of the withdrawal is over. Your body, however, continues to change and adjust to the chemical changes for months, maybe even years. At first, stay only with sugar abstinence. Let that become automatic, easy, second nature. Avoid large hunks of refined carbohydrates. Stay away from alcohol. When you are totally relaxed about sugar abstinence—six months or a year after withdrawal—then you can tighten your abstinence. Chapter 14 is about expanding abstinence to include certain carbohydrates and fats.

DECREASING DEPENDENCE ON FOOD TO ALTER FEELINGS

She comes home from work. She's spent. She gave and gave. She's empty. She comes through the door and heads for the kitchen. This is not thought out. Her action is automatic. She gets food. She eats. She fills the emptiness work created.

He's worried. There's another letter from the bank. Did he bounce a check? Is it another fee? Money pressure is breaking him. He shoves the letter under a stack of papers. He opens the fridge and starts to eat.

It's Saturday night. She's not going out. Nothing special is going to happen, no friends, no excited conversation, no laughter. It'll be an evening of TV reruns. She's lonely. She starts to eat. It'll get her through.

These are examples of using food to handle feelings and to cope with life. Our bond with food is strong. Abstinence from triggering foods will give you relief from the obsession, cut down cravings, increase energy, reduce binges, and clear your mind. But the bond with food will remain. Food has been a trusted friend—reliable, consistent, and effective. Food has given you a kind of control—control over your chemical functioning. Food has given you a way to vacation from problems and feelings. Food is nearly perfect.

People, on the other hand, are imperfect. Some aren't too healthy. Some can't be trusted. And some have hurt you deeply. Even the most wonderful person can't be there for you all the time. No wonder it's frightening to switch your reliance from food to people. Until you do, however, food will win when you need help. We all need help. If you don't turn to people, you'll turn to something else. The odds are enormous that the something else will be food.

Breaking the pattern of turning to food takes years. But in time, with practice, turning to healthy, supportive people looks better than food. You're not immune to slips, though. An hour after turning to human help you may still eat a little extra because of an unrealized anxiety.

Transferring your trust from food to people challenges nearly all the rules you made to survive your childhood. Obviously, this process cannot be taught or learned by a few months of classes about revising eating habits. If you've tried a weight-loss program that gave you the impression the classes would be enough to enable you to change your relationship with food, I hope now that you've read this book you'll see how absurd this expectation was. I hope you'll also see that if you gained any weight once the program was over, it was neither your failure nor your fault, but the fault of the program. Not even one year of such classes can bring about the profound systemic changes required if the bond with food is to be weakened.

A problem with many weight-loss programs is that they give the impression that all the changing can be done in your head. Their attitude is if you'll just change your thinking, your eating will change. But to try to lose weight only by thinking continues the deprivation of the soul we experienced as children when our inner selves were ignored. Difficult as it is, we escape our bondage to food only by reconnecting with our needs and feelings and by receiving care and comfort.

THE SPIRITUAL CONNECTION

Many of us are spiritual. We have prayed fervently that our need for food be lifted, only to believe that our petitions have gone unheard. Then we blame ourselves for lack of faith or inadequate piety.

We are spiritual yet human. Our soul is clothed by a body whose needs require attention. No matter how great our faith, very few of us could pray ourselves through a day of oxygen deprivation and emerge alive. In the same way, the needs we have had since childhood, the need for understanding and warmth, affection and comfort, assistance and healthy guidance must be met.

No matter how hard I pray, no matter how great my spiritual solace, my body still needs human interaction, exchange of ideas, hugs. For years I prayed for a miracle. When I entered recovery, I was astounded at the miracles awaiting me. Hundreds of times the exact help I needed appeared. Now I see that my prayers were answered, not with the lightning bolt I wanted, but by thousands of thoughtful acts and unearned gifts from human agents.

GOING THE DISTANCE

As abstinence lifts your food-caused anesthesia, feeling will come rushing back. During withdrawal you'll be bombarded. How are you going to handle all this feeling after years of eating to not feel? Recovering people can help you make it through withdrawal and restructure your life to maintain abstinence.

Why do I say recovering people? How many people have you fooled when you were hell-bent to eat? I can fool anybody—my mother, my therapist, my doctor, my mate. But I can rarely deceive my recovering support system. I've yet to fool my sponsor. My sponsor for recovery knows me. She knows my patterns, my tricks, and the stresses that make me vulnerable to food.

This is the crux of recovery—transferring your allegiance from food to people. It takes years. It may be the hardest thing you'll ever do. It may challenge most of the rules you live by. If you are a food addict or compulsive overeater, it's essential that you do so if you want to lose weight. The benefits are endless. Your inner self will finally get the attention she deserves. Long-standing wounds will get a chance to heal. Self-defeating patterns will be changed. You'll finally have the time and energy to pursue your purpose in life.

INCREASING METABOLISM

You're not eating trigger foods. You rarely use food as emotional support. Now what? The old metabolism needs stoking. This doesn't take much equipment. It takes less time than a binge. The method is simple. Fat is stored fuel. You can think of your stomach as a fuel storage tank. The way to get rid of fuel is to burn it.

Calories are the body's BTUs (British Thermal Units). It takes a certain number of BTUs to warm your house. It takes a certain number of calories to keep your body going. Exercise burns some calories but many more are burned to maintain basic body functioning. Breathing, sleeping, circulation, posture, and temperature maintenance are all fueled by the conversion of sugar or fat into energy. The *amount* of calories burned to maintain these basic activities is called the *basal metabolic rate*. The thermostat in your house operates much the same way as your metabolism. If it's set at sixty-five, it burns less fuel than if it's set at eighty. If your metabolism is low, you burn fewer calories when you sit, breathe, and bat your eyelashes than someone whose metabolism is higher.

The average woman burns 1,500 to 2,000 calories a day. A diet, however, slows the metabolic rate nearly 1 percent each day. The amount of possible weight loss is halved each month of the diet. The longer it lasts, the slower the metabolic rate. Thus, if you lose ten pounds the first month of the diet, you're likely to lose five pounds the second month and two-and-a-half pounds the third month.

The body regards this deprivation as famine and grows more efficient in response to it. Prior to your first diet, you may have used twenty-five calories a day to bat your eyelashes. After the diet, your metabolism may have dropped as much as 30 percent. By using calories more efficiently, your body figured out how to use only seventeen or eighteen calories to blink your eyes throughout the day. Metabolism recovers much more slowly than it drops. After you stop dieting, the body is slow to trust that the famine is truly gone. If you've cycled through dieting and nondieting a lot, the body may have settled rather permanently at a lower metabolic rate.

EXERCISE

What revs up your metabolism? Exercise. It not only burns calories but raises the metabolic rate for hours after the activity.[2]

Some of us, however, exercise compulsively, so much so that it becomes yet another addiction through which we abandon ourselves. And there's always the danger of injury.

Others have difficulty maintaining an exercise program. We are embarrassed to be seen in public and fearful of taunts. We simply may not enjoy exercise. It's your choice. If you want to lose weight, increased metabolism is what makes it happen. By working through the fears that keep you from exercising, you can free yourself to enjoy activities that will increase your metabolism.

Exercise strengthens your muscles, your lungs, and your cardiovascular system. It releases chemicals that help you feel more positive and optimistic. It lowers stress and gives you a healthy time-out. As long as you approach it moderately and with care—you don't need another injurious compulsion—it will give you more energy for the other things you want to do.

STOKING THE FURNACE

One way to exercise is by walking, but before you start, discuss the following plan with your doctor. Buy good walking shoes from a store that's knowledgeable about them and, if you like, get a tape player with earphones, one that's small, light, and will attach to a pocket or waistband. Tape players work better than radios—when you change direction, the reception stays consistent.

Some music tapes are made specifically for walking, with a beat that keeps you at a consistently brisk pace. These come with different tempos so you can pick a pace that suits your fitness level. Libraries often have stories or taped books you can listen to while walking. It's a nice way to get the benefits of reading and still have your eyes available for beauty. Portable television sound receivers are also available so that you can listen to a favorite program while walking.

Walking with a friend is excellent entertainment. You can talk out your problems and practically forget you're exercising. You can play mind games such as "Twenty Questions" or "Animal, Vegetable, or Mineral." You can play car travel games—find as many colors as possible; find things starting with letters of the alphabet; make up a story about who lives in the houses you're passing.

Wear loose, comfortable clothing. Natural fibers like cotton are cooler and more absorbent than synthetics. Wear layers so you can shed clothing as you warm up.

Be sure to warm up before you start. Raise your arms and stretch. Swing your arms in circles. Move your neck, your shoulders, your ankles, and your legs in circles. Lean forward with both palms against a wall and push back and forth as though you were doing a standing pushup.

Once you start, walk fast enough to warm up within about ten minutes but not so fast that you can't talk while walking. You shouldn't have to pant.

WALKING SCHEDULE

Weeks One and Two	Walk twenty minutes a day, three days a week.
Weeks Three and Four	Measure one-half mile from where you start walking (for example, starting from home, drive 0.5 miles). Attempt to get to the half-mile point within ten minutes.
Month Two	Attempt to get to the half-mile point and back within twenty minutes.
Month Three	Walk thirty minutes four times a week. Attempt to do a mile within the first twenty minutes.
Month Four	Walk forty minutes four times a week. Do one mile within the first twenty minutes.
Month Five	Walk fifty minutes five times a week. Aim for two miles within the first forty minutes.
Month Six	Walk sixty minutes five times a week. Aim for two miles within the first forty minutes.
Maintenance	Walk sixty minutes five times a week. Aim for at least three miles within that time.

If this schedule requires too much of you too soon, stretch it out. Take extra time with each increment. If the schedule keeps you at earlier levels too long, shorten the adjustment period by a week or two.

If you want to do something else, or if safe walking routes aren't available to you, then anything that makes you move will do. Would you like to swim, canoe, play badminton or softball? Have you always had a yen to learn belly dancing, country-western dancing, or sailing? Do it! Find out where you can learn. Learn what clothes, warm-ups, and cool-downs you should use. Find a friend who'll go with you the first couple of times if you're nervous about walking into a strange setting. Learn how to do it safely. Stick with it long enough to give yourself a real chance. Let go of the need to do it perfectly. The point is not to become an Olympic champion. The goal is for you to discover movement that you enjoy.

I am probably the worst cross-country skier in the world. I spend as much time on my back as on my feet. It's one of the few activities I'm willing to do that I do so terribly. I love it. It's excellent exercise. Even getting up again, which I do a lot, is good exercise.

If you make mistakes, so what? Have a good time. Enjoy learning. Meet new people. Become involved. You'll be exercising and hardly noticing because you'll be having so much fun. The goal is to be moving for an hour, five days a week. If your new sport is not one you can do daily, walk on the days you can't. Or pursue a second sport that has always interested you. The more forms of movement that you can develop, the easier it'll be to sustain an exercise program.

BODY GUARD

For some of us, extra weight performs a very critical function. It gives us a feeling of protection from sexual abuse or intimacy. Many of my clients who've had the greatest difficulty losing weight have been those who've been sexually or emotionally abused. Extra weight seems to be a way to take the body out of the attraction market. This seeming protection is more imagined than real. Many extra-weighted people are very attractive and have active social lives.

Extra size can be seen, however, as a way to avoid sexual feelings, to renounce sexual experience. Part of the safety comes from feeling less attractive to others—if no one wants us, we don't have to think about being sexual beings. But more of the safety comes from feeling unattractive to ourselves. When we feel unattractive, we behave differently than when we feel attractive. We are more shy, more guarded. We communicate nonverbally that we are closed to intimate interaction.

Women and men who have been abused may want to hold onto this safety forever. That is an option. If extra weight frees you to live without fear, this is fine. You know what the trade-offs are. To be absolutely clear, size isn't keeping you from intimacy. The need to avoid intimacy sends signals that keep potential partners at a distance. If you've examined the possibilities you're closing off and have chosen safety, full speed ahead and more power to you. It's your life and your choice.

But perhaps you are divided. You want to be safe and you want a fulfilling, intimate relationship. If fear keeps sabotaging you from finding an intimate partner, the loneliness can be horrible. You want someone special, yet you're afraid to put yourself in situations where you would meet someone. You spend evenings in front of the television, safe and lonely. You feel so sure no one would want you that when you are in a place where you could meet someone, you curtain yourself so that you aren't really seen.

Therapy offers a way out of this dilemma. Although recovering from sexual abuse takes time, a part of the recovery process is learning that you are safe and can protect yourself no matter how desirable or attractive you are. Developing the ability to say no, gaining a sense of your personal power, and coming into the certainty that you deserve to be treated well are all aspects of self-protection.

Are you afraid of your own sexual feelings? Is weight a way to keep from following up on attractions to others? Are you afraid you'd be promiscuous or addicted to sex if you felt attractive? You have such fears for a reason. You can discover these reasons and heal from the causes.

Sexual addiction is a sister disease to food addiction. Sex and sexual obsessions can be used as an escape from problems and feelings just as food can. The shame and secrecy surrounding obsessive sexual activity can also be crippling. Anonymous Twelve Step programs exist for those who suspect their sexual thoughts or activities are addictive or compulsive. Obsessions with sex and compulsive sexual activity are a common consequence of sexual abuse. We are sexual beings. Sexual harm has far-reaching effects.

Sexual addiction can harm us if it forces us to transgress our moral boundaries. We may harm others and pass on the abuse, thereby crippling another life. If you believe you are harming anyone, even mildly, I urge you to seek therapy. The needs and urges that force you into harmful activities can be dealt with. Please don't pass on abuse to others.

I guarantee this—if you are harming someone else, it's very likely you will eat or drink or drug over it. Most of us can't bear to truly hurt someone, so we escape the attendant shame or guilt with food, alcohol, or other drugs. So if for no other reason, it's practical to get therapy if you are harming others. Until you break the pattern, you probably won't be able to lose weight. This kind of recovery is profound and personal. It takes more than reading a book to heal from such deep harm.

If you want eventually to be open to intimacy, I hope you will dare to try therapy. The healing process is long and arduous, but imagine how wonderful it would be to be unafraid. The other side of the therapeutic process returns you to the wholeness someone took from you when you were small. You get your life back. And it can be safe to be a smaller size again.

ASSIGNMENT 15.1

Hold a pillow. Do you feel safer? Does that cushion give you a feeling of protection? Sit for fifteen minutes holding that pillow. Notice the feelings you have while you hold it. Drop the pillow. How does that feel? Do you feel exposed now? Less safe? Pick up the pillow and hold it again. Hold it whenever you want, day after day.

Do you like occasions that call for cloaking clothes? Do you like wearing a choir robe? Is winter better than summer because you can wear coats and sweaters? If you feel safer with the pillow, then extra weight likely protects you and makes you feel safe. If you have a therapist or a recovery group, talk about what you experienced as you read this chapter. If you don't have a therapist, consult your local newspaper for groups or workshops on recovery from sexual abuse.

BODY IMAGE

Do you need size to feel powerful? Are you afraid of success? Do you picture yourself as someone who doesn't finish things? These can be powerful reasons to keep eating. There are some excellent books on body image that can help you discover the role your size plays for you.

One technique used by weight-loss programs to change body image is *visualization.* As vividly as possible, visualize your body at your healthiest weight. See yourself dressing and moving through your day. Use all your senses. The point is to reprogram the negative images of fatness and failure in your brain.

Although we usually have little power over body functioning, images can mobilize the power of the brain to affect such functioning. Some believe, moreover, that visualization attracts positive spiritual forces that realign possibilities and create options—that negative thoughts and images block good, so positive thoughts and images attract good. Experiment for yourself.

◇

ASSIGNMENT 15.2

1. In an interruption-proof setting, sit in a comfortable chair that supports your head, neck, arms, and hands.

2. Breathe deeply. Mentally scan your body. Relax any tense areas.
3. *Option 1.* Picture yourself at your healthy weight. Dress yourself at that weight. Picture the activities you would enjoy. Imagine how your body would feel to you. How would it feel to take a shower, to run, to dance? What sports would you do? Imagine looking into the mirror. Imagine a photograph of yourself. Picture shopping for clothes and shoes.

   Option 2. Clip pictures from magazines showing people enjoying activities or wearing clothes you would like. Paste them on poster board in a collage format. Cut out pictures of your face and paste them onto the bodies of the people in your collage. Look at the images of you having fun and being active.
4. End the meditation by saying, "My body is healthy, energetic, active, and at a healthy weight."
5. Each morning for a few minutes before you get up, vividly visualize your healthy body. End the visualization with an affirmation similar to that in step 4.

LOVE YOUR BODY

Maybe you have been hating your body for a long time. You've been irritated and frustrated with it. Know that anger is part of grieving and that we, having suffered from this disease, have a good reason for grief. Any disease brings grief for the limitations it imposes. We also grieve the neglect and abuse we suffered as children. Know too, however, that anger toward your body is a part of hating yourself. Neither you nor your body deserves hatred. Maybe you're using your body as a scapegoat for not being happy with your life, but no matter how powerless you feel, your life can change if you get enough help.

If you've worked through the chapters and assignments of this book, you're well on your way toward accepting yourself. True acceptance is loving yourself regardless of the size of your body. If you abstain from triggering foods and raise your metabolism, you'll lose weight. Are you a significantly better person if you're five pounds lighter? Intellectually, you know being lighter or heavier doesn't change anything at all. If you feel worthwhile now, you will then. If you don't feel worth loving now, you won't then. Most of us want to be lighter so we'll feel better about ourselves. We want to feel whole, treasured, wanted. We want to belong. But we feel this way by learning to be good to ourselves, by learning to respond healthfully to our needs. We come to feel this way by being with people who show us we matter and by healing from the incorrect messages that taught us we were unworthy. When we draw such experiences to ourselves, we find acceptance regardless of our appearance. Being at home in our bodies and our lives comes not from having a perfect body, but from having a healthy life and healthy relationships.

ASSIGNMENT 15.3

This is a meditation exercise. I know it's hard to read this and meditate, too, but do the best you can. Take your time with each part, then move on to the next.

MEDITATION I

1. In an interruption-proof setting, sit in a comfortable chair that supports your head, neck, arms, and hands.
2. Breathe deeply. Mentally scan your body and relax any tense areas.
3. Picture your feet. Think about what your feet do for you. They hold you up. They take you where you want to go. They let you balance upright. Appreciate your feet.
4. Picture your legs. Think about what your legs make possible for you. Because they fold, you can sit and climb. You can walk through the house and the garden. Thank your legs.
5. Picture your sexual self. Think of the pleasure you've received. Perhaps that part of you has given you a beloved child. Appreciate the gift of your sexual body.

6. Picture your buttocks. Think of what they give you: a comfortable place to sit, a way to eliminate waste. The muscles in your buttocks enable you to walk and bend. Thank your buttocks.
7. Picture your abdomen and your stomach. Your abdomen contains vital organs. If you had no stomach or buttocks, skirts and pants would slide to the ground. Your stomach creates a lap to hold a kitten or a baby. Thank your stomach.
8. Picture your waist. Think of what your waist does for you. It lets you pick things up (you couldn't do that if you couldn't bend). It holds up your skirts and pants. It provides a place for your seat belt. Thank your waist.
9. Picture your back and front. Their muscles let you lift and carry. Your front gives you a place to hold a friend. Your back lets you lean against a wall or into a chair.
10. Your arms and hands are wonderful. Your hands can hold books. Your fingers can turn pages and dial phones. Your hands can pick flowers and pet puppies. They button and zip, bring liquid to your lips. They smooth and nurture. They pray.

    Your arms can hold bouquets and dear ones. They can reach for your camera on the shelf. They can bend so you can scratch your back and wash your hair. Appreciate your arms and hands.
11. Your shoulders hold up your shirts and blouses. They carry long packages. They enable you to hug and be hugged.
12. Appreciate your neck. It lets you look sideways without turning your body, handy when you're in a bus. Children can hold onto it when you carry them. It holds up your head and gives you a place from which to hang necklaces, ties, and scarves.
13. Your head contains your brain. Upon it lie your eyes, nose, ears, and mouth. Picture what they enable you to know and perceive. Thank your ears. Thank your eyes. Thank each gift on your head.
14. Surround your body with positive regard. Fill with gratitude for all the gifts of being physical.

MEDITATION II

1. In an interruption-proof setting, sit in a comfortable chair that supports your head, neck, arms, and hands.
2. Breathe deeply. Mentally scan your body. Relax any tense areas.
3. Think about your bones. They hold up everything. Your bones are the scaffolding that makes posture and movement possible. They are manufacturing plants for blood cells. Thank your bones.
4. Thank your skin. It holds you together. It stretches, wards off disease, and is remarkably strong and difficult to tear. Your skin is washable and flexible. Its color gives you a unique identity.
5. Thank your muscles. They make all movement possible. They take in and form your beating heart.
6. Thank your blood. It's rushing through your body carrying nutrients and transporting waste, oxygen, and the antibodies that fight disease.
7. Thank your immune system. It fights foreign invaders and remembers them should they ever come back.
8. Thank your brain, your senses, and your nervous system. Your nervous system alerts you to potential harm and maintains vital functions like breathing and body temperature.

   Your brain is the repository of all you know. There's no computer like it. It lets you make choices and makes it possible for you to change your life. Thank your brain and nerves.
9. Appreciate the marvel of your body. Surround it with positive regard.

ASSIGNMENT 15.4

1. Note how you reacted to the meditations. When you reached a certain part of your body, did you zone out? Did you have trouble thinking of any advantages for certain parts of your

body? Have you hated your stomach, for example, for so long that you couldn't think of anything good about it?

2. Draw a body shape. Use one color to shade the areas you like and feel good about. Use another color to shade the areas you don't like.
3. Let a part of your body be "Queen or King for a Day." For example: "Stomach, today is your special day. Today I will honor your contribution to this body." Tell that stomach about the good it does. Pat it now and then. Appreciate its shape. Make an effort to accept it as it is. If this is too hard, talk about your difficulty with a recovering person or in therapy.
4. Give a day to each part of the body you colored with dislike. At the end of each day, talk to a recovering person about your discoveries and feelings.
5. Give appreciation days to the parts of your body you like.
6. Now and then, focus on your entire physical body, notice its contribution, and appreciate it.

Eat to Even Blood-Sugar Level

Since the release of excess insulin keeps fat in storage and makes blood sugar drop so low that thinking gets cloudy and hunger starts, avoid triggering insulin release. Insulin is triggered by caffeine and high blood-sugar levels. High blood sugar results from eating high concentrations of sweet or starchy substances. By following certain guidelines, you can minimize excessive insulin release:

- Never skip a meal. Getting too hungry can cause you to eat too much. If you are desperately hungry, you are more likely to take whatever food you can find, even food from which you are normally abstinent.
- Plan a small snack whenever a meal is going to be delayed.
- Always eat something soon after you awaken. The worst thing you can do for your insulin level is to have coffee and a sweet roll for breakfast. Breakfast can be light if you prefer but eat at least a small amount of protein.
- Have a small amount of protein if you need a snack. A good snack combo is a piece of fruit and a small slice of cheese.

- Eat soup at least once a day before a meal. Because it is eaten slowly, soup has a gradual effect on blood-sugar level while lessening hunger, therefore enabling you to feel full sooner in the meal.
- Go for variety rather than big portions. At dinner, for example, try a cup of soup, a medium piece of meat, a small salad, a fresh vegetable, and a potato. This is distinctly different from one-food-at-a-time bingeing.

ASSIGNMENT 15.5

1. Think about your eating pattern during the past week. Draw a graph of the probable effect of your eating on your insulin and blood-sugar levels. For example, if you skipped breakfast or went long periods without eating, your blood sugar probably got pretty low. Symptoms are light-headedness, irritability, slow thinking, anxiety, and/or headache. If you skipped a meal and later ate a lot in a short time, your blood sugar probably rose and then dropped as the insulin level rose.
2. Today and tomorrow, pay attention to your body's signals. Try to pick up on the signals that tell you your blood-sugar level is getting low. Respond in kind by adjusting mealtimes.
3. Avoid eating in a way that triggers excessive insulin. Stretch mealtimes so you are taking longer to eat. Avoid eating a lot of food in a short time.
4. Notice the effect this attention has on intake. Are you feeling your stomach's fullness?

16

◇

FULLNESS

◇

We have been trying to get from food what we want from life—fullness. Many of us speak of an emptiness, a hollowness that we've attempted to fill with food. True fullness, however, is built bit by bit as we continue recovery.

The problem with food is that it's never enough. Even when our bellies are bulging, we'd eat more if we physically could. As with any drug, satiation moves further away and is shorter-lived. But as we become more receptive to alternatives, as we develop the ability to feel satisfied with life's gifts, we discover another kind of fullness that beats food hands down. Food, being physical, has a limited capacity to fill emotional and spiritual emptiness. Emotional and spiritual gifts, on the other hand, are unlimited in their power to fill the hollow spaces in our hearts.

Once you've followed the guidelines for building support and becoming abstinent, once you've become comfortable with abstinence and support, new rich pleasures await you. By then, too, you will already have increased your capacity for intimacy.

When you have learned to ask for help, when you have learned to talk about what you're feeling, when you have learned to tell your secrets and your fears, you will have become capable of receiving from others. Many of us are driven by an inward chant that says, "More, more, more." After two to five years of recovery (a recovery that includes facing some of your more pivotal life issues, especially those relating to your original family), you will become more open to experiencing enough. The exercises at the end of this chapter offer you a chance to experience enough. If you have not found support and abstinence, the exercises will probably not do much for you.

If you have been faithfully doing the previous exercises chapter by chapter, we have been together for months and you have a good chance at getting an inkling of the future. If you have returned to this chapter after a couple of years of recovery, abstinence, and support, full speed ahead! Let yourself restfully savor the inflowing of goodness.

Thank you for reading this book and for finding the courage to look at your own need for food. Every one of us who risks greater honesty and self-knowing gives the planet a better chance. Our integrity and health flow in ripples to touch those around us. As more of us become healthier, the ripples spread further. More lives have the opportunity to be inspired by our development. I wish for you tremendous fullness of spirit and life. May you be blessed with energy and purpose, joy and richness, fulfillment and completeness.

ASSIGNMENT 16.1

Stand up. Imagine you are a cat. Stretch slowly and sensuously. Reach upward. Feel yourself lengthen.

Stretch your waist. Sway in a slow circle like a willow tree next to a pond. Let your arms droop like the branches drawing circles on the pond's surface.

Be very still and quiet. Tune in to your body. Listen to it. Experience it. Take a slow, deep breath. Feel the pleasure from the stretch travel through you.

This is an experience of fullness.

ASSIGNMENT 16.2

1. Think of someone you trust a lot, someone you feel very safe with. Pick someone whose integrity you can trust absolutely.
2. Plan a time you can be together with no distractions (no children with needs, no phones that require answering). Explain that you would like her to tell you about your own worth. If she's willing, you might like to be held.
3. When you are together, ask her to quietly and confidently tell you about your goodness. Let her read the section below, which is a letter of instruction to her.

Dear Friend,
Your friend has asked for this time with you for a special purpose. She needs to be reminded of her basic worth. She trusts you quite a lot and she believes that you speak the truth. I ask you now to focus on the inner person in front of you. Picture how deep her goodness goes. Picture her worth, her value, her worthiness. She is special. She is unique. She has always deserved to have her needs met and to be well cared for. Even if that didn't happen, she deserved it. Even if other people made mistakes and hurt her, she never deserved to be hurt. She is a treasure. She is a special, worthwhile gift to the planet. She is so full of good. Tell her these things. Encourage her to sit comfortably with her eyes closed. Encourage her to allow herself to open as fully as possible to what you are telling her. For about ten to fifteen minutes, slowly and quietly repeat the above messages. If you are both willing, hold her the way you would a child. Mother her if you feel comfortable with this (that is, making soothing sounds or gently rocking). Let your warmth and care enfold her. Encourage her to be as open as possible to the comfort you are offering. Hold her for five to ten minutes or as long as is comfortable for both of you. Thank you. You have given her a great gift.

4. Be as open as possible to your friend's words and comfort. If you are comfortable, let her hold you and mother you with

soothing sounds or gentle rocking. When you separate, sit quietly apart with your eyes closed for a moment. Experience how nurtured you are. This is fullness.

5. Talk about the experience with your friend. Both of you share what the experience meant to you.

◇

ASSIGNMENT 16.3

1. On your day off, schedule four hours for yourself. Put this on your calendar and keep this appointment no matter what.
2. Go to a beautiful, safe place—a park, by the water, a forest, a mountaintop, an open vista. Stay apart from others. Be as private as it is safe to be.
3. Sit quietly with your eyes open. Take five slow, deep breaths. With each breath, pull the beauty and freshness of the place into you. Smell the wind. Let the wind blow into you. Let each breath freshen you.
4. Stand up and slowly move through the area. If it is a forest, look at the trees. Experience their tallness, their strength, their life. Pick a tree that seems special to you. Go right up to it. If you can reach a leaf, touch it. Leave it attached to the tree. Sandwich it in your hands and experience a mingling of your energy with the leaf's energy. Trace the veins with your fingers. Sense the texture. If you feel comfortable doing so, hug the tree. Let the tree's energy flow into your heart. Let your love flow into the tree. Sit with your back against the tree, like leaning against a friend. Let the wisdom of the tree enter your body. Feel how good it is to lean against a friend.
6. If you are by the water, experience the water in every way you can. If there's a dock or pier, sit at the end of it. Look deep into the water as far as you can see. If the water has waves, rock in time with their motion. Feel your kinship with the water. Let the water in you resonate with the motion and spirit of the water outside you. After a while, walk along the edge of the water and find a shell or a rock. Hold it in your hand. Let your fingers experience its texture, its solidness or

thinness. Let your hand absorb the experience of the rock or shell. Rub it against your face. Hold it against your heart. Let the energy of the rock or shell enter your heart.

7. No matter where you are, seek out the beauty around you. Study it from a distance. Let it imprint itself on your mind as if you were a painter's canvas. Then get close to it. Touch the beauty. Study it intimately. Lie down on the earth and hug the planet. Let the energy of the planet enter your heart. Let your love enter the planet. This is fullness.

NOTES

◇

CHAPTER 1

1. Steven Levenkron, author of *Best Little Girl in the World,* Warner Books, New York, 1979, in a speech at the convention of the International Association of Eating Disorder Professionals, 1988.

CHAPTER 2

1. Wurtman, J. J. 1987. Disorders of food intake. *Annals of the New York Academy of Sciences* 499:197–202.

2. Ashley, David. 1986. Dietary control of brain 5-hydroxytryptamine synthesis: Implications in the etiology of obesity. *International Journal for Vitamin and Nutrition Research* 29:27–40.

3. Silverstone, T., and E. Goodall. 1986. Serotoninergic mechanisms in human feeding: The pharmacological evidence. *Appetite* 7 (suppl.): 85–97.

4. See note 2 above.

5. Caballero, Benjamin. 1987. Brain serotonin and carbohydrate craving in obesity. *International Journal of Obesity* 11:179–183.

6. Zeisel, Steven. 1986. Dietary influences on neurotransmission, *Advances in Pediatrics* 33:23–48.

7. Ibid.

8. Bertiere, M. C., T. Mame Sy, F. Baigts, et al. 1984. Stress and sucrose hyperphagia: Role of endogenous opiates. *Pharmacology Biochemistry & Behavior* 20:675–679.

9. Rogers, P. J., and J. E. Blundell. 1980. Investigation of food selection and meal parameters during the developments of dietary induced obesity. *Appetite* 1:85.

10. Davis, J. M., M. T. Lowy, G. K. W. Yim, et al. 1983. Relationship between plasma concentrations of immunoreactive beta-endorphin and food intake in rats. *Peptides* 4:79–85.

11. Ostrowski, N. L., T. L. Foley, M. D. Lind, et al. 1980. Naloxone reduces fluid intake: Effects of water and food deprivation. *Pharmacology Biochemistry & Behavior* 12:431–435. Summarized in Bertiere, M. C., T.

Mame Sy, F. Baigts, et al. 1984. Stress and sucrose hyperphagia: Role of endogenous opiates. *Pharmacology Biochemistry & Behavior* 10:675–679.

12. See note 8 above.

13. Kral, J. G., L. Gortz, and L. Terenius. 1981. Endorphin-like activity in morbidly obese patients. A pilot study. *International Journal of Obesity* 5:539.

14. Awoke, S., N. Voyles, A. Wade, et al. 1982. Altered opiate levels in obese human subjects. *Diabetes* 31 (Suppl. 2):61A.

15. Louis-Sylvestre, Jeanine. 1984. Meal size: Role of reflexly induced insulin release. *Journal of the Autonomic Nervous System* 10:317–324.

16. Fullerton, Donald T., Carl J. Getto, William J. Swift, et al. 1985. Sugar, opioids, and binge eating. *Brain Research Bulletin* 14:673–680.

CHAPTER 7

1. As reported at International Association of Eating Disorders Professionals Convention, Orlando, Florida, November 1988.

CHAPTER 11

1. Steven Levenkron, M.A. and psychotherapist, is author of *Treating and Overcoming Anorexia Nervosa*, New York: Warner Books, 1982.

2. Yim, G. K. W., M. T. Lowy, J. M. Davis, et al. Opiate involvement in glucoprivic feeding. In *The Neural Basis of Feeding and Reward*, edited by B. G. Hoebel and D. Novin, 485–498. Brunswick, ME: Haer Institute for Electrophysiological Research, 1982.

3. Yim, G. K. W., and M. T. Lowy, 1984. Opioids, feeding, and anorexias. *Federation Proceedings*. (November) 43(14).

4. Ibid.

5. Marrazzi, Mary Ann. 1989. Presentation at convention of American Society for Pharmacology and Experimental Therapeutics. *The Eating Disorders Digest* (August) 17(5).

6. Kral, J. G., L. Gortz, and L. Terenius. 1981. Endorphin-like activity in morbidly obese patients. A pilot study. *International Journal of Obesity* 5:539.

7. See note 1 above.

8. Pirke, Karl. 1988. Biological disturbances in bulimia. Presentation at Third International Conference on Eating Disorders, New York. *The Eating Disorders Digest* (November) (1).

9. Plivy, Janet and Peter Herman. 1985. Dieting and Bingeing, A Causal Analysis. *American Psychologist* (February) 40:193–201.

10. Wooley, Susan, and Ann Kearney-Cooke. Intensive treatment of bulimia and body-image disturbance. In *Handbook of Eating Disorders: Physiology, Psychology, & Treatment*, edited by Kelly Brownell and John P. Foreyt. New York: Basic Books, 1986.

11. Ibid., p. 478.

12. Ibid.

13. Root, Maria, and Patricia Fallon. 1988. Victimization experiences as contributing factors in the development of bulimia in women. *Journal of Interpersonal Violence* 3(2):161–173.

14. See note 8 above.

15. Pike, Edwin J. The many faces of eating disorders. 1988. Presented at The International Association of Eating Disorders Professionals' Conference, October 1987. *The Eating Disorders Digest* (November) pp. 3–4.

CHAPTER 13

1. Thanks to Kathy Severson, MC, skilled therapist, for this definition.

2. The ideas in this paragraph come from Terence Gorski and Merlene Miller, *Counseling for Relapse Prevention,* Herald House, Missouri, 1982.

CHAPTER 15

1. Thanks to Amy Condon, Seattle therapist, for the term.

2. Caution to anorexics. If you are anorexic, this book is not for you. If you have been starving yourself for any length of time, your body has been burning body tissues to survive. After the fat was gone, it had to resort to burning muscle tissue and other proteins to keep you alive. Exercise is dangerous for you until the body tissues have been restored. Give this book to someone who really needs it and read a book that applies specifically to anorexia. Better yet, find a counselor who specializes in working with anorexics.

SOURCES OF HELP

EDAP
Eating Disorders Awareness and Prevention
255 Alhambra Circle, #321
Coral Gables, FL 33134
305-444-3731
[Sponsors Eating Disorders
Awareness Week]

FAA
Food Addicts Anonymous
4623 Forest Hill Blvd. #111-5
West Palm Beach, FL 33415-9121
407-967-3871
[Recovery support]

The Gurze Eating Disorders Bookshelf Catalogue
Gurze Books
PO Box 2238
Carlsbad, CA 92018
(800) 756-7533
[Has free catalogue of books & tapes]

IAEDP
International Association of Eating Disorders Professionals
123 NW 13th St. #206
Boca Raton, FL 33432-1618
(800) 800-8126
[Offers professional referrals]

OA
Overeaters Anonymous
World Services Office
2190 West 190th St.
Torrance, CA 90504
(213) 320-7941
[Local groups can be found in the phone book]

INDEX

◇

Abandonment, decreasing of, 92, 99
Abstaining food addict, support of, 118–123, 144–145, 148
Abstinence, *see also* Recovery; Withdrawal
  achieving of, 108–130
  as avoidance of dangerous drug, 111
  binge, 191–193
  definition of, to family, 117
  versus diet, 111
  and healing, 97
  and loved one, 149–150
  as only beginning, 81–83
  plan for, 110–112
  process of, 115–118
  refined carbohydrates as second, *see* Refined Carbohydrate abstinence
  sugar as first, 110–111, 112–114
Abstinent eating, guidelines for, 123–126
Abuse
  bulimia and, 165–166
  decreasing of, 92
  and listening to body, 198
  and low self-esteem, 52–53
  self-, stopping of, 98–99
  sexual, *see* Sexual abuse
Accuracy of feelings, 91–93
Acetylcholine, 31, 32, 33
Actions, identifying message through, 76
Addict(s)
  fat, test for, 9
  food, *see* Food addict(s)
  refined carbohydrate, test for, 8–9
  sugar, test for, 7–8
Addiction(s), 35–44
  food, *see* Food addiction
  genogram of, 47
  as illness, 11–20
  physical, 16–17, 141
  sexual, 215
  substitute, 125, 203
Addictive syndrome, 64–68
Affection, need for, 54
Agenda, for abstinence, 117–118
Al-Anon, 148, 150
Alcohol
  abstinence from, 111, 112, 124
  effects of, on brain, 35–36
  sugar in, 120
Alcoholics Anonymous (AA), 64, 100, 115, 124, 167
Allergy, brain, 109–110
Altering of feelings, dependence on food for, 207–208
Amino acids, 38–39, 126, 166
Anger, and weight, 202
Animal fat, 195
Announcement, of abstinence, 117

Anorexia, 155–163; *see also* Bulimia
  beta-endorphin and, 159–160
  as escape from feeling, 157–158
  obsession of, 161
  as retreat from maturity, 156–157
  stress and hunger and, 158–159
  treatment for, 161–163
Anorexics, caution to, 108
Attention, need for, 54
Avoidance, 64
Axon, 28, 30, 31
Axon terminal, 28, 30, 31

Bakeries, 123
Basal metabolic rate, 210
Belief relief, 89–91
Beta-endorphin, 25–26, 40–41, 42
  two sides of, in anorexia, 159–160
Binge abstinence, 191–193
Black/white thinking, 66
  and stress, 175, 176
Blood-brain barrier, 38
Blood-sugar level, eating to even, 221–222
Body
  listening to, 197–199
  love of, 217–222
Body image, 216–217
Bonding, to parents, 57
Boundaries
  need for, 54
  during withdrawal, modeling of, 118
Brain
  chemicals that feel good to, 34–35
  effects of alcohol on, 35–36
Brain allergy, 109–110
BTUs (British Thermal Units), 210
Bulimia, 163–168; *see also* Anorexia
  and abuse, 165–166
  diets and, 164
  psychological consequences of, 166–167
  recovery from, 167–168
  as rejection of femaleness, 164–165
Bulimics Anonymous (BA), 115, 131, 150, 167

Caffeine, 124
Calories, 210
Carbohydrates, 37, 39, 43, 44; *see also* Starch
  refined, *see* Refined carbohydrate *entries*
Caretaking role, 66
Cerebral cortex, 33
Certification, 134, 135
Certified Eating Disorders Counselor (CEDC), 134
Certified Eating Disorders Therapist (CEDT), 134
Chemicals, that feel good to brain, 34–35
Chemical triggers, 205–207
Chemistry, of food addiction, 21–47
Childhood issues, working through of, stress and, 176
Choice(s), 169–173
  of foods, loss of control over, 13–14
Choosing, of therapist, 136
Churchill, Winston, 185
Codependence, 98
Codependents Anonymous, 148, 150
Commitment to support, 144–145, 148
Communication, need for, 54
Compliance, 67
Compulsions, substitute, 125, 203; *see also* Addiction(s)
Conscious cravings, 19
Conscious refusal to know or feel, 182–185

Consequences
financial, 105–106
identifying message through, 77
minimizing of, 66
moral, 106
physical, 105
psychological, of bulimia, 166–167
of recovery, 171–172
social, 105
spiritual, 106–107
threats of, 20
Contact
with healthy people, 93–94
with people who want your well-being, 92, 176
with recovering people, 94, 176, 177, 209, 221
Control, loss of, 13–15
Control efforts, 19–20, 104
Converting
to other whole grains, 191
to whole-wheat eating, 189–190
Coping skills, learning of, 93
Corn flour, 191
Corn syrup, 112–113
Cortex, 33
Cortisol, 162
Cravings, conscious, 19

Day, of food addict, 139–140
Defiance, 67
Dendrites, 28, 30, 31
Dependence
on food, to alter feelings, 207–208
physical, 16–17, 141
Dependency, feelings of, 66–67
Deprivation, 48–69
and addictive syndrome, 64–68
assignment concerning, 68–69
and breaking rules, 62–64
case history of, 49–52
decreasing of, 92
and failure of diets, 60–61
light, 75
minimum and, 48–49, 52–53, 57, 58–59
overeater's story of, 52–58
and survival techniques, 61
Developmental tasks, need for support in working through, 54–55
Diabetics, caution to, 108
Diet(s)
abstinence versus, 111
and bulimia, 164
failures of, 60–61, 75
recovery versus, 145–146
Difficulty stopping eating, 14
Disease inventory
genogram of addiction in, 46–47
messages about food in, 75–78
projection of future in, 172–173
self-honesty regarding food addiction in, 102–107
Dopamine, 31, 32, 41
Drug, abstinence as avoidance of dangerous, 111
Dynorphin, 40
stress and, 41, 44, 59, 92, 159

Eating
abstinent, guidelines for, 123–126
difficulty in stopping, 14
to even blood-sugar level, 221–222
at inappropriate times or places, 14
knowledge of, through labels, 122–123
minimizing of, 66
powerless, progression of, 104
whole-wheat, converting to, 189–190
Eating Disorders Anonymous (EDA), 115, 131, 150, 167
Emotional needs, 71, 81–94; *see also* Feeling(s)

Emotional needs (*cont.*)
basic, 53–58
neglecting of, stress and, 175, 176
reconnecting with, 97
understanding of, by loved one, 141
Enablers, 116, 133, 148
Endorphins, 24, 25–26, 32, 39–42
and feelings, 33, 34
manipulating level of, 42–45
Energy
overeating and deficit in, 75
recovery and, 170
Enkephalins, 26, 32, 33, 39–40
Equal, 112, 113, 120
Escape, 70–80
anorexia as, 157–158
Excessive quantities, 14
Exercise
anorexia and, 159
bulimia and, 163, 167
as substitute compulsion, 203
weight loss and, 146–147, 210–213
Exposure, *see* Contact
Extreme measures to obtain particular food, 14–15

Failure(s)
of diets, 60–61, 75
setting up for, 11–13
Falling in love, 124–125
Fat(s)
animal, 195
and endorphins, 41, 42, 45
moderating of, 194–196
Fat addict, test for, 9
Fat prejudice, 151–154
Fear(s)
exposure of, 92
recovery and, 170
Feeling(s), 81–94; *see also* Emotional needs
accuracy of, 91–93
altering of, dependence on food for, 207–208
anorexia as excape from, 157–158
conscious refusal of, 182–185
demonstration of, 85–87
endorphins and, 33, 34
following of, 83–84
good, chemicals causing, 34–35
healthy ways to handle, 54
process of, 87–89
reconnecting with, 97
self as, 99–101
unsafe, identification of, 92
Feelings quiz, 78–80
Femaleness, rejection of, bulimia as, 164–165
Financial consequences, adverse, 105–106
Food(s), *see also* Substances
choice of types of, loss of control over, 13–14
containing refined carbohydrates, 122
dependence on, to alter feelings, 207–208
extreme measures in obtaining particular, 14–15
with high natural sugar content, 121
Food addict(s)
abstaining, support of, 118–123, 144–145, 148
loved one of, 137–150
and minimum, 52–53, 58–59
Food addiction
causes of, 37–39
chemistry of, 21–47
nature of, 13–20, 138–139
process of, 24–33
Friend, support, *see* Support friend
Fullness, 223–227

Genogram of addiction, 47
The Gods Must Be Crazy, 95

Grains, whole, converting to, 191
Grief, recovery and, 171
Group
  support, *see* Support group
  therapy, *see* Therapy group
Guilt, 58

Happiness, and real living, 5
Healing, 95–107
  internal processes of, 97–99
Healthy people, contact with, 93–94
Help, 131–136; *see also* Support *entries;* Therapeutic *entries;* Treatment
Heredity, 44–47
Hierarchy of needs, 72–74
Higher Power, 184
Hitting bottom, 172
Home, safe, creation of, 116–117
Honesty
  of adults, need for, 54
  self-, 102–107, 170
House changes, for abstinence, 117
Hunger, stress and, and anorexia, 158–159
Hypothalamus, 33, 159

Identification
  of message, 76–77
  of unsafe feelings, 92
Illness, addiction as, 11–20
Impulsiveness, 66
Inappropriate times or places, eating at, 14
Independence, appearance of, 66–67
Individuality, need for, 54
Inner self, telegrams from, 84–85
Insulin, 39, 75, 108, 124, 164, 204, 205, 221–222
Insurance, 136
International Association of Eating Disorders Professionals, 134
Interpretations, 56–57
Intimacy, weight as protection from, 213–217
Inventory, disease, *see* Disease inventory
Isolation, 66

Kindness, self-, 62
Knowledge
  conscious refusal of, 182–185
  in eating, 122–123

Labels, 122–123
Levenkron, Steven, 15, 157, 161
Light deprivation, 75
Lipoprotein lipase, 204–205
Listener, good, 83; *see also* Support friend
Listening, to your body, 197–199
Life
  finding of, 6–7
  importance of, 5–6
Living, real, happiness and, 5
Loss
  as consequence of choice, 171–172
  of control, 13–15
Love
  falling in, 124–125
  of your body, 217–222
Loved one, of food addict, 137–150
Lying, 14

Manipulation, 14
Maslow, Abraham, 72–74
Maturity, retreat from, anorexia as, 156–157
Max Planck Institute, 166
Meditation, 218–220; *see also* Visualization
Melting the cocoon, 204–205

Membrane, of neurons, 35–36
Menus, 123
Message, identifying of, 76–77
Metabolism, increasing of, 209–210
Minimizing, of eating and its consequences, 66
Minimum, 48–49, 57
  food addicts and, 52–53, 58–59
Moderting fats and oils, 194–196
Monamines, 32
Moral consequences, adverse, 106

Nature's telegrams, 81–94; *see also* Feeling(s); Needs
Need ranking, and overeating, 73–75
Needs, *see also* Feeling(s)
  emotional, *see* Emotional needs
  hierarchy of, 72–74
  physical, neglecting of, stress and, 175, 176
Negative people, protection from, 92, 94
Nerves, workings of, 26–31
Nervous system, sympathetic, 41, 159
Neurons, 28, 29, 35
Neurotransmitter receptors, 31–33
Neurotransmitters, 28–29, 30, 31, 34, 35–36, 166
Norepinephrine, 31, 32, 159
Nucleus, 28
Nutrasweet, 112

Obsession, of anorexia, 161
Obtaining particular food, extreme measures in, 14–15
Oils, moderating of, 194–196
Opiate helpers, 159–160
Overeater, story of, 52–58
Overeaters Anonymous (OA), 115, 124, 131, 148, 150, 167
Overeating, need ranking and, 73–75

Pain, sensitivity to, 44–46
Parents, bonding to, 57; *see also* Heredity
Peaceful coexistence, violence versus, 197
Perfectionism, 66
  and stress, 175, 176
Personal power, need for, 54
Physical addiction, 141
Physical consequences, adverse, 105
Physical dependence/addiction, 16–17
Physical needs, neglecting of, and stress, 175, 176
Physical survival
  brain systems for, 33
  need for, 53
  as pleasure, 34–35
Pike, Edwin, 166
Plan, for abstinence, 110–112
Pleasure, survival as, 34–35
Power, personal, need for, 54
Powerless eating, progression of, 104
Prejudice, fat, 151–154
Priorities, *see* Hierarchy of needs
Properly proportioned portions, 194
Protection
  from negative people, 92, 94
  of self and others, during withdrawal, 117–118
  from sexual abuse or intimacy, weight as, 202, 213–217
Protective structures, against stress, 176–177, 182
Prozac, 126
Psychological consequences, of bulimia, 166–167
Punishment, self-, 66

Quantities, excessive, 14

Quiz, *see also* Disease inventory; Test
  feelings, 78–80
  review, 128–130

Ranking, of needs, and overeating, 73–75
Reactions, 71; *see also* Feeling(s)
Receptors, neurotransmitter, 31–33
Reconnecting with feelings and needs, 97
Recovering people, contact with, 94; *see also* Sponsor
  and meditation difficulty, 221
  stress and, 176, 177
  withdrawal and, 209
Recovery, *see also* Abstinence
  from bulimia, 167–168
  versus dieting, 145–146
  gifts of, 170–171
  therapists in, 135
Refined carbohydrate abstinence, 111–112, 114–115, 187–194, 197–199
  binge abstinence in, 191–193
  converting to other whole grains in, 191
  converting to whole-wheat eating in, 191
  nature of, 188–189
  properly proportioned portions in, 194
Refined carbohydrate addict, test for, 8–9
Refined carbohydrates, 59
  foods containing, 122, 189–190
  forms of, 121, 188–189
Refusal to know or feel, conscious, 182–185
Rejection of femaleness, bulimia as, 164–165
Relapse, 174–186
  anatomy of, 177–182
  conscious refusal to know or feel and, 182–185
  loved one and, 149–150
  progression of, 183–185
  protective structures against, 176–177, 182
  stress and, 175–176
Relationship, need for, 54
Relationship skills, learning of, 93
Rest, during abstinence, 126
Retreat from maturity, anorexia as, 156–157
Review quiz, 128–130
Rules, survival, *see* Survival rules

Sabotage, 143–144
Safe home, creation of, 116–117
Safe places, for breaking survival rules, 92–93
Safety, need for, 54
Secretiveness, 66
Self
  feeling, 99–101
  inner, telegrams from, 84–85
  protection of, during withdrawal, 117–118
  testing of, 7–10
Self-abuse, stopping of, 98–99
Self-acceptance, 13
Self-esteem, low
  abuse and, 52–53
  extra weight and, 200–202
Self-honesty, 47, 102–107, 170
Self-kindness, 62
Self-punishment, 66
Sensitivity, to pain, 44–46
Serotonin, 24, 25, 26, 31, 32, 33, 37, 38, 39, 43, 44–45, 126
Setting up to fail, 11–13
Sexual abuse, 56–57, 98
  and listening to body, 198
  weight as protection from, 202, 213–217
Sexual addiction, 215
Shame, 58, 59
Sharing discoveries, 77–78
Shopping, as substitute compulsion, 125, 203
Sleep, *see* Rest

Social consequences, adverse, 105
Spiritual consequences, adverse, 106–107
Spirituality, and weight loss, 208–209
Sponsor, and relapse list, 186; *see also* Recovering people; Support friend
Starch, and endorphins, 40–42, 45, 46; *see also* Refined carbohydrates
Starving, as stress, 160
Stimulation, need for, 54
Stimulus, to nerve, 30
Stopping eating, difficulty in, 14
Story, of overeater, 52–58
Stress
  and dynorphin, 41, 44, 59, 92, 159
  and endorphins, 42
  factors that increase, 175–176
  and hunger, and anorexia, 158–159
  starving as, 160
Structures, protective, against stress, 176–177, 182
Struggle, of food addict, 141
Substances, containing sugar, 120–121; *see also* Foods
Substitute addictions/compulsions, 125, 203
Substitution(s)
  for fats and oils, 196
  of substance for real need, 64–65
Sugar
  blood-, eating to even level of, 221–222
  and endorphins, 40–43, 44–45, 46
  as first abstinence, 110–111, 112–114
  foods with high natural content of, 121
  forms of, 119
  substances containing, 120–121
Sugar addict, test for, 7–8
Sugar Twin, 120
Support
  of abstaining food addict, 118–123, 144–145, 148
  in working through developmental tasks, need for, 54–55
Support friend, *see also* Sponsor
  calling of, to talk, 94, 101–102
  fat prejudice risk activity with, 154
  and fullness exercise, 225–226
  and second abstinence, 199
  sharing discoveries with, 77–78, 103, 172, 173
  and stress, 177, 182
Support group, 94; *see also* Therapy group
  and fat prejudice risk activity, 154
  and stress, 176–177, 182
Support system, developing strong, 93–94, 101–102, 115–116
Survival, physical
  brain systems for, 33
  need for, 53
  as pleasure, 34–35
Survival rules, 89
  breaking of, 62–64, 92–93, 98, 176
  exposure of, 92
  and future, 173
  and stress, 176
Survival techniques, 61
Survivors, withdrawal, 127–128
Sweet-'n'-Low, 120
Symbolizing, 82–83
Sympathetic nervous system, 41, 159
Synapses, 28, 29, 31, 35
  experience and, 96

Taking the rap, 92
Talbott, Douglas, 109
Telegrams, *see also* Emotional needs, Feeling(s)
  from inner self, 84–85
  nature's, 81–94

Test, addiction, 7–10; *see also* Disease inventory; Quiz
Therapeutic process, 132–134; *see also* Treatment
Therapist(s)
  bulimia and, 167, 168
  choosing of, 136
  and fat prejudice risk activity, 154
  and meditation difficulty, 221
  and protective weight, 216
  in recovery, 135
  and second abstinence, 199
  sharing discoveries with, 77, 103, 172, 173
  and stress, 176
Therapy group, 94; *see also* Support group
  bulimia and, 167
  nature of, 132–136
  and relapse list, 186
  and second abstinence, 199
  sharing discoveries with, 77, 103, 173
  and protective weight, 216
  and stress, 176, 186
Timing, 169–173
Tradition, need for, 54
Transference, 133–134
Traveling, 124
Treatment, of anorexia, 161–163; *see also* Therapeutic *entries*
Trust, need for, 54
Tryptophan, 37, 38, 39, 44, 126
Twelve Step programs, 131–132, 167–168, 215
Types of food chosen, loss of control of, 13–14

Understanding, of food addict, 141
Unfinished business, 92
Unmanageability, 104–105

Validation, need for, 54
Vesicles, 30, 35
Violence, versus peaceful coexistence, 197
Visualization, 216–217; *see also* Meditation

Walking, 211–213
Walking schedule, 212
Weight, 200–222
  anger and, 202
  loving your body and, 217–222
  melting cocoon of, 204–205
  as protection from sexual abuse or intimacy, 202, 213–217
  substitute compulsions and, 203
Weight loss, 146–148
  exercise and, 146–147, 210–213
  going the distance in, 209–210
  healthy, 205–208
  spiritual connection in, 208–209
Well-being, contact with people who want your, 92, 176
White flour, 189–190
Whole grains, converting to, 191
Whole-wheat eating, converting to, 189–190
Wiring, nerves as, 28–31
Withdrawal, *see also* Abstinence
  big ten days of, 126–128
  description of, 117
  going the distance in, 209–210
  preparation for, 118
  survivors of, 127–128
Words, identifying message through, 76
Work, as substitute compulsion, 125, 203
Working through
  of childhood issues, stress and, 176
  of developmental tasks, need for support in, 54–55

ABOUT THE AUTHOR

◇

Anne Katherine, M.A., CEDT, CMHC, is the author of *Boundaries: Where You End and I Begin.* She has a Master of Arts in Psychology from Peabody College and a Certificate in Addiction Studies from Seattle University. She is a Certified Eating Disorders Therapist by the International Association of Eating Disorder Professionals, and a Certified Mental Health Counselor. She has 14 years of personal recovery from binge eating and 23 years of experience as a psychotherapist. Based on her studies of brain functioning, she has created a recovery program that combines the knowledge, skills, and practices that, in concert, bring about lasting recovery from binge-eating and food addiction. Her practice, with Associated Recovery Therapists, is in Seattle.

Order Form

Anatomy of a Food Addiction is available at bookstores and libraries. It may also be ordered directly from Gürze Books.

FREE Catalogue

The Gürze Eating Disorders Bookshelf Catalogue has more than 80 books and tapes on eating disorders and related topics, including body image, size-acceptance, self-esteem, feminist issues, and more. It is a valuable resource that is handed out by therapists, educators, and other health care professionals throughout the world.

Please send me:

____ **FREE** copies of the *Gürze Eating Disorders Bookshelf Catalogue*

____ copies of ***Anatomy of a Food Addiction***
$12.95 each (1-4 copies)
plus $2.50 each for shipping and handling

____ copies of ***Anatomy of a Food Addiction***
$10.95 each (5+ copies)
plus $1.95 each for shipping and handling

Quantity discounts are available on large orders.

NAME ______________________________

ADDRESS ______________________________

CITY, ST, ZIP ______________________________

PHONE ______________________________

Mail a copy of this order form to:

Gürze Books (AFA)
P.O. Box 2238
Carlsbad, CA 92018
www.gurze.com

Order by phone: 800/756-7533